IMPRESSIONS OF
THEODORE ROOSEVELT

THEODORE ROOSEVELT AT WORK
From a photograph taken in 1912 at his desk in the office
of the *Outlook*

Impressions
of
Theodore Roosevelt

By
Lawrence F. Abbott

Garden City   New York
Doubleday, Page & Company
1919

TO

MY FATHER

WHOM THE MORAL LAW COMMANDS ME TO
LOVE BUT WHOM OF MY OWN VOLITION
I LIKE AS THE MOST DELIGHTFUL AND
DESIRABLE OF FRIENDS AND COMPANIONS

PREFACE

This book makes no pretense of being a biography of Theodore Roosevelt. Nor will the reader find in it a chronological narrative of the events of his career. Those who wish to know these chronological facts are referred to his own Autobiography; to the forthcoming "Life and Letters" by Mr. Joseph Bucklin Bishop, who was named by Mr. Roosevelt as its authorized editor; to the introduction, notes, and appendices which I furnished for his volume of "African and European Address"; and to the article on Theodore Roosevelt which I contributed to The Eleventh Edition of the Encyclopædia Britannica.

The purpose of the present volume is to record some personal impressions which this great American made upon me in the course of an acquaintanceship of twenty-two years, during the latter half of which our relations were those of intimate association and friendship. It is with the hope of supplying some useful details for the final portrait which will be painted by the historians of the future that this simple, informal, and free-hand sketch is undertaken.

LAWRENCE F. ABBOTT.

The *Outlook* Office,
  New York,
    July 30, 1919.

CONTENTS

ix

LIST OF ILLUSTRATIONS

LIST OF ILLUSTRATIONS

ROOSEVELT'S CHIEF WRITINGS, EXCLUDING NEWSPAPER ARTICLES AND STATE PAPERS

"African and European Addresses." New York: G. P. Putnam's Sons, 1910.

"African Game Trails." New York: C. Scribner's Sons, 1910.

"America and the World War." New York: C. Scribner's Sons, 1915.

"American Ideals and Other Essays Social and Political." New York: G. P. Putnam's Sons, 1904.

"A Book-lover's Holidays in the Open." New York: C. Scribner's Sons, 1916.

"Fear God and Take Your Own Part." New York: G. H. Doran Company, 1916.

"The Foes of Our Own Household." New York: G. H. Doran Company [cop. 1917].

"Good Hunting in Pursuit of Big Game in the West." New York: Harper and Brothers, 1907.

"Gouverneur Morris." Boston: Houghton, Mifflin and Company. [1st pub. 1888.] (American statesmen.)

"The Great Adventure; Present-day Studies in American Nationalism. New York: C. Scribner's Sons, 1918.

"History as Literature, and Other Essays." New York: C. Scribner's Sons, 1913.

"Hunting Trips of a Ranchman: Sketches of Sport on the Northern Cattle Plains." New York: G. P. Putnam's Sons, 1885. [Also other editions.]

"Life of Thomas Hart Benton." Boston: Houghton, Mifflin and Company, 1887. (American statesmen.)

"National Strength and International Duty." Princeton: Princeton University Press, 1917 (Stafford Little lectures for 1917.)

"Naval War of 1812; or, The History of the United States Navy During the Last War with Great Britain." New York: G. P. Putnam's Sons, 1882. 8th edition.

"New York." New York: Longmans, Green and Company, 1903. (Historic towns.)

"Oliver Cromwell." New York: C. Scribner's Sons, 1900.

"Ranch Life and the Hunting-trail." New York: Century Company, 1896.

"The Rough Riders." New York: C. Scribner's Sons, 1899.

"The Strenuous Life: Essays and Addresses." New York: Century Company, 1900.

"Theodore Roosevelt; an Autobiography." New York: Macmillan Company, 1913.

"Through the Brazilian Wilderness." New York: C. Scribner's Sons, 1914.

"The Wilderness Hunter." An account of the big game of the United States and its chase with horse, hound, and rifle. New York: G. P. Putnam's Sons, 1893.

"The Winning of the West." 4 volumes. New York: G. P. Putnam's Sons, 1889-96. Various editions; Standard library edition, 4 volumes each; Sagamore edition, 6 volumes each.

Roosevelt, Theodore, and Heller, Edmund.
"Life Histories of African Game Animals." New York: C. Scribner's Sons, 1914. 2 volumes.

ROOSEVELT CHRONOLOGY

Born in New York City, October 27, 1858

Graduated from Harvard, 1880

Elected to New York Legislature, 1881, 1882, 1883

Republican candidate for Mayor of New York, 1886

Civil Service Commissioner, 1889

Police Commissioner, 1895

Assistant Secretary of the Navy, 1897

Lieutenant-Colonel and Colonel, Rough Riders, 1898

Governor of New York, 1899-1900

Elected Vice-President, November 4, 1900

Became President on death of President McKinley, September 14, 1901

Elected President of the United States, 1904

Became associated with the *Outlook* in spring of 1909

Sailed for Africa in March, 1909

Organized Progressive Party and was Progressive Party Candidate for President, 1912

Shot at Milwaukee, in October, 1912

Visited South America, October, 1913-June, 1914

Resigned from the *Outlook* in 1914, and later became special contributor to the *Metropolitan Magazine* and the Kansas City *Star*

In the autumn of 1918 he had a recurrence of the jungle fever which he contracted in South America

Died at Sagamore Hill, January 6, 1919

Buried at Oyster Bay, January 8, 1919.

IMPRESSIONS OF
THEODORE ROOSEVELT

IMPRESSIONS
OF
THEODORE ROOSEVELT

CHAPTER I

ACQUAINTANCESHIP

I FORMED the Roosevelt habit early. In the autumn of 1881 Theodore Roosevelt was elected as a Republican to the Legislature of the State of New York. The story of that election is a characteristic and amusing one and will be referred to in more detail in the next chapter. On taking his seat in the lower house, or Assembly, of the Legislature he became at once a prominent if not a national figure. He was reëlected in 1882 and 1883 and was selected by his party in the Legislature as its candidate for Speaker. All this happened when he was less than twenty-four years old. Naturally his success—based as it was on high standards and enduring, even pugnacious, courage, combined with human sympathy and democratic interest in all sorts of men, when they

3

were real men—attracted the attention of hundreds of young Americans of his own age. They felt, somehow or other, that he was a symbol of what young America could do if it tried.

I was living in New York at the time, working as a clerk in a publishing office, and the picture of this young college man—a graduate of Harvard in the Class of 1880, scarcely a year older than myself, fighting for decency and honesty in politics at a time when American political morals were at a pretty low ebb—appealed to my imagination, and I followed his political career with intense interest.

But I was not, I think, altogether blinded by my admiration, for although I was born and brought up a Republican of a somewhat strict sect, I voted for Cleveland in the presidential election of 1884 as a protest against the forces behind Blaine, while Roosevelt, having opposed as strongly as he could the nomination of Blaine in the Republican National Convention, nevertheless voted for him as his party's regular candidate. And wisely, I think. For Roosevelt had deliberately chosen politics as his career, intended to make politics, if possible statesmanship, his profession; and in a two-party government like ours the political administrator and statesman must work with his party except in a crisis of the utmost national import. The ordinary citizen, on the other hand, may, and often should, use his vote as an independent instrument to serve as a check upon the unwise policies or unwholesome tendencies of the party in power.

It is difficult to look back over a span of thirty-five years and recall all the details of one's feelings, even in the field of politics where, generally, the emotions, prejudices, and passions of antipathy or devotion are developed and manifested in their strongest form. But apparently my difference of opinion with Roosevelt in the Blaine campaign could not have been very deep-seated, for, in 1886, when he ran as Republican candidate for Mayor of New York City, I supported and voted for him with ardour. It was a "three-cornered campaign," Abram Hewett being the Democratic (and successful) candidate while Henry George, the distinguished apostle of the single tax doctrine, represented the Radicals. Although Roosevelt ran third in the race his personality as a candidate made a deep impression upon me, and I remember that campaign as the starting point of a political career in which I have taken a constant and, whenever I could, an active interest. Whether it was because this mayoralty contest was a complete defeat or because Roosevelt's managers made it one of partisanship rather than of fundamental principles I do not know, but the fact is that it made little impression on him and apparently did not especially interest him as one of the milestones of his political progress, for I never heard him talk about it—as he was glad to do about his other political experiences—and he does not even mention it in his autobiography!

It was in this way that the foundations were laid for my later personal friendship with Roosevelt and for my sympathy with his political philosophy. But I did not make his personal acquaintance until 1895 when he was president of the Board of New York Police Commissioners.

William L. Strong, a well-known and public-spirited merchant of New York City, had been elected mayor on an anti-Tammany fusion ticket in 1894. One of the factors in his election was the work done by the "Good Government Clubs" which were organized in various districts of New York City. As a result of the impetus which I have received from the political work and qualities of Theodore Roosevelt, I entered with enthusiasm this Good Government Club movement and served as a watcher at the polls on Election Day in one of the toughest Tammany districts in what was known as the gas-house quarter on the East Side.

The election was being carried on under a new

Mr. Roosevelt as president of the Board of Police, New
York City, 1895–97

law, which I had taken the pains to study. While at the outset the Tammany "heelers" and even the Tammany policemen endeavoured to browbeat and obstruct me, I found before the night was over (because they became convinced that I intended to be fair and was unwilling to throw out ballots on mere technicalities) that they were appealing to me for help in the canvassing; finally, they accepted both my advice and my decisions. This experience convinced me that Theodore Roosevelt's doctrines of political management and administration were workable. And so, when Mayor Strong appointed him one of the four police commissioners and he became president of the Board, I watched with more than ordinary interest his endeavours to make the police system of the city an honest and effective one.

One day Jacob Riis—at that time a representative of, I think, the *Evening Sun* at Police Headquarters—came into my office, when I told him of an experience that I had had with a drunken police officer, whose number I had taken the precaution of noting in my memorandum book. Riis asked me whether I had any objection to his telling the story to Roosevelt. On my assent he evidently related the incident to the new commissioner with all the colour and picturesqueness that characterized his work as a writer. For, in a day or two he came back and said that Commissioner Roosevelt wanted me to come down to Police Headquarters and make a complaint against the disreputable policeman. I went down, was ushered into Mr. Roosevelt's presence, and there met him for the first time. He had in the room to meet me the policeman whose number I had given to Mr. Riis. I recognized and identified the man and, at Mr. Roosevelt's request, made the proper complaint. The affair resulted in a police trial at which one of Mr. Roosevelt's colleagues, Commissioner Parker, presided. Commissioner Parker was not in sympathy with Mr. Roosevelt's efforts to take the police force out of corrupt politics, and although he was superficially courteous he made the day that I spent in the trial room one of the most uncomfortable of my life. What finally was the disposition of the case I do not know, for Commissioner Parker suspended judgment at the conclusion of the trial. But I have never regretted that day, miserable though it was, because it proved to be the beginning of an acquaintanceship with Theodore Roosevelt which later became an intimate one and developed into what was, to me, a deep and delightful friendship.

One of the most readable and entertaining chapters of Mr. Roosevelt's autobiography is his account of his work as Police Commissioner. He not only tells of some of his difficulties but relates stories of particular officers, like those of Otto Raphael and Captain Bourke that are as lively and as absorbing as any novel. His final estimate of his work with the police is as follows:

Let me again say that when men tell me that the police are irredeemably bad I remember scores and hundreds of cases like this of Bourke, like the case I have already mentioned of Raphael, like the other cases I have given above. It is useless to tell me that these men are bad. They are naturally first-rate men. There are no better men anywhere than the men of the New York Police force; and when they go bad it is because the system is wrong, and because they are not given the chance to do the good work they can do and would rather do. I never coddled these men. I punished them severely whenever I thought their conduct required it. All I did was to try to be just; to reward them when they did well; in short, to act squarely by them. I believe that, as a whole, they liked me. When, in 1912, I ran for President on the Progressive ticket, I received a number of unsigned letters inclosing sums of money for the campaign. One of these inclosed twenty dollars. The writer, who did not give his name, said that he was a policeman, that I had once had him before me on charges, and had fined him twenty dollars; that, as a matter of fact, he had not committed the offense for which I fined him, but that the evidence was such that he did not wonder that I had been misled, and never blamed me for it, because I had acted squarely and had given honest and decent men a chance in the Police Department; and that now he inclosed a twenty-dollar bill, the amount of the fine inflicted on him so many years before. I have always wished I knew who the man was.

It was through his work as police commissioner that I first began to realize Theodore Roosevelt's deep-seated human sympathy and his understanding of human character. He was an indefatigable worker then as he was in every phase of his life. He was not too busy to ask me, a citizen unknown to him and holding no public position, to come down and make a complaint which might help in the work he was trying to do. Since his death, an old boyhood friend of mine, a practising physician in New York City, Dr. Matthew Beattie, has sent me fifteen letters which Commissioner Roosevelt wrote to him between August, 1895, and December, 1896. They are only a few of a much larger number, nearly forty in all.

Dr. Beattie gives me the following interesting account of his experiences with Mr. Roosevelt as to police reform:

Mr. Roosevelt had been in office only a few days when I called on him at Police Headquarters and told him that No. —— and No. —— on the block on which I lived were, and had been for a long time, houses of ill fame. Quick as a flash he replied with this question: "Doctor, will you wait here until I get your police captain?" Of course I said "yes." Immediately Captain S.—— of the West —— Street station was summoned. He was hardly seated and informed of my complaint when Mr. Roosevelt walked up rather close to him and said, with great determination: "Captain, I will give you just five days to close those three houses."

In three days all three houses became vacant and were respectable boarding houses for the following sixteen years to my personal knowledge.

A druggist, living about half a mile from my office, wrote to me asking me to use my influence with Police Commissioner Roosevelt to curb or punish a drunken policeman, named M——, who often insulted women in his drug store and on the near-by streets. I presented the case to Mr. Roosevelt who at once asked me to aid him in a little detective work to catch officer M——. I was glad to do so, and secured the help of Professor Harry Cushing, then of Columbia College, who lived in my house. . . . M—— was found guilty of being off post and fined on that count. Cushing and I, however, had not *proved* the character of the house of ill fame which we saw him enter. Therefore, he could not be dismissed from the force on our complaint, but I was informed that he was dismissed two weeks after the trial, on another charge.

Two of these letters to Dr. Beattie are typical of Mr. Roosevelt's methods. The first illustrates the directness with which he went to the point:

DEAR DR. BEATTIE:
I am very doubtful indeed about the captain in question, but keep a close eye on him.
As to your questions:
  I. Continue to make reports to me.
  II. Grant the request.
  III. Carry a pistol and apply for a permit to the Chief.
Very truly yours,
THEODORE ROOSEVELT.

The second letter illustrates his fairmindedness. The Captain S—— who had been summoned to Mr. Roosevelt's office, on Dr. Beattie's complaint, to close three disorderly houses apparently did his duty so well, after he found that he had a real backer in the new commissioner, that he brought down on his head the wrath of the powers of corruption. When Mr. Roosevelt found that he could be relied upon for honest work he supported him, as will be seen from the second letter:

December 7, 1896.

MY DEAR DR. BEATTIE:

Your letter gave me sincere pleasure. I have reason to believe that Captain S—— has been persecuted, not for his failings, but for his efficiency, and especially because of the way he has acted in support of you and your representatives —conduct that has cost him much bitter hostility. I trust you will be willing to appear as a witness to testify in his behalf if he is put on trial.

Sincerely yours,

THEODORE ROOSEVELT.

Beginning with his police commissionership I came into contact with Mr. Roosevelt occasionally, but it was not until he was about to leave the White House that the real association began upon which these impressions are based.

Not long after Mr. Roosevelt's election to the Presidency in 1904 he announced that he would not be a candidate for a second consecutive term. In

the summer of 1905 I began to turn over in my
own mind one day what Mr. Roosevelt would do
when he left the Presidency. It seemed to me that
after he retired from official life he must have some
organized means of expressing his views and exert-
ing his influence on public questions. He was not
a lawyer by profession, as so many other ex-Presidents have been, and he could not go into active industrial or financial business. That had been tried
by one ex-President, General Grant, with disastrous
consequences. Since Mr. Roosevelt was not only a
statesman but a man of letters, I wondered whether
some form of journalism in which he could take
part in discussions on social, economic, and political questions would not be appropriate. Would
it be possible to have him associate himself with
the *Outlook?* With this idea in mind, I worked
out a plan—coining the phrase "contributing
editor"—and it was put before him. How he met
it is described in a letter to me, dated March 5,
1917, from which I quote:

It was your father and you yourself who personally brought
to my attention the idea of my joining the *Outlook* as a contributing editor. This was in the White House at the beginning of the year 1906. I spoke of it again with your
father that summer and in the following year, but I came to
no definite decision until the spring or early summer of 1908,
when you came to see me at Sagamore Hill, and I agreed

definitely to go in with you on practically the basis on which I afterward did go in. It was your father who was the decisive factor in getting me to accept. I *might* have accepted your request alone; but I have a peculiar feeling for your father. I regard him and have long regarded him as a man who in a way stands entirely apart from all others in our national life, and, if the expression does not seem exaggerated, my regard for him has in it a little of that feeling of reverence which is perhaps the finest feeling an old man can inspire in younger men—even when these younger men, like myself, become old men! I felt honoured to be associated with him, and I was also very glad to be associated with the rest of you.

The result of these negotiations was that on the 7th of November, 1908, the *Outlook* was able to announce that "on and after the 5th of March, 1909, Theodore Roosevelt will be associated with the *Outlook's* editorial staff as special Contributing Editor." From that day until June, 1914, he was in a very real sense a member of our staff. He made his office with us and he regularly attended our weekly editorial conferences.

According to our mutual agreement he was to be free to express his own views over his own name and the *Outlook* was equally at liberty to state its opinion even when it varied from his on public questions. We rarely differed, but when we did he accepted the difference of opinion with perfect loyalty to the understanding which was the basis of our joint work. He believed in what he called

Roosevelt in cowboy costume during his early years as a ranchman

"team-work," and practised his belief. He listened to the views of his colleagues, and often modified his own as a result of the interchange of opinion. He never wrote an article that he did not, before publication, submit to one of us, and he almost invariably accepted our suggestions, sometimes with regard to verbal expressions and sometimes with regard to change of ideas or views of the article. I do not mean to give the impression that he altered his mind frequently. On matters of principle he could be as fixed as adamant. But in methods of putting a principle into effect he habitually sought counsel and was eager to adopt suggestions. Not only did he contribute to our pages articles over his own name, but his wide experience, his comprehensive knowledge of men and affairs, and his unique ability as an interpreter of political and social movements found expression in our own editorials through the comments and suggestions which he made at the weekly conferences.

One of the first results of his prospective connection with the *Outlook* was that I had the very unusual, if not the unique, experience of attending a semi-official cabinet meeting in Washington. Mr. Taft was running for the Presidency against Mr. Bryan, and in the latter part of the summer of 1908 there was great anxiety among the Republican managers lest Mr. Bryan might be elected on the anti-corporation "trust-busting" issue. He was, it is true, defeated by so large a majority that these anxieties now seem hardly credible, but at the time they were very real. Governor Haskell of Oklahoma was the treasurer of the National Democratic Committee and Mr. Bryan's right-hand man in managing his campaign. The *Outlook* had learned that the university professors and educators of Oklahoma were very much upset by Governor Haskell's management of the educational system of that state. They felt that he was trying to prostitute it to partisan political ends. During a visit which my father had made to the State of Oklahoma shortly before the campaign of 1908 he was urged to defend in the *Outlook* the university and schools of Oklahoma against the political machinations of Governor Haskell. My father was very glad to do this and the *Outlook*, supported by documents and other proof, took up the issue with some vigour. For when political bosses endeavour to turn a state educational system into a political machine they are guilty of perhaps the worst form of political corruption. To debauch the public schools in this way is to pollute the very springs of our national life. Mr. Roosevelt knew and approved of the part which the *Outlook* had been taking in this controversy.

One September Saturday afternoon, while playing golf at my summer home on the Hudson about fifty miles from New York, the following telegram was repeated to me by telephone from my office in the city:

The White House, Washington, September 26, 1908.
Lawrence F. Abbott
  The *Outlook*
    New York City
Letter received. If you want to write on Haskell I have many records to show you which you ought to see. Come on to see me this evening or to-morrow (Sunday) afternoon or evening. Don't forget the expression used by one of the Oklahoma senators in championing Haskell that Haskell is merely Bryanism in action.
                                THEODORE ROOSEVELT.

In reply I telegraphed that I would report at the White House the next morning, Sunday, at nine o'clock. Reluctantly I left my game of golf, hastily packed a bag, and got a train for New York which enabled me to take the midnight express over to Washington.

When I presented my card at nine o'clock at the White House the doorman was a little dubious, owing to the very unusual hour of the call, but it was sent to the President who summoned me to join him. I found him at breakfast with Mrs.

Roosevelt at a small round table on the back verandah overlooking the pleasant garden with the towering Washington Monument in the distance. He explained that he and Mrs. Roosevelt were accustomed to breakfast alone on Sunday mornings, without even other members of the family, because in this way they could take one of the very few opportunities they had for an hour of uninterrupted companionship.

Mr. Roosevelt informed me that he was in the process of an exchange of open letters with Mr. Bryan on issues of the campaign; that he had written the first one; that Mr. Bryan had replied; and that he was about to write his second letter that afternoon. With the astute wisdom which he showed in all practical matters, Mr. Roosevelt had picked out the Monday morning newspapers as the medium for his open letters. Daily newspaper editors are always glad to get some striking feature for Monday morning since the Sunday issue has used up everything of sensational value in hand.

At the President's invitation I returned to take luncheon with him and afterward went up into his study, where a table was covered with documents and records of all kinds regarding the campaign. At three o'clock those members of the Cabinet who were then in Washington came to the room by appointment and Mr. Roosevelt began to dictate the open letter to Bryan, walking up and down the room as he talked to the stenographer in a characteristic fashion. Finally he came to a criticism of Mr. Bryan himself and was making the application of this criticism somewhat personal and vigorous, whereupon a member of the Cabinet remarked: "Mr. President, it does not seem to me wise to make a personal attack upon Mr. Bryan and certainly not upon Mr. Bryan's integrity, for such an attack, in my judgment, would react in his favour." Mr. Roosevelt stopped and answered: "Mr. Secretary, I want to dictate this letter based on these documents and facts before me with perfect freedom of expression. I want you to listen and form your own judgment and to come back at nine o'clock this evening prepared to make any suggestions or modifications that occur to you." He then went on with his dictation and finished the article or open letter, which I should imagine would have taken the space of a column and a half or two columns of a daily newspaper. At the conclusion of the session which was attended by Secretary Cortelyou of the Treasury, Secretary Straus of the Department of Commerce and Labour, Secretary Meyer of the Navy, and, I think, one other member of the Cabinet whose name I cannot recall (these gentlemen being the only members of the Cabinet in town at the time)—I went back to my hotel much impressed with the fact that I had been a spectator of what was at least an informal Cabinet meeting in action.   I was also impressed with the conviction that the secretary who raised the question about a personal criticism of Mr. Bryan was right in his judgment; and yet I thought I understood, from my conversations with him, Mr. Roosevelt's own point of view. I therefore wrote, and sent to the White House by special messenger, a note something like this:

My Dear Mr. President:
   May I venture to say that it seems to me that Secretary —— was right in deprecating anything that appears like an attack upon Mr. Bryan's personal integrity, but on the other hand I do not understand that you desire to make such an attack.   Is it not your purpose to point out that Mr. Bryan's close association with Governor Haskell, whose methods have been dishonourable, shows not a lack of honour but a lack of wisdom and sound judgment.   What you wish to say to the American people, as I understand you, is that if Mr. Bryan can make so lamentable an error of judgment as to appoint a political spoilsman like Governor Haskell as his right-hand man and lieutenant in this campaign, what guarantee have they that he will not, if elected President, make a similar mistake of judgment in appointing the members of his Cabinet and other officers of the Government ?

Five minutes after this note had gone I would have given a good-sized cheque to get it back.

"What have I done?" I said to myself. "With only a limited acquaintance with the President, I have ventured to send him a letter of advice in a matter in which his Cabinet are his proper advisers! He is reported to carry 'a big stick.' What will happen to me when I go back to him this evening?" For he had invited me to return at nine o'clock to be present when the letter was revised.

I dined with Secretary Meyer and went back to the White House at nine o'clock. As I entered the little study in which this piece of work was done I literally trembled in my shoes. The President was sitting at his desk, in a swivel chair, with his back to the door. He swung around, greeted Secretary Meyer, said good evening to me, and added: "Thank you for your note, Abbott. I was glad to get it. You are right. I shall modify the passage about Mr. Bryan accordingly."

He then asked the three or four members of the Cabinet who had heard him dictate the letter to sit down, and requested each one to read the type-written transcript of the dictation, sheet by sheet, and to make their criticisms. I was also asked to read the pages as they left the hands of the last Cabinet officer. Suggested modifications were freely made by the Cabinet members (I, of course, was merely a silent observer) and were incorporated by Mr. Roosevelt with his own pen, until some of the pages were black with interlineation. Each revised page was sent out to be freshly copied, brought in for the President's final visé, and then sent to the telegraph office downstairs for immediate transmission through the Associated Press. Every suggestion, with one exception, was adopted by Mr. Roosevelt. I think it was Mr. Straus who asked for the modification of one sentence or phrase on the ground that it was a little too severe. The President turned to him and said: "No, Mr. Secretary, I think it should stand as it is. You must remember that this is a poster, not an etching!"

This incident seems to me to be worth recording somewhat fully because it illustrates what was one of Roosevelt's striking characteristics and yet a characteristic which the general public, I think, was not aware of. I mean his constant practice of seeking the facts and complete information about a given matter from any source that he thought would be serviceable. It was this motive that led him to summon me—a comparatively unknown man, holding no public or cabinet position—that we might be able mutually to help each other in giving the public the facts about Governor Haskell. From this incident the reader will also get the impression, and I think it is the correct impression, that Mr. Roosevelt in all his public acts sought advice and followed suggestions. In this instance he summoned those members of his Cabinet who were available, had them give personally and collectively three or four hours' consideration to a newspaper-campaign letter, and invited and adopted their modifications and advice. It was these qualities of coöperation which made his public career on its human side so preëminently successful, and they have always seemed to me to be important traits of his character—so important that I shall recur to them more than once as I proceed.

Roosevelt was not only a staunch advocate of the doctrine of military preparedness—to which, by the way, he gave expression at the age of twenty-two in his "Naval History of the War of 1812," referred to more fully in a later chapter—but practised preparedness in every activity of his life. His desk was always clear, although he wrote more letters probably than any other man of his time. His articles were always finished on the day and the hour when they were promised—often a little beforehand. He pressed his work instead of being pressed by it, and was never confused or worried by an accumulation of duties. He was the busiest man I ever knew, and yet he never seemed to be hurried. In other words, he was a remarkable executive, partly because he knew how to handle men and get them to work, but very largely, I think, because he practised preparedness.

For example, he took with him into the African wilderness a supply of stationery, with sheets of carbon paper like those that are used on the ordinary typewriter, and indelible pencils, and wrote in duplicate by means of the carbon paper, under what to most men would have been impossible conditions, some of his book, "African Game Trails," and at least one of the important addresses that he delivered in Europe. He was distinctly what some of my Yankee forbears would have called "forehanded."

A significant instance of this forehandedness was his first editorial act as a member of the staff of the *Outlook*. He relinquished the Presidency on March 4, 1909, and sailed for Africa on March 23rd. In characteristic fashion, he instantly turned from the work of President to that of editor. Indeed, while still President he had written half a dozen editorial articles and had them all ready for publication. Wednesday, March 10th, was his inauguration day as one of the editorial board. When it came his turn to suggest a topic for editorial consideration he said: "I wonder whether you would be willing to tell the story of the Government's prosecution of the Sugar Trust for its criminal attempt to evade paying customs duties? The Government, in the face of incredible difficulties, has won its case, and the Sugar Trust has been convicted of smuggling sugar by the daily use of a fraudulent device extending over a period of some years. Unfortunately, for mysterious reasons which it is not wholly difficult to explain, the New York daily press has practically ignored the Government's victory and its dramatic incidents, and the public therefore does not know all it should about the crime, and the success of the Government in ferreting it out and punishing it. There may be good reasons why you do not want to go into this matter, but if you do I shall be glad to see that you are supplied with all the facts in the case."

Of course we instantly said that we should be glad to take the matter up and would do all we could, with his help and direction, to make the case public. With a smile he responded: "I rather thought that would be your decision, and so I have taken the liberty of asking United States District Attorney Stimson and his assistant, Mr. Denison, to come here this morning; they are now outside in the reception room with a large bag full of documents and other interesting pieces of evidence that we used in the trial."

Mr. Stimson and Mr. Denison were instantly invited to join us, and they related one of the most dramatic stories of fraud and prosecution that I have ever listened to. They had with them some of the incredibly ingenious and delicate mechanical devices which the Sugar Trust had used in making the scales on the pier where the sugar was unloaded register false weights. The result of this story led us to take the matter up with care, and Mr. Harold J. Howland, of our editorial staff, wrote an article—after a very careful study of the case, aided by both Mr. Stimson and Mr. Denison—entitled: "The Case of the Seventeen Holes." It was published in the *Outlook* a month later, and created something of a sensation. It may be added that Mr. Stimson later became Secretary of War in the Cabinet of President Taft; and Mr. Denison became Secretary of the Interior of the Philippine Islands and member of the Philippine Commission.

It seems worth while to make these brief records of Mr. Roosevelt's essays in journalism because probably it was the first time in the history of the United States that an ex-President had chosen journalism as his professional career on returning to private life. After leaving the *Outlook* in 1914,

Mr. Roosevelt became editorially associated with the *Metropolitan Magazine*, and, still later, an editorial contributor to the Kansas City *Star*. Thus he was engaged in active journalism for ten years from the time he ceased to be President in 1909 until his death. Indeed, he wrote editorials for the Kansas City *Star* almost up to the very hour of his death, for one of his last acts, the evening before he suddenly and unexpectedly passed away, was to correct the proof of a *Star* editorial. His success as a journalist is only another striking illustration of his almost unmatched versatility. Historians say that he might have been a historian; biologists and zoölogists, that he might have been a scientific naturalist; soldiers, that he would have made a great professional soldier. It is equally clear that if the environment of his early life had so influenced him he might have become a great newspaper editor. He had the instinct for news and the faculty for interesting the public in it. He also had what is more important, but too often lost sight of in modern journalism: definite views as to the moral standards which ought to apply to the trade or profession of newspaper men as rigorously as the ethics of the medical profession or the obligations of the Hippocratic oath apply to doctors. In his first editorial he used these words of one of the banes of American newspaper life:

Yellow journalism deifies the cult of the mendacious, the sensational, and the inane, and, throughout its wide but vapid field, does as much to vulgarize and degrade the popular taste, to weaken the popular character, and to dull the edge of the popular conscience, as any influence under which the country can suffer. These men sneer at the very idea of paying heed to the dictates of a sound morality; as one of their number has cynically put it, they are concerned merely with selling the public whatever the public will buy— a theory of conduct which would justify the existence of every keeper of an opium den, of every foul creature who ministers to the vices of mankind.

To these words he added the comment upon his new editorial associates that "it is perhaps not especially to their credit that they have avoided this pit; fortunately they are so constituted that it is a simple impossibility for them to fall into it." He defined his journalistic creed as follows: "It is not given to humanity never to err"; but the right-minded editor "makes a resolute effort to find out what the facts actually are before passing judgment." He "believes that things in this world can be made better," but he "does not indorse quixotic movements which would merely leave things worse." He "feels a peculiar desire to do all that can be done for the poor and the oppressed, and to help upward those struggling to better themselves"; but he "has no sympathy with moral weakness or sentimentality." All that he can he "does and will do for the cause of labour;" but he "will in no shape or way condone violence or disorder." He "stands for the rights of property, and therefore against the abuses of property." He "believes in a wise individualism, and in encouragement of individual initiative; and therefore all the more . . . in using the collective force of the whole people to do what, but for the use of that collective force, must be left undone."

It may not be inappropriate to conclude this chapter of journalistic reminiscences with one of the amusing incidents connected with Mr. Roosevelt's new journalistic venture; I say "amusing," although at the time it was vexatious and disturbing.

The late James Stillman, one of the foremost railway financiers and bankers of the United States, had been for more than thirty years a personal friend as well as a neighbour of my father and had aided him in the purchase of the journal which later became the *Outlook*. The result was that he was a stockholder in the *Outlook* Company although he owned less than a tenth interest.

In becoming a stockholder he had simply performed a generous act for a personal friend and he had never in any way attempted to influence the policy of the paper. He had never even attended a stockholders' meeting either in person or by proxy. He was in 1909 closely associated with the Standard Oil Company both through family and financial connections. A New York daily newspaper in search of a sensation announced that Mr. Stillman was a stockholder of the *Outlook* and that, therefore, Mr. Roosevelt had connected himself with a journal controlled by the Standard Oil Company. In view of Mr. Roosevelt's attitude at that time toward the great corporations and the proceedings at law which his administration had instituted against the Standard Oil Company, the newspapers took this piece of gossip up and it created a lively though temporary furore. The facts were frankly stated in the pages of the *Outlook*, and Mr. Roosevelt himself, in November, 1908, made the following statement through the public press:

The President has not the slightest concern with the question as to who are the stockholders of the *Outlook*. His concern is with the general policy of the paper, which is and has been consistently admirable in every respect. The President will be responsible only for what he himself writes;

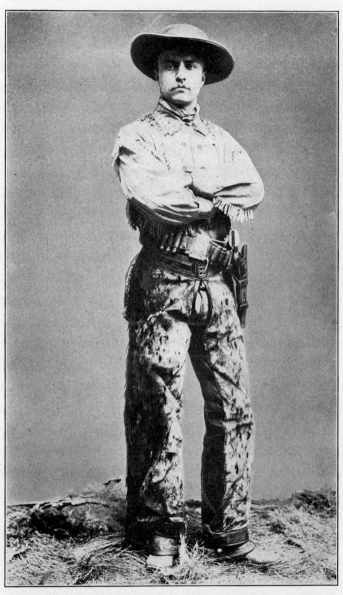

Theodore Roosevelt in 1885. This picture was taken in
North Dakota four years after Joe Murray started Mr.
Roosevelt's political career

and his probable future attitude must be judged by his action
in the past.

Referring to this episode President Roosevelt
wrote me from the White House on November 14,
1908:

> You need not be in the least sorry. I was not caused the
slightest annoyance by the statement about the Standard
Oil control of the paper. On the contrary, the only effect
was to give the heartiest enjoyment to the entire Cabinet at
the Cabinet meeting—and the Cabinet meetings are rarely
melancholy anyhow! I wanted very much to issue a statement to the effect that if the Standard Oil really controlled
the *Outlook*, I thought they must have experienced a change
of heart when they hired me to write editorials for it! But
I thought it was not worth while. Last summer your father
told me substantially what you tell me now, namely, that
. . . Mr. Stillman who was an old friend and neighbour
. . . owned less than a tenth of the stock, and never
made any effort to influence the course of the paper. It was
on the tip of my tongue to say that that was self-evident
from all I had seen in the paper, but I did not say so because
I was afraid your dear father might think I was speaking
a little harshly of Mr. Stillman. Let me say that I have
never heard anything to Mr. Stillman's discredit.

The spirit of this note is one that actuated Theodore Roosevelt in all his journalistic relations.
He was quick to see the good in every man and
while in controversy he often "got mad," to use
the vivid expression of boyhood, he never stayed

mad nor cherished resentments of any kind.   He
was always ready to renew friendly relations with
an antagonist unless they had been broken because of some fundamental vicious streak in his
opponent which could not be remedied by any kind
of readjustment.

CHAPTER II

POLITICS

THEODORE ROOSEVELT was born into the Republican party as inevitably as Woodrow Wilson was born a Democrat, a fact which may well arouse some curious and interesting speculation about the influence of birth and heredity upon statesmanship and national history. If Roosevelt's father had been a Southerner, as his mother was, and Theodore had been born at "Roswell," the maternal family homestead in Georgia, it is quite possible, perhaps even probable, that he would have become a member of the Democratic party. But his ancestry and surroundings in New York being what they were, it was as natural for him to attach himself to the Republican party as it was to go to Harvard College. In fact, in his autobiography he intimates as much himself in these words:

At that day, in 1880, a young man of my bringing up and convictions could join only the Republican party, and join it I accordingly did. It was no simple thing to join it then. That was long before the era of ballot reform and the control of primaries; long before the era when we realized that the Government must take official notice of the deeds and acts of party organizations. The party was still treated as a private corporation, and in each district the organization formed a kind of social and political club. A man had to be regularly proposed for and elected into this club, just as into any other club. As a friend of mine picturesquely phrased it, I "had to break into the organization with a jimmy."

Had Theodore Roosevelt become a scientific naturalist, as Father Zahm thinks he might have, or a historian and man of letters, as Brander Matthews almost wishes he had, he would doubtless have habitually voted the Republican ticket although his energies would never have been devoted to political administration. But since his career was that of a statesman it is interesting to know how it happened that, at twenty-two years of age, he became a Republican office-holder and thus entered upon an active political life.

Various people have claimed the honour of first suggesting his name as a Republican candidate for the New York Legislature. The matter, however, is easily settled on Theodore Roosevelt's own authority. He says that the man who launched him into practical politics was Joe Murray, a Republican leader—"lesser captain" Mr. Roosevelt calls him —in the twenty-first district Republican Association in the City of New York. In one of the most

entertaining and readable chapters of his autobiography Mr. Roosevelt tells the story and testi-
fies to his respect and friendship for Joe Murray.
Joe Murray's version of this important episode in
the life of the future President of the United States
has never yet, so far as I know, been publicly told,
and I am fortunate in being able to reproduce it
here. I came into possession of the story, which
I shall proceed to relate in Mr. Murray's own
words, in this way.

In 1910, when Theodore Roosevelt returned from
his memorable trip through Africa and Europe, he
was appealed to by a group of younger men in the
Republican party to aid them in attempting to
wrest the party control from the hands of the so-
called "Old Guard." He somewhat reluctantly
consented, as will appear hereafter, and went to
the State Republican Convention at Saratoga as
an ordinary delegate from Nassau County. I happened to be elected to the same convention as an
alternate delegate from my own county, Orange. I
went from New York to Saratoga in company with
Mr. Roosevelt. On the train he introduced me to
a strong, vigorous, ruddy-faced man of about sixty,
saying: "I want you to know my friend, Joe Murray. He started me in politics. Take him into the
smoking room and get him to tell you the story."

Whereupon Murray and I went into the smoking compartment of the parlour car and he told me in a most entertaining fashion how he happened in 1881 to pick Theodore Roosevelt as a candidate for the Legislature. The main points and the agreeable flavour of Joe Murray's story have remained with me ever since. But in order to be verbally accurate I got him to come to my office not long after Mr. Roosevelt's death and tell me the story again. I am sure that Mr. Murray will not object to my giving his colloquial and intimate language just as it fell from his lips, for it constitutes, I think, a human document of both charm and importance in the record of Theodore Roosevelt's political career. Incidentally, it reveals some of the methods of American politics at the time when Roosevelt was getting his first impressions of the need of social, industrial, and political reforms. This is the story, *verbatim et literatim*, taken down stenographically as Joe Murray told me how he first met young Roosevelt:

JOE MURRAY'S STORY

In 1881 Jake Hess was the leader in the Republican Twenty-first Assembly District organization of this city, the boundaries of which were the north side of Fortieth Street, the south side of Fifty-ninth Street, the east side of Seventh Avenue, and the west side of Lexington Avenue. Its headquarters were Morton Hall at Fifty-ninth Street and Fifth Avenue, on the southeast corner. At that time a hotel had been started there by Tweed, but was never completed. The iron frame-work was partitioned off, and our organization occupied a portion of it, with stores underneath. The portion which we occupied was known as Morton Hall.

In those days I believed in the organization and I do now to a very large extent, but I did not think it was infallible. It makes mistakes. I believe to keep the party strong it is necessary to keep it pure.

In 1881, after the district was portioned off, we elected a man for the Legislature. The newspapers made a rather severe attack on him, and Major Bullard, who was one of the leaders in our organization, and myself had an idea that if he was renominated it would be necessary for us to have a defensive campaign, which is not a good thing for a Republican candidate. This Assemblyman had supported Platt and Conkling, the state bosses, in the previous Legislature, and they wanted him renominated, if he desired it, as a reward for his loyalty. Major Bullard and myself did not think he could be elected, and we considered that it would be a disaster to the Republican party to have the Twenty-first District go Democratic. Jake Hess wanted to follow the wishes of the State bosses, Platt and Conkling, and intended to nominate this man even if he couldn't be elected.

Hess was at that time one of the Commissioners of Charities and Corrections, and was of course a very influential man in the party, while I was more or less insignificant compared to him. He and Major Bullard and I got together to arrange a ticket for the coming primaries.

What Hess and Bullard and myself had to do was to pick out the delegates to be elected to the conventions, including the Assembly Convention which was going to nominate our candidate from the district. Hess wanted me as a delegate to the Congressional Convention and also to the Senatorial Convention because I was familiar with the routine; but I wanted, although I did not say so, to have a part in the Assembly Convention in order to prevent the renomination of this weak candidate that I have already spoken of. I assented to Hess's wishes and was a delegate, but I paid no attention to either the Senatorial or the Congressional Convention. Of course we knew beforehand that William Waldorf Astor was to be our Congressional candidate. What I wanted to give my special attention to was the Assembly Convention, although I was not a regular delegate. As a matter of fact, while I was not a delegate to the Assembly Convention, Major Bullard and I named fifteen out of the twenty-five delegates to this convention among our personal friends on whom we could depend.

Major Bullard, like myself, was a veteran of the Civil War. He and I went down to see Hess at the office of the Commissioner of Charities on Third Avenue, and there we met the candidate who represented the district the year previous and was seeking renomination. We took a walk over to the Sinclair House to get a drink. Bullard and Hess walked ahead, the Assemblyman and I were behind them. On the way over the Assemblyman says to me: "Joe, don't you think I ought to get a larger vote this year than I did a year ago?" I says: "For what?" He says: "For the Assembly, of course. You know I am better known now than I was then." I says: "Well, you're certainly better known. The fact of it is that anybody who knows you wouldn't vote for you." He says: "You'd vote for me, wouldn't you?" "Billy," I says, "I know a trick or two better than that. I wouldn't do anything of the kind."

So after we got to the bar-room he was particularly anxious to get away from me in order to talk to Hess. (Up to this time Hess knew nothing about this or about the position which Bullard and I were taking. But the delegates had been picked and he could not do anything.) After awhile, however, the prospective candidate got away. He went over to Hess, and after talking with him a very short time I

Mr. Roosevelt as a member of the New York Assembly

Theodore Roosevelt, Civil Service Commissioner, 1889 to 1895

saw Hess look over at me. We had our drink and went out.
Hess then says to me: "Billy tells me that you are opposed
to him." I says: "Yes." "Well," he says, "he will be
nominated anyway. You don't amount to anything." I
says: "No? Well, I don't amount to much, but if Billy goes
up to the Legislature he certainly will not be indebted to Joe
Murray!"

Of course Hess had a copy of the list of delegates selected—
the primary ticket—and he sent a man named Jake Weller
and his brother Charlie around to see the different delegates.
Some of them told these men that they had not made up
their minds; but the majority of them said: "Charlie, I
should like to do you a favour very much, but I promised Joe
Murray to vote for his candidate." When we had reached
this point Major Bullard and I were sure of the convention.
Now the thing to do was to get a candidate.

A night or two after this talk at the Sinclair House Mr.
Roosevelt came around to a regular meeting at Morton Hall
to enter his protest against the renomination of the candidate
that the county organization desired to have renominated.
So I spoke to young Roosevelt that night. I told him that
I was also opposed to the renomination of the regular candidate and that I was looking around to try to get a suitable
candidate. I had seen young Roosevelt at the meetings of
the organization. My first interest in him was that of a vote-
getter. It was later that I became interested in him as a man.

At that time Columbia College was in the district. His
father figured more or less prominently in philanthropy, and
the name was a good one. In addition to that, I thought
I would interest the football team of Columbia, the baseball
team, and the other different athletes connected with the
College, together with the professors, among the most prominent of whom was Professor Van Amringe. Later, this professor got out and worked like a beaver.

When I asked young Roosevelt if he would take the nomination, he says: "No, I wouldn't dream of such a thing. It

would look as though I had had selfish motives in coming around to oppose this man." "Well," I says, "get me a desirable candidate." "Oh," he says, "you won't have any trouble." "Well," I says, "it looks kind of easy, but so far I have not been able to get a candidate—the kind of a candidate that the Major and I think is a suitable one. We want to get the strongest one we can."

So finally he promised to look around. By that time I made up my mind that it was Theodore Roosevelt or no one. Of course I did not tell him so. We parted that night, and I met him by appointment the next night. I forget now whether he asked me if I had a candidate or whether I asked him if he had found any one. Neither one of us had one. I says: "The convention meets in a couple of nights and we have got this man beaten, but we have no candidate. What excuse can we give to the organization for not renominating this man when we have no candidate?"

"We won't have any trouble in getting a candidate," says Roosevelt.

I says: "I hope not, but Mr. Roosevelt, in case we can't get a suitable candidate, will you take the nomination?"

He hesitated a moment, and says: "Yes, but I don't want it. In the meantime, I want you to promise me that if you can find a suitable man, have no hesitancy about nominating him and do not take me into consideration."

I says: "All right, I'll do it." But I knew what I was going to do. So I met him the next night, and I reached out to shake hands with him, and instead of taking one hand he grabbed both hands.

He says: "Mr. Murray, I have done you a great injustice. I had an idea that you were guying me. I met our friend, Mr. Edward Mitchell [afterwards United States District Attorney and one of the Trustees of Columbia College at the time] this morning. I had a talk with him, and I told him about my conversation with Mr. Murray. He said: 'Mister Murray? Do you mean Joe Murray?' I said,

'Yes.' He said: 'Mr. Roosevelt, did he tell you he would nominate you?' I said 'Yes.' And Mitchell answered me and said: 'Well, Joe is not in the habit of making statements that he cannot make good. There is one thing I'll tell you. You have fallen into very good hands.'"

"Oh," I says, when Mr. Roosevelt finished his story about Mitchell, "that's all right." Afterward he made me say that I should have no hesitancy about pulling him out if I could get another candidate.

The Convention met a couple of nights after that. Hess started around to capture my delegates. I had an idea that two could play at that game. Therefore while he was trying to capture four or five of my delegates, I happened to capture one of his; so, instead of the vote being fifteen to ten, it was sixteen to nine.

After his nomination Theodore Roosevelt, Hess, Bullard, and I went out on a personal canvass. It was the custom in those days to visit the gin-mills, the stores, and places of business. The first place we happened to go into was the lager-beer saloon on Sixth Avenue, near Fifty-fifth Street kept by a German named Fischer. Hess introduced Mr. Roosevelt to the proprietor as the candidate for Assembly. Mr. Fischer says to him: "Well, Mr. Roosevelt, the liquor interest has not been getting a square deal. We are paying excessive taxes. I have no doubt that you will try to give us some relief when you get up to the Legislature." (One of the grievances of Mr. Fischer was that the license was too high.) Mr. Roosevelt asked him: "Mr. Fischer, what is the license now?" Mr. Fischer named the figure—what he had to pay—and Mr. Roosevelt says, "Well, that's not right. I don't think you pay enough. I thought it would be at least twice as much!"

After that we hustled him out and told him that he had better see to the college boys and his friends on Fifth Avenue, the society folks; that Hess, Bullard, and I would do the other end.

I took charge of his canvass. Mr. Roosevelt referred a great many of his friends to me to find out what they could do, among them being Professor Van Amringe—I recollect him because he was more active than the others. Quite a few of the football team, two-thirds of the baseball team, and the boxing club and the wrestlers came down to see what they could do. I told them to go around to see their friends. They wanted to know, however, what they could do on Election Day. I told them that they could stand at the booths and ask their friends, irrespective of politics, to vote for Roosevelt. But a very large majority wanted to know where the tough districts were. I wanted to send them to the dude districts where they belonged, as I thought, but they thought they would be of more service where there was more fighting to be done. So the districts that we considered difficult to carry were the ones that were particularly well manned. In fact, we had ten men where under ordinary circumstances we would only send one. There were no special difficulties in the election, for the simple reason that the Tammany men knew what was coming to them if they started any rough house.

Some of Mr. Roosevelt's friends who had "inside information," as they thought, came around and told him that I was an organization man, and that we wanted to elect Mr. Astor at all hazards; that he was simply put up for trading purposes in order to get votes for Astor from the Democrats, while in return we would vote for the Democratic candidate for Assembly. There were twenty-five election districts, and we only carried twenty-three out of the twenty-five for Roosevelt. It did not look, therefore, as though we had done much trading. The fact of the matter is there might have been some trading, but if there was we did not get the worst of it. As Mr. Roosevelt has said in his autobiography, it was a question between Jake Hess and Joe Murray. If Mr. Roosevelt was beaten Mr. Murray was beaten, and Joe could not afford to have himself beaten.

Is it not a matter of satisfaction, a source of a
kind of affectionate pride to those who believe in
American democracy, that Theodore Roosevelt
had this kind of introduction, thus described by
Joe Murray, into the career which was eventually
to make him one of the great figures of world history? There is certainly a distinctively American
flavour in the fact that the Irish immigrant of simple origin and the native American of aristocratic
lineage thus formed a political and personal acquaintanceship which ripened into a friendship
that lasted until the day of the ex-President's
death. It reveals a certain endearing human quality in Theodore Roosevelt to know that he often
expressed his sense of indebtedness to Murray
as though the latter had been one of his earliest
preceptors in the practice and philosophy of politics. Indeed, he says of Murray in his autobiography:

We never parted company excepting on the question of
Civil Service Reform, where he sincerely felt that I showed
doctrinaire affinities, that I sided with the Pharisees. We
got back again into close relations as soon as I became Police
Commissioner under Mayor Strong, for Joe was then made
Excise Commissioner, and was, I believe, the best Excise
Commissioner the city of New York ever had. He is now a
farmer, his boys have been through Columbia College, and
he and I look at the questions, political, social, and industrial,

which confront us in 1913, from practically the same stand-point, just as we once looked at the questions that confronted us in 1881.

Theodore Roosevelt's political creed was indeed, from the very beginning, a distinctively human one. He liked men of all sorts and conditions of life so long as they were really men. He was not a "hail fellow well met" of the shoulder-slapping variety. No man knew better than he how to command respect and how to preserve his own dignity. But when he formed a friendship—and no man of our time has had wider, deeper, or more varied friendships—his personal relations with his friends were natural, simple, and confident. For him, a fundamentally good quality in a man covered, like charity, a multitude of sins, which would have repelled a more austere and exacting judge. At the same time his own standards were extraordinarily high and consistent. Yet he was often accused of associating and working with political publicans and sinners—by men whom it is perhaps not unfair to call political Pharisees. This apparent anomaly was clearly seen to be no anomaly at all by those who understood his own doctrine of political association. It was once expressed by him to his intimate friend, Jacob Riis, in a picturesque and illuminating fashion: "I suppose,"

he said, speaking of his earliest experiences in the
New York Legislature, "that my head was swelled.
It would not be strange if it was. I stood out for
my own opinion alone. I took the best 'mugwump' stand—my own conscience, my own judgment were to decide in all things. I would listen
to no argument, no advice. I took the isolated
peak on every issue, and my associates left me.
When I looked around, before the session was well
under way, I found myself alone. I was absolutely
deserted. The people didn't understand. The
men from Erie, from Suffolk, from anywhere, would
not work with me. 'He won't listen to anybody,'
they said, and I would not. My isolated peak had
become a valley; every bit of influence I had had
was gone. The things I wanted to do I was power-
less to accomplish. I looked the ground over, and
made up my mind that there were several other
excellent people there, with honest opinions of the
right, even though they differed from me. I turned
in to help them, and they turned to and gave me a
hand. And so we were able to get things done.
We did not agree in all things, but we did in some,
and those we pulled at together. That was my
first lesson in real politics. It is just this: if you
are cast on a desert island with only a screwdriver,
a hatchet, and a chisel to make a boat with, why,

go make the best one you can. It would be better if you had a saw, but you haven't. So with men. Here is my friend in Congress who is a good man, a strong man, but cannot be made to believe in some things in which I trust. It is too bad that he doesn't look at it as I do, but he *does not*, and we have to work together as we can. There is a point, of course, where a man must take the isolated peak and break with all his associates for clear principle: but until that time comes he must work, if he would be of use, with men as they are. As long as the good in them overbalances the evil, let him work with them for the best that can be obtained."

One of the common virtues that most strongly appealed to him, socially as well as politically, was dependability. He was chary of making promises himself but when he did make them he kept them and he expected other men to do so, too. No Republican leader of the late eighties was more generally charged with being pastmaster in all the arts and finesse of reactionary and corrupt machine politics than Senator Matthew Quay of Pennsylvania, popularly known as "Matt" Quay. Now Roosevelt had not the slightest toleration for corruption of any kind, but I have heard him more than once defend "Matt" Quay against attacks on the ground that when Quay made a promise to perform a certain act or to take a certain course that he could be depended upon to carry out that promise no matter what the political cost to his own interests might be. And I have also heard him in the same spirit criticize with almost extravagant severity a great leader of the Republican party, whom the people at large regarded as a shining exemplar of uprightness and high principles, because this leader would make a promise and then fail to carry it out loyally and energetically.

McKinley

There naturally was never a warm friendship between this leader and Mr. Roosevelt, a lack of friendship which by Mr. Roosevelt's critics was sometimes ascribed to jealousy—a wholly mistaken diagnosis, in my judgment. There was not a tinge of jealousy in Theodore Roosevelt's disposition. He was, however, attracted by loyalty and dependability and repelled by what he thought to be austere or selfish aloofness.

As an illustration I may perhaps without impropriety refer to his relations with Senator Root who was Secretary of War and Secretary of State in the Cabinet of President Roosevelt, and whom Mr. Roosevelt often named as one of the ablest, wisest, and most patriotic statesmen that the country has ever produced. In 1912, when Roosevelt left the Republican party after being defeated for the presidential nomination by methods which he thought were unjust and un-American, and by an unparalleled stroke of political skill formed the Progressive party and became its presidential nominee, his political and personal relations with Mr. Root were severed. But while in that hot and bitter campaign he denounced others among his political opponents in terms that sometimes had the flavour of primitive man, I never heard him once, either in private or in public, utter a personal criticism of Mr. Root. Indeed he defended Mr. Root against the criticisms of his (Roosevelt's), own friends who felt resentment that Mr. Root's rulings as chairman of the Republican National Convention had deprived Roosevelt of the nomination which the people at large really wished him to have. More than once I have heard him say when Mr. Root's "steam-roller" methods of seating and unseating delegates at the Convention were denounced as inexplicable disloyalty to his former Chief: "No, you are wrong. It was not disloyal. Elihu Root has the legal temperament developed to a high degree. His first duty he conscientiously believes is to his client. When he was a practising lawyer before going into the Government the corporations were his clients, and he was for the corporations. When he became a

member of my Cabinet the United States was his
client, and he was for the United States and against
the corporations. As chairman of that convention
the Republican party and its managers were Root's
clients, and he was for them and against me."

The fact is that Roosevelt respected, I think it
may be even said that he admired, this quality of
loyalty in Mr. Root, although he believed it to be
misdirected in the campaign of 1912 and felt that
he was unjustly a sufferer from the misdirection.

Theodore Roosevelt's career both as a politician
and a statesman—I say politician and statesman
because I think there is a real distinction between
the two which I shall try to make clear in a later
chapter—was consistent, coherent, and coördinated.
This statement may be challenged. For his public
life was broken up, so to speak, into so many brilliant and dramatic episodes that these episodes, to
the observer, sometimes seemed to be wholly unre-
lated and not infrequently antagonistic.

For example, in 1884 Roosevelt was a delegate
to the National Republican Convention which
nominated James G. Blaine for the Presidency.
He opposed that nomination and fought vigorously
in behalf of the candidacy of Senator George F.
Edmunds of Vermont. But Mr. Blaine was nominated. In spite of his ability and brilliance there

were some financial incidents in his political career which were repellent to a large wing of the Republican party who were then, as Mr. Roosevelt was, working for the reënforcement of the principle of common honesty in practical politics. This group of Republicans bolted the nomination, forming what was then known as the "mugwump" group, and supported Mr. Cleveland, the Democratic candidate. Although Roosevelt was only twenty-five years old he had made himself a figure in the convention as well as in the party. It was thought by the leading "mugwumps" that he would sympathize with them and join them in their support of Cleveland. They were mistaken, however. He supported Blaine, and gave his reasons for so doing in the following public statement:

I intend to vote the Republican Presidential ticket. A man cannot act both without and within the party; he can do either, but he cannot possibly do both. Each course has its advantages, and each has its disadvantages, and one cannot take the advantages or the disadvantages separately. I went in with my eyes open to do what I could within the party; I did my best and got beaten, and I propose to stand by the result.

Was his action in the Blaine campaign consistent with his action in 1912 when he bolted the nomination of Mr. Taft, formed the Progressive party, and ran as a candidate for President himself? The consistency, it seems to me, is a very real one. It is found in the statement made to Jacob Riis which I have quoted earlier in this chapter: "There is a point where a man must take the isolated peak and break with all his associates for clear principle: but until that time comes he must work, if he would be of use, with men as they are. As long as the good in them overbalances the evil let him work with them for the best that can be obtained."

In 1884 he believed that it was his duty to work with the Republican organization. In 1912 he believed the time had come to take to the "isolated peak" and to summon his supporters to join him. Both actions, seemingly so contradictory, were based upon, and were the logical result of, a fundamental political and moral philosophy. I propose in the next chapter to try to outline why Theodore Roosevelt was led to create the Progressive party and to oppose the candidacy of Mr. Taft—the most dramatic and outstanding event in his career as a political manager.

CHAPTER III

THE PROGRESSIVE PARTY

WHEN Roosevelt emerged from the African wilderness in March, 1910, I met him at Khartum in the desert on the edge of the jungle, fifteen hundred miles up the river Nile from Cairo. He had no sooner discarded the trappings of the jungle—and rather ragged and dilapidated trappings they were—and resumed the garb of the civilian *en grand tour*—in his case this garb was always simple and unaffected though appropriate—than he was confronted with all sorts of invitations to take up politics again. These invitations were conveyed by letter, cablegram, and even by personal delegation. He was asked to become a candidate for mayor of the City of New York and for senator from the State of New York, for example. All these invitations he declined with decision and without discussion. In more than one conversation he declared that his greatest desire, his sole ambition, was to return to his home at Sagamore Hill, Oyster Bay, for which I know, as do all his friends, that he had a deep and abiding affec-

tion.   There it was his plan, he said, to live the life
of a country gentleman, spending his time out of
doors in the countryside which he knew so well,
and his time indoors in study, reading, and in writing on historical, scientific, or political questions,
with such occasional public speaking as might be
appropriate.   I am reminded of what Roosevelt
said at that time by an incident related by Brander
Matthews in a note which I received from him after
Roosevelt's death:

I think it was in February, 1893, that we spent a week
in Washington.   We dined one night with the Roosevelts.
I made some pleasant allusion to his future in public life.
He looked at me, seriously and almost sadly. (Roosevelt
was then Civil Service Commissioner.)   Then he said: "My
future?   How can I have a future in public life?   Don't you
know as Civil Service Commissioner I have made an enemy
of every professional politician in the United States?   I can't
have any political prospects."
I retorted that he would be President sooner or later.
Whereupon he smiled and asked, "Then what will you want?"
And then I smiled and answered: "I think I would rather go
to London."

In this same vein Roosevelt said to me in Khartum: "My political career is ended.   No man in
American public life has ever reached the crest of
the wave as I appear to have done without the
wave's breaking and engulfing him.   Remember
Dewey."

In reply I told him I did not think the two cases were at all parallel; that the American people knew him, Roosevelt, after thirty years of trial in the whitest kind of light; that his acts, achievements, and character were tested and understood; and that the people had taken him into their confidence and affection permanently, for better or for worse. On the other hand, I argued that Dewey had suddenly been seized upon as a kind of idol by the American people, not because they knew him very well, but because of one great dramatic episode; and that when he did something which they disliked they discarded him, although unjustly, without any wrench or sense of personal loss. "No," insisted Roosevelt, "I am going down like Dewey." More than once during our journey through Europe he referred to this assumed parallel in his career and that of the hero of the Naval Battle at Manila. "Remember Dewey" became almost a slogan or shibboleth in our political conversations, although Roosevelt used it not jocosely but very seriously.

Coming back on the steamer from Southampton to New York in June of that year, the usual entertainment given in the saloon, for the benefit of some seamen's fund or other, took the form of a "chalk talk" by the late Homer Davenport, then one of the foremost of American newspaper cartoonists. The passenger list of the ship was a very large one, many people choosing this particular steamer because Roosevelt was on it, and the saloon

"He's good enough for all of us!"

A Davenport cartoon of the presidential campaign of 1904 in which Mr. Bryan was thought to be not wholly averse to Judge Parker's defeat

on the evening when Davenport spoke was crowded to its extreme capacity. Davenport's "chalk talks" consisted of a series of stories, usually humorous, each one being illustrated by a picture or a portrait which he rapidly drew with black crayon on a very large-sized pad of brown paper placed on an easel in sight of the audience. On this particular evening the last story which he told was one about Admiral Dewey. The story, somewhat condensed, ran about as follows:

At the time when Admiral Dewey was being bitterly attacked in the newspapers, and criticized throughout the country because of the disposition which he made of the house presented to him in honour of his victory at Manila, I published in one of the newspapers a cartoon in his defense. I thought the Admiral was most outrageously treated, and I rather laid myself out to make the cartoon a striking and effective one. A few days after it was published a friend of mine who knew Dewey met me on the street in New York and said: "Dewey has seen your cartoon and wants to see you. Will you go over to Washington?" "Sure," I replied. We went over, and my friend took me to the Admiral's house. We entered the drawing room; I was presented to Mrs. Dewey; and just as the Admiral came forward to give me his hand, he burst into tears and threw himself upon a sofa in a paroxysm of weeping. Mrs. Dewey apologized and said: "You must excuse the Admiral, Mr. Davenport. He has been wrought almost to a pitch of nervous prostration by the unjust attacks made upon him. We had decided to go to Europe, never to set foot on American soil again, and had actually packed our trunks when we saw your cartoon. It was the first ray of light, and made us change our minds, and we have decided to remain in America, although some of our trunks are still upstairs just as we packed them for our departure."

Davenport thereupon rapidly sketched a portrait of Admiral Dewey and his talk or lecture was finished. There were calls for Mr. Roosevelt. He rose:

"Mr. Davenport," said he, "may I ask if the story you have just related of Admiral Dewey is accurate in all its details, or have you taken the pardonable liberty of an artist and put in a little colour?"

"No," answered Davenport, "the incident is just as I related it, in every detail."

Whereupon Mr. Roosevelt paid an eloquent tribute to Dewey, defending him from the attacks that had been made upon him, and, after thanking Davenport, sat down. I happened to be next to him, and immediately on taking his seat he turned to me, and—recalling the numerous times in the month or two preceding in which he had remarked that he was "going down like Dewey"—said, *sotto voce*, "Lawrence, they may treat me like Dewey, but I'll tell you one thing, I shall neither weep nor shall I go to Europe!"

Unhappily first the country and then the Government did treat him like Dewey, but he neither wept nor did he abandon his country. He did not even show resentment or disappointment, but kept up his fight to the very end, in the greatest good spirits. His buoyancy, his capacity to rise superior to all external disappointments, was, I think, one of his greatest qualities.

When Roosevelt arrived in New York in June, 1910, after more than a year's absence, and after President Taft's Administration had been in power for more than a year, he found the Republican party in a condition of chaos, if not completely disrupted. He believed that under the leaders then in control the party was going backward, that instead of being a party of progress it was becoming a party of reaction. His foresight was confirmed in the autumn by the Democratic victories and especially by the loss to the Republican party of Ohio, President Taft's own state. The disruption was caused by "Cannonism" the term used to describe Speaker "Joe" Cannon's control of party councils and party legislation, by the controversy over the Ballinger case and by Mr. Taft's apparent indecision and inconsistent public utterances on the tariff question. This domination of the reactionary group led some of the younger and forward-looking men in the party to make a protest. It was rebellion, and was in fact called the Insurgent Movement. It is well to remember that the Insurgents (so-called) of 1910 were the direct political progenitors of the Progressives of 1912.

It is, of course, a fact that not long after his return from Europe in 1910 Mr. Roosevelt did plunge into active politics again, was elected a delegate to the State Republican Convention at Saratoga, and made himself the leader of that convention, not by "steam-roller methods"—for he did not possess the power of official authority—but by the sheer force of his personal influence and persuasive argument. He not only did not shut off debate but contended that the "Old Guard," or Reactionary Group, should have complete freedom of discussion and the right to vote untrammelled by any technical procedure. It was the most open and, in the best sense of the word, the most democratic convention that New York had seen for a long time. Roosevelt's candidate for governor, Mr. Henry L. Stimson—later from 1911 to 1913 Secretary of War—was nominated for governor although he was defeated for election in the autumn by Mr. Dix, the Democratic candidate. Mr. Stimson's defeat at the polls was regarded as a defeat for Roosevelt, and his opponents asserted that it meant the elimination of his active influence or authority in American politics. But in this judgment they were as mistaken as he himself had been when he compared himself to Admiral Dewey.

How is it possible to reconcile Mr. Roosevelt's professions that he wished to keep out of active politics and had no ambition for political preferment, with his political activities in the summer of

1910, his organization of the Progressive party in 1912, and his candidacy for President under the auspices of that party? It was commonly said at the time, and is perhaps now believed by some people, that his course was prompted by the desire to destroy Mr. Taft politically because of rancour and antagonism that had sprung up between them. Fortunately I have in my possession a document which may throw some light upon this question.

I had known through intimate association with Mr. Roosevelt of all the incidents which had led to the estrangement between himself and Mr. Taft. In the various political contests between 1910 and 1912 people had not infrequently come to me and asked for the facts, or had made statements to me that I knew were not accurate. I finally went to Mr. Roosevelt and asked his permission to describe the situation as I knew it, permission being necessary, I thought, because my knowledge had been acquired through confidential relationships. For example, when he left New York for Africa, in March, 1909, I went with him, by invitation, to the steamer on which he sailed. Just before the ship pulled out into the stream I asked whether there were not something I could do of final service. "Yes," he said, "I wish you would send a telegram to Taft." I thereupon sat down at a table in the suite of rooms which he was to occupy and took down in long hand, at his dictation, a message—which I later despatched myself to Mr. Taft—a cordial and warm-hearted telegram bidding his old friend, now his successor in the White House, good-bye.

I later learned that Mr. Roosevelt never received any reply or acknowledgment of his telegram, and that the first communication which came to him from Mr. Taft was not received until a year and three months later, when he arrived in London, although friends and acquaintances, and even strangers, had sent him, when he reached Khartum, cablegrams and letters of congratulation on his success in passing through the dangers of his African journey. This letter from Mr. Taft, written in his own hand, was received by Roosevelt in London in June, 1910. It stated the political difficulties into which the Republican party had been plunged and asked Mr. Roosevelt's counsel and help in extricating the party from those difficulties.

On receiving Mr. Roosevelt's permission to make public, as I saw fit, such facts as these and others I wrote in January, 1912, for the weekly paper in my own home town—the Cornwall, New York *Local Press*—an article which was stated by the editor to give "some facts concerning the personal relations of President Taft and Mr. Roosevelt presidential timber, and in my judgment would have made a great President, but there was at that time throughout the country such a feeling of antagonism towards the great corporations and so-called trusts,that it was believed that Mr Root's reputation as a great corporation lawyer might endanger his election This was especially feared in view of the fact that Mr Bryan was likely to make an anti-corporation campaign.

It is easy enough now to look back and feel that probably any high-minded Republican could have been elected, but those who remember the activities of the campaign of 1908 will also remember that there were times when even the Republican managers felt that Mr Bryan's chances of election were altogether too good for their comfort.

When it was finally decided that the nomination of either Mr. Hughes or Mr. Root, was out of the question for the reasons I have given above.

Mr. Taft was left as the most available;I may almost say, the only available candidate. It has been sometimes said that his candidacy was forced upon the party by Mr Roosevelt. This is not so. He was the free choice of the party. He had won a deservedly national reputation through his administration of the Philippine Islands; he had been a successful and popular Secretary of War; he was believed to understand intimately Mr Roosevelt's philosophy and principles of Government and to be in sympathy with them; he was a warm personal friend of Mr. Roosevelt; and his nomination gave satisfaction not only to the party but to the country. Mr. Roosevelt entered into the campaign for Mr Taft's election with his characteristic enthusiasm and tireless vigor. His speeches, his letters, his knowledge of conditions, and his political experience contributed so largely to the successful result of the election that his critics have said that he alone nominated and elected Mr. Taft.

Unfortunately, some of Mr. Taft's advisors took this mistaken view of

the care and between the date of his election and his inauguration in 1909, urged him to separate himself as thoroughly from any Roosevelt associations, that his administration could create its own policies, and that thus he might be renominated and re-elected in 1912 on his own individual merits "without any taint of Rooseveltism."

When Mr. Roosevelt succeeded to the presidency on the death of Mr McKinley he promised to carry out Mr McKinley's policies. This he did loyally He retained in his Cabinet not all of the members of Mr. McKinley's Cabinet, and it was not until he was elected in 1904 that he began to shape the Government upon the policies, in contra-distinction to those of Mr McKinley, which have now become historically associated with his administration. Mr. Taft, on his election, no doubt wished to carry on the work of his predecessor, and, if not publicly, often privately said that it was his desire and intention to retain those Cabinet colleagues of Mr Roosevelt who had contributed so much to the re-creation of the Republican party. But this intention became gradually modified during the winter of 1908-09. Only one member of the Roosevelt Cabinet was retained, and the one member who was Mr. Roosevelt's most intimate associate and on whom he depended more than on any one else in his struggle to take the Government out of the control of 'big business,'—the one member of all others whom he would have preferred to see retained was not retained. I refer, of course, to Mr James Garfield, Mr. Roosevelt's Secretary of the Interior. In the Ballinger controversy which has had so disastrous an effect upon the Taft administration another of Mr Roosevelt's intimate colleagues, Mr Gifford Pinchot, was practically dismissed. It was perfectly manifest from these and many other occurrences of which these are only examples that Mr. Taft preferred to "go it alone." No one has ever accused Mr. Roosevelt of being dull in his perceptions. He quickly found that Mr. Taft wished to be relieved of any intimate Roosevelt associations, and he cheerfully and promptly acquiesced. One of the reasons that he went to Africa, to bury himself in the wilds for nearly a year, was to remove any possible ground for the charge that he was interfering with Mr Taft's administration. People have said to me sometimes. "Why is it that Mr. Roosevelt, who was such an intimate friend of Mr. Taft's, ceased to maintain that intimacy after Mr Taft got into the White House!" I should

A photographic reproduction of a portion of the "Local Press" article, show-

suppose it would be apparent to any one who stops to think, that Mr Roosevelt refrained from imposing himself upon the new President, from the highest sense of delicacy The ex president of a college who remains on the Board of Trustees, and constantly attempts to advise or correct or meddle with his successor is one of the most unpleasant persons in the world

Mr Roosevelt has never failed to respond quickly and cordially to the slightest wish expressed by Mr Taft for his company or his views. Take for instance one incident in the political campaign of last autumn when Mr Roosevelt was carrying on his almost single-handed fight in the State of New York. One stormy day Mr Roosevelt jumped into a motor boat at Oyster Bay, crossed the Sound, and had a private interview with Mr Taft at New Haven, when the latter was attending a meeting of the Corporation of Yale University The following day the newspapers announced—very unfortunately with the apparent acquiescence of those nearest to Mr Taft—that the meeting was sought by Mr Roosevelt for the purpose of getting some help in his contest with the "Old Guard" of the State Republican Machine The facts are—and I have learned them, not from Mr Roosevelt, but from a friend of Mr Taft who knew all the circumstances—that Mr Taft sent word to Mr Roosevelt, asking him to come in order that he (Mr Taft) might get the benefit of Mr Roosevelt's advice regarding the serious split in the national affairs of the Republican party which resulted from the fight of the "progressives" in Congress against so-called "Cannonism." The newspapers, not knowing the facts, said, "Aha! this is just like Roosevelt. He has neglected Mr Taft, but the moment he gets into trouble he runs to him for help." The exact contrary is true, and when Mr Taft called on Mr Roosevelt he quickly and generously responded to the call. These facts have never been published, for, of course, Mr Roosevelt could not publish them, he simply had to grin and bear it, as he has borne a good many other unjustifiable criticisms. I am stating them now on my own responsibility and without consultation with Mr Roosevelt simply as an example of the misinterpretation which every man in public life has often to undergo.

Let me now turn to the question of Mr Roosevelt's political ambitions When he emerged from Africa, I met him at Khartum, one thousand miles up the Nile, in the center of Africa. He received scores, yes hundreds of letters and telegrams, urging him to come back to the United States and enter public life again. Some wanted him to become a candidate for United States Senator some wanted him to become candidate for Mayor of New York some wanted him to help save the Republican Party from the disasters with which it was threatened by Cannonism and bad tariff legislation To all these correspondents he said that his political activity had come to an end when he left the Presidency that he was a private citizen and preferred to live the life of a private citizen To me he said over and over again that not only was his political career finished, but his popularity was at an end that he had reached the crest of the wave and that the wave inevitably was about to break He referred more than once to the experience of Admiral Dewey and expressed his belief that, like Dewey, he was bound to meet with a revulsion of popular feeling. Very vigorously, but in perfect good humor, he asserted that he had accomplished his mission in American political life, and that others not only would, but must, take the center of the stage One evening at a public lecture on the steamer which brought us home from Southampton to New York, when Homer Davenport, the cartoonist, told a story of Admiral Dewey's being overcome by tears at the treatment he had received from the American people and of the revolution he at one time formed of going to Europe to live, never to set foot on American soil again, Mr Roosevelt turned to me and said They may treat me like Dewey but I tell you one thing, I shall neither weep nor shall I go to Europe"

He arrived in New York about the middle of June, 1910, and began at once to devote himself to his editorial work on The Outlook. The gubernatorial campaign of the State was in full swing Some of the younger leaders in the party came to him and asked him to go into the campaign He declined. They said to him that it was not fair to decline, that the Republican Party had heaped honors upon him and that now in the time of its tribulation and danger when they were honestly trying to purge it of some of the corrupt elements he ought not to desert them. "If that is the way you feel about it," was his reply, "I will take hold and do what I can, but I warn you that there is hardly a fighting chance for success and that we shall all probably go down to ignominious defeat together."

It was in this spirit that he went into the campaign. He was elected as a delegate from Nassau County to the Saratoga Convention, was chosen temporary Chairman participated in the free nomination of Mr Stimson as candidate for Governor, gave his opponents the "Old Guard, the fullest and fairest opportunity to make their fight on the floor of the

ing Roosevelt's autographic comments
on the Presidential Campaign of 1908

never before published." The issue in which this paper appeared was that of January 4, 1912. I did not consult Mr. Roosevelt while writing the article, but after it was printed I cut it out, pasted it on some sheets of white paper with wide margins, and showed it to him. These margins contain annotations, in his own hand. written with an indelible pencil.

It seems to me that the best way I can interpret Mr. Roosevelt's course from 1908 to 1912 is to quote here the essential portions of that article giving especially his own notes upon my statements. I do this with some reluctance because Mr. Taft and Mr. Roosevelt resumed friendly relations before the latter's death, and because I personally share in the country's affection for Mr. Taft's genial kindliness of spirit. But my purpose, indeed my duty is to interpret Mr. Roosevelt, and that can only be done by frankly stating the facts connected with the Progressive campaign of 1912.

THE "LOCAL PRESS" ARTICLE WITH MR. ROOSEVELT'S ANNOTATIONS

In order to understand the present political situation [January 1912] with regard to the presidential nomination next summer it may be interesting to review Mr. Roosevelt's connection with National politics during the last three years.

In 1908 Mr. Roosevelt declined the Republican nomination which he could very easily have had. In fact, the party tried everything in its power to make him take it. But he stood by his public statement, made in 1904, that he would not take the nomination in 1908 even if it were offered to him. In keeping this promise it is quite within the bounds of truth to say that he worked harder to prevent his nomination in 1908 than most presidential candidates have to work to capture a nomination. [This statement was one that Roosevelt made to me in more than one conversation.]

Mr. Roosevelt having eliminated himself, it was necessary for the Republican Party in 1908 to find a candidate who would be considered by the country as capable of carrying out the uncompleted programme of the Roosevelt Administration. The chief feature of this programme was the establishment of successful principles and methods by which the great railway and industrial corporations of the country could be brought under government control.

The three prominent figures in the Republican Party at that time, next to Mr. Roosevelt, were Governor Hughes, Secretary Root and Secretary Taft. Governor Hughes had not then won the great national confidence which he afterward enjoyed. It was thought by the political managers, unjustly no doubt, that he did not possess those qualities of personal magnetism, the lack of which defeated President Harrison in 1892.

Mr. Root, a great lawyer and a great Secretary of State, was a man of presidential timber, and in my judgment would have made a great President, but there was at that time throughout the country such a feeling of antagonism toward the great corporations and so-called trusts, that it was believed that Mr. Root's reputation as a great corporation lawyer might endanger his election. This was especially feared in view of the fact that Mr. Bryan was likely to make an anti-corporation campaign. [Note by Mr. Roosevelt: *"I found that the westerners would not stand Root."*]

It is easy enough now to look back and feel that probably any highminded Republican could have been elected, but those who remember the activities of the campaign of 1908 will also remember that there were times when even the Republican managers felt that Mr. Bryan's chances of election were altogether too good for their comfort.

When it was finally decided that the nomination of either Mr. Hughes or Mr. Root was out of the question for the reasons I have given above, Mr. Taft was left as the most available, I may almost say, the only available candidate. It has been sometimes said that his candidacy was forced upon the party by Mr. Roosevelt. This is not so. He was the free choice of the party. [Note by Mr. Roosevelt: *"But it is so! I could not have nominated an extreme progressive or an extreme conservative but I could by a turn of the hand have thrown the nomination to either Taft or Hughes. The only way to prevent my own nomination was for me actively to champion and to force the nomination of some one else; I chose Taft rather than Hughes, and I still think I was wise."*] He had won a deservedly national reputation through his administration of the Philippine Islands; he had been a successful and popular Secretary of War; he was believed to understand intimately Mr. Roosevelt's philosophy and principles of government and to be in sympathy with them; he was a warm personal friend of Mr. Roosevelt; and his nomination gave satisfaction not only to the party but to the country. Mr. Roosevelt entered into the campaign for Mr. Taft's election with his characteristic enthusiasm and tireless vigour. His speeches, his letters, his knowledge of the conditions and his political experience contributed so largely to the successful result of the election that his critics have said that he alone nominated and elected Mr. Taft.

Unfortunately, some of Mr. Taft's advisers took this mistaken view of the case and, between the date of his election and his inauguration in 1909, urged him to separate himself so thoroughly from any Roosevelt associations that his administration could create its own policies and that thus he might be renominated and reëlected in 1912 on his own individual merits "without any taint of Rooseveltism."

When Mr. Roosevelt succeeded to the presidency on the death of Mr. McKinley he promised to carry out Mr. McKinley's policies. This he did loyally. He retained in his Cabinet all of the members of Mr. McKinley's Cabinet and it was not until he was elected in 1904 that he began to shape the government upon the policies, in contra-distinction to those of Mr. McKinley, which have now become historically associated with his administration. [Note by Mr. Roosevelt: *"No; the mere force of events had made me strike absolutely my own note by October 1902, when I settled the coal strike and started the trust control campaign. In 1903 I took Panama."*]

Mr. Taft on his election no doubt wished to carry on the work of his predecessor, and, if not publicly, often privately said that it was his desire and intention to retain those Cabinet colleagues of Mr. Roosevelt who had contributed so much to the re-creation of the Republican Party. [Note by Mr. Roosevelt: *"He told me so, and authorized me to tell the Cabinet, specifically Garfield, Straus and Luke Wright."*] But this intention became gradually modified during the winter of 1908-09. Only one member of the Roosevelt Cabinet was retained, and the one member who was Mr. Roosevelt's most intimate associate and on whom he depended more than on any one else in his struggle to take the government out of the control of "big business," the member of all others whom he would have preferred to see retained, was not retained. I refer, of course to Mr. James Garfield, Mr. Roosevelt's Secretary of the Interior.

In the Ballinger controversy, which has had so disastrous an effect upon the Taft Administration, another of Mr. Roosevelt's intimate colleagues, Mr. Gifford Pinchot, was practically dismissed. It was perfectly manifest from these and many other occurrences, of which these are only examples, that Mr. Taft preferred to "go it alone." No one has ever accused Mr. Roosevelt of being dull in his perceptions. He quickly found that Mr. Taft wished to be relieved of any intimate Roosevelt associations, and he cheerfully and promptly acquiesced. One of the reasons why he went to Africa, to bury himself in the wilds for nearly a year, was to remove any possible ground for the charge that he was interfering with Mr. Taft's administration. [Mr. Roosevelt often told me that this was one of his motives for his African trip.]

People have said to me sometimes, "Why is it that Mr. Roosevelt, who was such an intimate friend of Mr. Taft's, ceased to maintain that intimacy after Mr. Taft got into the White House?" I should suppose it would be apparent to any one who stops to think that Mr. Roosevelt refrained from imposing himself upon the new President, from the highest sense of delicacy. The ex-President of a college who remains on the Board of Trustees, and constantly attempts to advise or correct or meddle with his successor is one of the most unpleasant persons in the world.

Mr. Roosevelt has never failed to respond quickly and cordially to the slightest wish expressed by Mr. Taft for his company or his advice. Take for instance one incident in the political campaign of the autumn of 1910 when Mr. Roosevelt was carrying on his almost single-handed fight in the State of New York. One stormy day Mr. Roosevelt jumped into a motor boat at Oyster Bay, crossed Long Island Sound, and had a private interview with Mr. Taft at New Haven, when the latter was attending a meeting of the Corporation of Yale University. The following day the newspapers announced—very unfortunately with the apparent acquiescence of those nearest to Mr. Taft—[as a matter of fact the announcement was made in an official despatch from the presidential train on which Mr. Taft was travelling] that the meeting was sought by Mr. Roosevelt for the purpose of getting some help in his contest with the "Old Guard" of the New York State Republican Machine. The facts are—

and I have learned them not from Mr. Roosevelt but from a friend of Mr. Taft's who knew all the circumstances, that Mr. Taft sent word to Mr. Roosevelt asking Roosevelt to come in order that he, Mr. Taft, might get the benefits of Mr. Roosevelt's advice regarding the serious split in the national affairs of the Republican Party, which resulted from the fight of the "progressives" in Congress against so-called "Cannonism." The newspapers, not knowing the facts, said, "Aha! This is just like Roosevelt. He has neglected Mr. Taft but the moment he gets into trouble he runs to him for help!"

The exact contrary is true and when Mr. Taft called on Mr. Roosevelt he quickly and generously responded to the call.

These facts have never been published, for, of course, Mr. Roosevelt could not publish them; he simply had to grin and bear it, as he has borne many other unjustifiable criticisms. I am stating them now on my own responsibility without consultation with Mr. Roosevelt, as an example of the misinterpretation which every man in public life has often to undergo. [Note by Mr. Roosevelt: *"My personal feeling about Taft's relations with me never influenced by one iota my public course; it took 18 months to convince me that he was a first-class lieutenant, but no leader, with no real conviction on or appreciation of the magnitude of the really vital problems before this country."*]

. . . .

He [Mr. Roosevelt] arrived in New York about the middle of June, 1910, and began at once to devote himself to the editorial work on the *Outlook*. The gubernatorial campaign of this state was in full swing. Some of the younger leaders in the party came to him and asked him to go into the campaign. He declined. They said to him that it was not fair to decline; that the Republican Party had heaped honours upon him and that now in the time of its tribulation and danger when they were honestly trying to purge it of some of the corrupt elements he ought not to desert them. "If that is the way you feel about it," was his reply, "I will take hold and do what I can, but I warn you that there is hardly a fighting chance for success and that we shall all probably go down to ignominious defeat together." [Note by Mr. Roosevelt: "*Hughes in especial asked me.*"]

The result of the campaign is a matter of record. Mr. Roosevelt was defeated. For a time he suffered from a most pronounced reversal of popularity and his opponents and his critics rejoiced in their openly expressed belief that he was permanently down and out. He made no complaint but went on with his editorial work, discussing questions of politics and public importance with zest and without repining. As the year 1911 came into its last quarter, the people of the State, even some of the most enthusiastic supporters of Governor Dix, began to perceive that what Mr. Roosevelt had said in his public speeches during the campaign was true. The defeat of Mr. Stimson meant the saddling of Tammany upon the whole political machinery of the State.

What Mr. Roosevelt does or says will be interpreted by some critics to his disadvantage. In the building where the *Outlook* has its offices there are two elevators, one in the main hall and one in the side hall. Mr. Roosevelt once said with a laugh during the campaign of 1910 when the *Outlook* office was crowded with people who came to consult him: "If I go down in the front elevator, my critics call it ostentation; if I go down in the side elevator, they call it secretiveness!"

If Mr. Roosevelt is ever elected President again it will not be because he seeks or wants the office; it will be because the

Colonel Roosevelt and a party of Republicans who came to tell him that he was their nominee for President

The Inaugural Address of 1904

country wants him in the office to perform a certain job. He has had all the political and official honours that any normal man can possibly want. He accepted a nomination for the Vice-Presidency in 1900 when such a nomination was thought to be equivalent to political oblivion, and although he wanted to run again for governor of the State of New York in order to complete some important work in that office. But his friends told him that it was his duty to sacrifice himself in order to strengthen Mr. McKinley's nomination and the campaign for sound money and the financial honour of the Nation. He accepted the nomination on that ground, although at the time both his friends and his enemies said it would mean the end of his political career. But instead of plunging into oblivion it brought to him an election to the Presidency in 1904 by one of the largest popular and electoral majorities ever received by an American President. This is what his critics call "Roosevelt luck."

In 1908 he not only declined, but put a stop to his nomination at a time when such a nomination was equivalent to an election. He has a European reputation as a statesman which has never been surpassed by any other American in political life and he appears to-day to be as popular among his own countrymen as he ever was. What possible incentive can there be to a man with such a record of achievements and honours to enter the arduous, disagreeable and often disastrous contests into which the candidate who struggles for the Presidency is inevitably plunged.

To be understood properly the notes which Roosevelt made upon the document here reproduced need some interpretation. He wrote them briefly and categorically because he was aware that I would understand them without amplification.

When he says: "I could have nominated Hughes

more easily than Taft" or: "I could not have nominated an extreme Progressive or an extreme Conservative," he means, of course, not that he was acting as a dictator but as the acknowledged leader of his party to whom not only the party managers but the delegates themselves came for advice. What they wanted was that he should tell them whom they should vote for in the convention if not for him. It was his moral and personal leadership and not his dictatorial and official power that made him the arbiter of the nomination.

The same interpretation is to be given to his phrase: "In 1903 I took Panama." Of course he could not have taken it in the sense in which Philip II of Spain took the free cities of the Netherlands. The meaning of the phrase will be more clear if it is paraphrased in this way: "In 1903 *I took action*, guided almost solely by my own judgment of what was wise and proper, that resulted in the building of the Panama Canal." The fact that the inhabitants and the government of Panama itself were the most enthusiastic supporters and approvers of this action is proof that Roosevelt did not use the verb "to take" in the sense of seizure or conquest.

What he says about Mr. Taft being "a first-class lieutenant but no leader, with no real convictions

on or appreciation of the magnitude of the really
vital problems before the country" is perhaps sufficiently explained later in this article.   He did not
mean that Mr. Taft had no convictions of any kind.
On the contrary, I am convinced that he believed
Mr. Taft's convictions on legal and judicial questions were of a very high order.   In a later chapter
of the book from which this article is taken I quote
in full Roosevelt's own statement of the reasons
that led him to become a Progressive.   From the
time of his governorship of the State of New York
he had been slowly but steadily coming to the conviction that there needed to be a thorough-going
reform of the relations of government to industry
both as regards capital and as regards labour.   He
felt that the country was approaching a crisis in its
social and industrial conditions, a feeling that the
outcome of the European war has more than confirmed.   His belief was that Mr. Taft did not share
this conviction and did not appreciate the magnitude and imminence of the crisis.   The cleavage
between the two men was due not to friction in
their personal relations but to a fundamental difference in their point of view.   The personal friction
was not the cause but the result of the difference in
their political philosophies.   I hope it is not pre-
sumptuous in me to say that I think Mr. Taft's at-

titude toward these social and human problems has changed since 1912, and that he and Roosevelt found themselves much more in agreement during the last year of the European war. Mr. Taft's vigorous and broadminded leadership in support of the plan for a League of Nations against the bitter opposition of powerful members of his own party discloses those qualities of statesmanship in matters of national and international procedure which originally drew him and Roosevelt together during the years of the latter's Presidency.

The statement that "Hughes in especial asked me" refers to these facts: Mr. Hughes at the Harvard Commencement of 1910 added his urgency to that of the younger Republicans who were begging Roosevelt to go into the state campaign of that year. Mr. Hughes put this request on the ground that the Direct Primary cause which he had inaugurated needed Roosevelt's backing. Roosevelt assented and went into the fight, but somewhat to his chagrin Mr. Hughes then failed to give him any active support in the contest.

As the *Local Press* article was commented upon by Mr. Roosevelt and in that way received the stamp of his personal approval it may be taken as a fair indication of his state of mind as to politics at the opening of the campaign of 1912. The dissatisfaction of the Liberals or "Progressives" in the Republican party with the course of Mr. Taft's administration had steadily grown during 1911. Early in 1912 President Taft made a speech at Cleveland in which he reviewed and defended his Administration. The *Outlook* made the following comment on that speech, and as Mr. Roosevelt was then a member of the editorial staff I know that its comment was not inharmonious with his own view.

Why is it that there should be wide-spread popular discontent with the Administration, not only on the part of the President's political opponents, but also within the ranks of the President's own party?

In the first place, the President [Mr. Taft] has allowed himself to become identified in the public mind with those elements in his party which have been frankly opposed to progress. It was not, for example, merely his defense of the Payne-Aldrich Tariff Act, as made in his Winona speech, that set the Progressive element in his own party to questioning his attitude; it was even more the evidence that in the conferences over the tariff he seemed to find most congenial to him those leaders in the party who had been most opposed to real tariff reform. Another illustration of this point was the famous Norton letter, in which it was admitted that the President had used Federal patronage against the Progressives in Congress. This feeling on the part of the Progressive element in the party has been confirmed by many expressions of the President himself. A notable illustration occurs in the closing sentence of his Cleveland speech:

"On this, the natal day of William McKinley, let us take new vows in behalf of the Grand Old Party, standing by the Constitution, standing by the rights of liberty and property of the individual, and willing to face defeat many times in behalf of the cause of sound Constitutional government."

This might have been said in exactly these words by Mr. Cannon or any of the so-called standpatters who believe that the prime function of party government is to promote material prosperity or mere money-making. In such a sentence there is no hint of that feeling for which the Progressive element of Mr. Taft's party stands, that feeling which is growing more and more throughout the country—that in the end when human rights clash with property rights, human rights should prevail. In this sentence there is no hint of really sympathetic understanding of that movement which has changed the complexion of Congress and which has put the reactionary element in both parties on the defensive.

The Progressive element, for the reasons thus set forth, was busily seeking for a candidate representing the Liberal wing of the Republican party who could be put in nomination against Mr. Taft at the National Republican Convention at Chicago in June. The Liberal leaders were in constant consultation with Mr. Roosevelt, and his office was daily crowded with people. It was a veritable political headquarters. When urged to accept the titular leadership of the Liberal wing he steadily declined, and more than once I heard him say during this period that, while he was glad to help in any way he could, Senator La Follette of Wisconsin was the man on whom the Liberals must probably depend. This was not because of his personal admiration for Senator La Follette, about whom there was much which was not sympathetic to Roosevelt, but because he thought that justice to Senator La Follette required recognition of the sacrifices he had made in fighting the champions of reaction, for the Senator had devoted himself for many years with unflagging energy to the cause of popular government as opposed to special privilege.

But in February, 1912, Senator La Follette collapsed in an aggravated attack of nervous prostration. This collapse came in a dramatic and tragic fashion while he was making a speech at the annual dinner of the Periodical Publishers' Association in Philadelphia, a speech which I happened to hear and which culminated in one of the most painful public spectacles I have ever witnessed. As a result of that unfortunate episode, during which for two hours the Senator rambled on, sometimes violently, sometimes incoherently, his friends and political managers announced his withdrawal as a presidential candidate.

The pressure upon Mr. Roosevelt then became greater than ever. He finally said that if there was any evidence that a considerable body of the Republican party wanted him to be a candidate he would agree to follow their wishes. Whereupon seven Republican governors, of the states of West Virginia, Nebraska, New Hampshire, Wyoming, Michigan, Kansas, and Missouri, addressed a letter to Mr. Roosevelt urging him to be a candidate and saying:

We feel that you will be unresponsive to a plain public duty if you decline to accept the nomination coming as the voluntary expression of the wishes of a majority of the Republican voters of the United States through the action of their delegates in the next National Convention.

Even before this letter was sent to Mr. Roosevelt steps had been taken in various parts of the country to elect Roosevelt delegates to the National Convention. Mr. Roosevelt believed that this letter of the seven governors was voicing a common popular demand and he replied, agreeing to become a candidate. In his letter he said:

One of the chief principles for which I have stood and for which I now stand and which I have always endeavoured and always shall endeavour to reduce to action, is the genuine rule of the people; and, therefore, I hope that so far as possible the people may be given the chance, through direct primaries, to express their preference as to who shall be the nominee of the Republican Presidential Convention.

On the publication of the letter of the seven governors and Roosevelt's reply the campaign began with a full swing. Indeed, in so far as Mr.

Theodore Roosevelt addressing a street audience with characteristic gesture and emphasis

Roosevelt's political principles and policies were concerned, it had begun some weeks before, for early in February he had been invited to address the Constitutional Convention in Columbus, the capital city of Ohio, and had there stated certain principles which he called "A Charter of Democracy." He announced his belief in the short ballot; in direct nominations by the people including preferential primaries for the election of delegates to the national nominating conventions; in the election of United States senators by direct vote; in the initiative and referendum "which should be used not to destroy representative government, but to correct it whenever it becomes misrepresentative"; and finally he promulgated a theory which, because it was misinterpreted and misunderstood, raised a tremendous storm in the campaign—the theory of "The Recall of Judicial Decisions." Briefly, he asserted that under this doctrine the voters at the ballot box should have an opportunity of saying whether a law nullified by the courts as contrary to the Constitution was in fact unconstitutional or not. On reading the speech it is apparent he had in mind the application of this principle or doctrine only to the individual states with regard to laws affecting social justice and that he doubted whether it could be adopted with regard to decisions of the United States Supreme Court.

Not long after this address, which was popularly known throughout the campaign as the Columbus speech, he made another at Carnegie Hall in the City of New York. It was delivered on March 20, 1912, under the auspices of The Civic Forum, a non-partisan organization. The Carnegie Hall speech was notable for two or three things. In it he took issue with Mr. Taft for the first time in public. He said:

Mr. Taft's position is the position that has been held from the beginning of our government, although not always so openly held, by a large number of the reputable and honourable men who, down at bottom, distrust popular government, and, when they must accept it, accept it with reluctance, and hedge it round with every species of restriction and check and balance, so as to make the power of the people as limited and as ineffective as possible. Mr. Taft fairly defines the issue when he says that our government is and should be a government of all the people by a representative part of the people. This is an excellent and moderate description of an oligarchy. It defines our government as a government of all of the people by a few of the people. Mr. Taft, in his able speech, has made what is probably the best possible presentation of the case for those who feel in this manner.

He reaffirmed the creed which he had uttered before the Ohio Constitutional Convention saying:

I stand on the Columbus speech. The principles there asserted are not new, but I believe that they are necessary to the maintenance of free, democratic government. The part of my speech in which I advocated the right of the people to be the final arbiters of what is due process of law in the case of statutes enacted for the general welfare will ultimately, I am confident, be recognized as giving strength and support to the courts instead of being revolutionary and subversive.

The Carnegie Hall speech contains a good example of Roosevelt's enjoyment in occasionally treating his own foibles humorously, in poking fun at himself, so to speak. William Draper Lewis, Dean of the Law School of the University of Pennsylvania, who afterward became intimately associated with Roosevelt in the Progressive campaign, had, in a newspaper article, referred to the recall of judicial decisions with approval on the whole. He had commended the plan as being not only in favour of popular rights but as entirely harmonious with the best-established legal principles, adding, however:

I think it unfortunate that it should have been proposed by Colonel Roosevelt. He is a man of such marked characteristics and his place in the political world is such that he arouses intense enthusiasms on the one hand and intense animosities on the other. Because of this, the great idea which he has propounded is bound to be beclouded and its adoption to be delayed. It is a pity that anything so important should be confounded with any man's personality.

During his speech Roosevelt read Dean Lewis's entire critique of the plan and said with that characteristic intonation of voice which indicated his sense of humour:

> As regards the Dean's last paragraph I can only say that I wish somebody else whose suggestions would arouse less antagonism *had* proposed it; but nobody else *did* propose it and so I *had* to. I am not leading this fight as a matter of æsthetic pleasure. I am leading because somebody must lead, or else the fight would not be made at all.

The Carnegie Hall speech contained one of the most eloquent and moving passages in the whole range of Roosevelt's public utterances. Toward the conclusion of the speech he uttered these words:

> Friends, our task as Americans is to strive for social and industrial justice, achieved through the genuine rule of the people. This is our end, our purpose. The methods for achieving the end are merely expedients, to be finally accepted or rejected according as actual experience shows that they work well or ill. But in our hearts we must have this lofty purpose, and we must strive for it in all earnestness and sincerity, or our work will come to nothing. In order to succeed we need leaders of inspired idealism, leaders to whom are granted great visions, who dream greatly and strive to make their dreams come true; who can kindle the people with the fire from their own burning souls. The leader for the time being, whoever he may be, is but an instrument, to be used until broken and then to be cast aside; and if he is worth his salt he will care no more when he is broken than a soldier cares when he is sent where his life is forfeit in order that the victory may be won. In the long fight for righteousness the watchword for all of us is "Spend and be

spent." It is of little matter whether any one man fails or succeeds; but the cause shall not fail, for it is the cause of mankind.

The audience, recognizing the personal implication of these words, responded by instinctively rising to their feet and bursting into a storm of applause. I happened to be sitting in a box and could look down upon the people who filled every available seat in the body of the hall. I noticed William Barnes of Albany, the well-known leader of the "Old Guard" faction in the Republican party, a typical reactionary, who had fought Roosevelt in the gubernatorial campaign of 1910 and who was later to engage in a bitter libel suit with him as a result of their political antagonisms. But Barnes rose and applauded with the rest. A friend told me that when Barnes later in the evening at one of the clubs was twitted for this public tribute to his arch-enemy he replied: "Why, I was on my feet before I knew it. Roosevelt, confound him, has a kind of magnetism that you cannot resist when you are in his presence!"

It is not necessary here to go into the historical details of the Progressive campaign. Roosevelt was the popular candidate for the Republican nomination. He was seeking not merely the nomination, but to establish the free primary system by which the people at large could exercise their choice directly in the National conventions. At the Republican Convention in Chicago delegates who were elected to vote for his nomination were refused credentials and delegates whom he and his friends believed did not represent popular will but who were pledged to vote for Mr. Taft were seated. Roosevelt felt that this was not merely an injustice to himself but that it was a corrupt and brazen violation of popular rights. How close he came to the nomination was related as follows by one of my associates on the staff of the *Outlook*, Mr. Travers Carman, who accompanied Roosevelt to the Republican Convention as a personal friend and aide.

It was known that Mr. Roosevelt lacked twenty-eight delegates (my recollection is that this was the number) to secure the nomination. The most memorable conference I ever attended (and I was there merely in the capacity of "doorman") was held that night at the Colonel's headquarters on the second floor of the Congress Hotel, and attended only by those most concerned in the success of Mr. Roosevelt's campaign. The entire situation was carefully discussed, analyzed, and dissected. By questionable means the Colonel would not, and by fair means apparently he could not, secure the nomination, and then came the memorable climax; a delegate to see Mr. Roosevelt, on a vitally important matter, who, when admitted to the conference, announced with ill-concealed excitement that he represented thirty-two Southern delegates to the Republican Convention who would pledge themselves to vote for the Colonel as the Presidential candidate, provided that they would be permitted to vote with the old-line Republicans on all motions with reference to party organization, platform, etc. Here were thirty-two votes, and all that Mr. Roosevelt needed was twenty-eight.

Without a moment's hesitation and in the deathlike silence of that room the Colonel's answer rang out, clearly and distinctly: "Thank the delegates you represent, but tell them that I cannot permit them to vote for me unless they vote for all progressive principles for which I have fought, for which the Progressive element in the Republican party stands and by which I stand or fall."

Strong men broke down under the stress of that night. Life-long friends of Mr. Roosevelt endeavoured to persuade him to reconsider his decision. After listening patiently he turned to two who had been urging him to accept the offer of the Southern delegates, placed a hand on the shoulder of each, and said: "I have grown to regard you both as brothers; let no act or word of yours make that relationship impossible."

While the formalities of Mr. Taft's nomination were as yet incomplete the delegates supporting Mr. Roosevelt, who were convinced that they were a true majority of the Republican Convention, gathered almost spontaneously in Orchestra Hall and nominated Roosevelt for the Presidency. The Progressive party was thus born. It was completely organized in every state in the Union during the next few weeks and cast more than four million votes in November. It was a political achievement, solely the fruit of Roosevelt's extraordinary personality, unparalleled in the history of this country—or any other for that matter.

The Progressive campaign was one of very deep feeling and earnestness and of some bitterness, although I do not think that the bitterness was greater—perhaps it was even less—than that of the presidential campaigns of my boyhood and early manhood. Possibly the very fact that they had formerly been close friends led both Mr. Taft and Mr. Roosevelt to feel especially strongly about the personal contest in which they had become involved. This peculiar feeling of antagonism found vent in two speeches, both made in New England, one by Mr. Taft, and one by Mr. Roosevelt, in which some invective was employed on both sides. I think it is only fair to Mr. Roosevelt's memory to say that it was not he who cast the first stone, but that he struck back only when he felt that he had been himself "hit below the belt." And during the rest of the campaign, although his own motives were repeatedly attacked, he never resorted to aspersing the motives or personal character of his opponents.

That, however, is happily an episode of the past, and it is a satisfaction to all their friends, many of whom shared their friendship with each man, that the two ex-Presidents were reconciled before the end came. Whatever harshness óf language Mr. Roosevelt may have employed in the one speech to which I have referred, acrimony was not at all characteristic of him. Indeed, there may well be repeated of him what Lord Rosebery, in his life of William Pitt, said of Charles James Fox:

The mastering passion of Fox's mature life was the love of liberty; it is this which made him take a vigorous, occasionally an intemperate, part against every man or measure in which he could trace the taint or tendency to oppression; it is this which sometimes made him speak with unworthy bitterness; but it was this which gave him moral power, which has neutralized the errors of his political career, which makes his faults forgotten and his memory sweet.

During the entire summer of 1912, while he was involved in a contest that cost him friendships and associations that meant much to him, he preserved his poise and equanimity in a very marked degree. He went through the National campaign of 1912 as he went through the state campaign of 1910, in a vigorous, alert, undismayed, and actually happy frame of mind. I think he was sustained by the knowledge that there were thousands upon thousands of Americans, whom he had never seen or spoken to, who liked him and trusted him. My brother who once made a campaign trip with him, during the period in which the Progressive party was gradually developing, has described as follows, for a French periodical, this affection of the plain people for the man whom they delighted to call "Teddy":

It was my fortune to accompany him on this journey in a private car. He was not then President, for he had retired from office the year before; he was not a candidate for election. He was simply a private citizen; but everywhere people came in throngs to greet him. He was their man. I remember one night, while the train was rushing through one of the great central prairie states, I looked out of the window just before I went to sleep and saw in the lighted doorway of one isolated farmhouse a little family group gathered and waving a flag; as I watched, another farmhouse flashed by and there was another little group waving their salute. It was as if they had waited up to bid a welcome and a good-bye to a brother, though they knew in advance he would be unseen and unseeing. And in the morning I waked up very early; it was scarcely dawn; but as I looked out the people were up and greeting their friend. All night long, apparently, these friends of Theodore Roosevelt whom he never saw, one family group after another, had been giving him their benediction.

Another day on this same journey stands out in my memory. It was a Sunday. Mr. Roosevelt had stated positively that he would make no speeches that day. The special train was to run from the morning until almost dusk without a stop. It had not run far when I heard a strange sound. It swelled suddenly into a confusion of voices and then subsided. I looked out. We had just passed a railway station in a wide stretch of country. Around the station I saw a crowd of people. Where had this crowd come from? Every farmhouse for miles must have contributed its entire household. Again as we passed another station came the *crescendo* and *diminuendo* of the sound of voices. Mr. Roosevelt came out from his stateroom where he had been reading. He could not pass these friends of his, friends he had never before seen, but friends who had cared so much for him that they had driven for miles over the rough country roads, in all sorts of vehicles, simply in order to be beside the track as his train went by. So thirty times that day the sound of cheering voices swelled, thirty times the train stopped, thirty times Mr. Roosevelt left his reading to be out on the rear platform and greet those who had for the most part never seen him, and had no hope of seeing him, but who came just to show their friendship.

I am reminded, by my brother's account of Roosevelt's genius for friendship, of an incident which came under my own observation.

During the gubernatorial campaign of 1910, which resulted in the defeat of Mr. Roosevelt's object, a defeat which I think he foresaw, he maintained his good spirits and even gayety of humour, although it must have been a very trying summer. The days that he spent at his office were constantly interrupted by an interminable procession of callers with all of whom he was patient, although in only a few cases could he have had any interest in seeing them. One day while I was seated in his private office, which was a fairly good-sized room, his secretary announced Senator Carter of Montana. The Senator was shown into the room. He was dressed, as I recall it, in a gray frock coat. His round face, surmounted with red hair, shone with pleasure.

To my intense amazement Mr. Roosevelt leaped out of his chair, seized the Senator by the hands and they began dancing back and forth across the room, chanting the following doggerel in unison:

> "Oh, the Irish and the Dutch
> They don't amount to much,
> But huroo for the Scandinoo-vian!"

After Senator Carter had left, Mr. Roosevelt, amused at the look of surprised interrogation on my face, volunteered the following explanation: "Tom Carter is a good friend of mine, although we have often disagreed radically on political principles and issues. He is something of a standpatter and I am afraid he sometimes thinks I am something of a visionary crank. Some years ago, during a political campaign, he and I were scheduled to speak on the same occasion in a town of the Northwest. When we came out of the hall and were walking along the boardwalk of the little village to our hotel we met a huge Swede or Norwegian who was somewhat exhilarated from pouring too many libations in honour of the Republican party. As he zigzagged his way along the narrow sidewalk, we had to step aside to avoid a collision. He was singing at the top of his lungs that song about the Irish and the Dutch. Now Senator Carter is Irish and I am Dutch and we thought it was a very good joke on us. So every time we have met since, unless there are too many people about, we are apt to greet each other as we did just now. It has become a kind of ritual."

The Progressive campaign of 1912, with its exhausting work and its depressing disappointments, was a severe test for any man. Roosevelt came through it with two of his marked and engaging personal qualities unimpaired—his capacity for friendship and his unquenchable sense of humour.

CHAPTER IV

STATESMANSHIP

THEORETICALLY, the words "statesman-ship" and "politics" are synonymous. The primary meaning of "politics" is given in the Century Dictionary as: "The art or science of government"; and the same authority defines "statesmanship" as: The qualifications of "a man who is versed in the art of government." But the development of democracy among English-speaking peoples has given rise to secondary meanings of the terms which involve a marked differentiation between them. The Century Dictionary adds to its first definition of "statesmanship" that it is: "Political skill in the *higher sense*," and asserts that "politics" usually means, in American practice at least, "the art or vocation of guiding or influencing the policy of a government through the organization of a party among its citizens; the art of influencing public opinion, attracting and marshalling voters; in an evil sense, the schemes and intrigues of political parties, or of cliques or individual politicians." The same lexicographers who tell us that the word "politics" is derived from the Greek word πολίτης, citizen, emphasize the degraded side of politicians. Is this because of the instinctive distrust of democracy on the part of the French and English intellectuals who made our earliest dictionaries?

For some reason or other, which it would be interesting to inquire into but which is not germane to my purpose, mankind has always looked somewhat superciliously upon the mechanics of any art. The poet is more highly honoured than the grammarian, the painter than the chemist, the violinist than the physicist, the aviator than the machinist. And yet we could not have the poetry of Keats without the men who have grubbed out the rules of syntax and prosody; the paintings of Monet without the workers who have toiled over the chemistry of colours and the laws of light; the music of Fritz Kreisler without those who have discovered in the workshop and laboratory the principles of harmonies and resonance; the heroic "aces" on the western front without the grimy artisans in overalls who adjusted and tuned up the engines of the battle-planes. So, too, we could not have statesmen if there were no politicians to create the machinery without which statesmanship would be inoperative. Nevertheless, it has long been the fashion to treat politics and politicians as if they were necessarily contemptible. James Russell Lowell once said: "I always hated politics in the ordinary sense of the word." James Bryce, in his classic and monumental "American Commonwealth," speaks of "the local and dirty work of politics," and gives one of his chapters the significant title: "Why the best men do not go into politics."

Now with this secondary—although, unfortunately, customary—interpretation of the terms "*politics*," "*politicians*," "*political parties*," Theodore Roosevelt had no sympathy whatever. He knew, of course, that politics is often corrupt; that politicians are often ignorant, selfish, and dishonourable; that political parties are often narrow, hide-bound, and short-sighted. But he did not believe that these evils are essential to and inseparable from politics any more than reactionary dogmatism and inquisitorial cruelty are essential and irremediable characteristics of the Church. He believed that politics and political activity in the administrative sense—in the *machine* sense, so to speak—are the very basis of democracy. Politics meant citizenship to him and he thought that every citizen should take some part in political activities. Moreover, he believed that deliber-

A rear platform speech to a group of citizens in Ohio

ately to make politics a profession, a means of live-
lihood, is no more unworthy or undignified than
to make a living from the practice of medicine or of
law, provided that the professional politician puts
service to the State as his main object. There are
doubtless quacks among the doctors, pettifoggers
among the lawyers, and hypocrites among the
clergy, but we do not for that reason condemn all
men who choose Law, Medicine, or the Church for
their life work and are supported by the proper
emoluments of their services.

It is necessary to understand this point of view
in order properly to interpret Theodore Roosevelt's life-long attitude toward what is too often
contemptuously called "practical politics." The
very mainspring of his tireless activities was statesmanship—the framing, shaping, administering,
and maintaining of those great policies of national
and international relations that make civilized
society a permanent, vital, and progressive organ-
ism. He lived, however, not in the clouds but
with both feet on the ground, and he knew that
great State policies cannot be obtained unless the
political machine that produces them is kept in
good running order. Statesmanship is like a valuable and beautifully patterned silk; politics is the
intricate loom on which it is woven. Roosevelt's

eye was always on the silk; that is what he was ultimately striving for; but he was never bored, or
irritated, or disgusted, as statesmen of the highly
sensitized type of James Russell Lowell or John
Hay often are, by the necessity of tinkering with
the loom, or of soiling his hands with the lubri-
cating oil, or of spending tedious hours in replacing
broken or worn-out parts. He felt a zest to the
very last for this mechanical side of statesmanship.

Among my papers I find a letter written to my
father by Mr. Roosevelt and dated the White
House, February 23, 1906. It discloses, it seems
to me in a way pertinent to what I am contending
for in this chapter, Roosevelt's own attitude of
mind toward the machinery of politics. The circumstances that prompted the letter are as follows:

In the November elections of 1905 the defeat of
machine-made tickets in both the Republican and
Democratic parties in various states was so marked
that the *Outlook* gave a large amount of space to
the phenomenon calling it: "The Rout of the
Bosses." Massachusetts was nearly lost to the
Republican party. In commenting upon this surprising reversal of form in a banner Republican
state, the *Outlook* said editorially:

Senator Lodge is a boss of agreeable personality—a gentleman of culture, a "scholar in politics"—against whose personal integrity no suspicion has ever been uttered, but he has undertaken to tell the people of Massachusetts what they ought to wish instead of asking them what they do wish, and every vote for Mr. Whitney was less a vote for reciprocity than a vote against the spirit and methods of a political dictator.

This drew from Mr. Roosevelt the letter above referred to, in which he said:

You would be surprised to know how many men have spoken to me about the article on Lodge. Lodge has violent enemies. But he is a boss or the head of a machine only in the sense that Henry Clay and Webster were bosses and heads of political machines; that is, it is a very great injustice to couple his name with the names of those commonly called bosses, in any article. I know Massachusetts politics well. I know Lodge's share in them, and I know what he has done in the Senate. He and I differ radically on certain propositions, as for instance on the pending Rāte Bill and on the arbitration treaties of a couple of years ago; but I say deliberately that during the twenty years he has been in Washington he has been on the whole the best and most useful servant of the public to be found in either house of Congress. I say also that he has during that period led politics in Massachusetts in the very way which, if it could only be adopted in all our states, would mean the elimination of graft, of bossism, and of every other of the evils which are most serious in our politics. Lodge is a man of very strong convictions, and this means that when his convictions differ from mine I am apt to substitute the words "narrow" and "obstinate" for "strong"; and he has a certain aloofness and coldness of manner that irritate people who do not live in New

England. But he is an eminently fit successor of Webster and Sumner in the senatorship from Massachusetts.

In other words, Roosevelt believed in political organizations; he believed that those organizations must have managers, often miscalled "bosses," just as every business man of common sense knows that factories and ranches and railroads must have foremen or bosses. The political manager, however, must exercise his function in order to get the best product out of the machine, which is the general welfare not merely of the party but of all the citizens.

Nowhere else in his writings, so far as I know, has Roosevelt expressed so clearly his buoyant enjoyment of his work, of its very obstacles and rebuffs, as he did spontaneously in an address to the students of the University of Cambridge on May 26, 1910, when he received the honorary degree of LL.D. His discourse on this occasion, as I have said in a preface of his collected "African and European Addresses" published by the Putnams, was not like his Romanes lecture at Oxford, part of the academic ceremony connected with the conferring of the honorary degree. It was spoken to an audience of undergraduates when, after the academic exercises in the Senate House, he was elected to honorary membership in the Union

Society, the well-known Cambridge debating club which has trained some of the best public speakers of England. At Oxford the doctors and dignitaries cracked the jokes—in Latin—while the undergraduates were highly decorous. At Cambridge, on the other hand, the students indulged in the traditional pranks which often lend a colour of gayety to University ceremonies at both Oxford and Cambridge. Mr. Roosevelt entered heartily into the spirit of the undergraduates, and it was evident that they, quite as heartily, liked his understanding of the fact that the best university and college life consists in a judicious mixture of the grave and the gay. The honour that these undergraduates paid to their guest was seriously intended, was admirably planned, and its genuineness was all the more apparent because it had a note of pleasantry.

Mr. Roosevelt spoke as a university student to university students and what he said—although brief, extemporaneous, and even unpremeditated— was the genuine expression of his philosophy of life. The speech was frequently interrupted by the laughter and applause of the audience, and the theory that Mr. Roosevelt propounded, namely, that any man in any walk of life may achieve genuine success simply by developing ordinary qualities to a more than ordinary degree, was widely quoted and discussed by the press of Great Britain. I quote the following passage from that speech because it confirms the point I am endeavouring to make.

We have in the United States an organization composed of the men who forty-five years ago fought to a finish the great Civil War. One thing that has always appealed to me in that organization is that all of the men admitted are on a perfect equality, provided the records show that their duty was well done. Whether a man served as a lieutenant-general or an eighteen-year-old recruit, so long as he was able to serve for six months and did his duty in his appointed place, then he is called Comrade, and stands on an exact equality with the other men. The same principle should shape our association in ordinary civil life.

I am not speaking cant to you. I remember once sitting at a table with six or eight other public officials, and each was explaining how he regarded being in public life—how only the sternest sense of duty prevented him from resigning his office, and how the strain of working for a thankless constituency was telling upon him—and that nothing but the fact that he felt he ought to sacrifice his comfort to the welfare of his country kept him in the arduous life of statesmanship. It went round the table until it came to my turn. This was during my first term of office as President of the United States. I said: "Now, gentlemen, I do not wish there to be any misunderstanding. I like my job, and I want to keep it for four years longer." [Loud laughter and applause.] I don't think any President ever enjoyed himself more than I did. Moreover, I don't think any ex-President ever enjoyed himself more. I have enjoyed my life and my work because I thoroughly believe that success—

the real success—does not depend upon the position you hold, but upon how you carry yourself in that position. There is no man here to-day who has not the chance so to shape his life after he leaves this university that he shall have the right to feel, when his life ends, that he has made a real success of it; and his making a real success of it does not in the least depend upon the prominence of the position he holds.

The spirit lying back of these words explains, it seems to me, the real joy he had in his rows with the United States Senate—rows which almost drove Secretary John Hay to his grave—or in contests with political bosses like Senator "Tom" Platt.

I remember an occasion when I was one of a luncheon party at the White House—one of those never-to-be-forgotten luncheons at which President Roosevelt was in the habit of collecting all sorts of interesting guests from all parts of the world. The place of honour was filled by an official of the British Government who was visiting the United States for the first time. I was seated two or three places away from the President, next to Governor Curry of New Mexico, who had been a member of Roosevelt's "Rough Riders" in the Spanish War, had lived a somewhat tempestuous career on the western frontier (where he had shot and killed one or two desperadoes in pursuance of his duty as sheriff), and was now filling honourably and admirably the high office to which the President had appointed him. Roosevelt was then engaged in one of his periodical contests with the Senate over some important legislation of reform connected with the "Predatory Trusts" or Conservation—I forget which—and, being much interested in the contest, I had that morning visited the Senate Chamber, where I had happened especially to notice Senator Platt of New York, the arch-enemy of all progressive Republicans, sitting inert like a death's head, with sunken eyes, and appearing to be in the last stages of physical decay.

Soon after we sat down at the table the President leaned over and said: "Lawrence, I want you to know Governor Curry; he's well worth knowing in spite of his homicidal tendencies!"

"I have already introduced myself to Governor Curry, Mr. President," I replied, "and I wish you would persuade him to go over to the Senate Chamber, from which I have just come, and exercise his homicidal skill upon the senators from my state!"

"A good suggestion!" was the President's retort. "In fact," he added, showing his teeth in a characteristic smile, "he could take a pot shot at the whole lot of them without doing a great amount of harm to the country!"

Colonel Roosevelt in his English Academic Robes

This is believed to have been Colonel Roosevelt's favourite
photograph of himself

The undisguised amazement of the British guest of honour showed that he did not understand, as everyone else at the table did, that this was merely a symptom of that high good humour in which Roosevelt gave and took political blows in contests the like of which completely embittered President Andrew Johnson, led President Cleveland to make serious protests, and even upset the equanimity of so philosophical a temperament as that of Washington. Roosevelt, however, was not a philosopher; he was simply human. He took the hard knocks of life, not with resignation but with a kind of boyish zest and joy. When attacked he hit hard in return, but without bitterness or rancour. And, in spite of his not-infrequent conflicts with Congress, his opponents had a kind of subconscious fondness for him even when they were exchanging blows.

E. L. Godkin—the brilliant editor of the New York *Evening Post* and founder of the *Nation* (the present character of which must almost make him turn in his grave)—and Theodore Roosevelt were at swords' points for many years. Godkin, the older man of the two, who professed and doubtless did have a faith in theoretical democracy but actually detested democratic affiliations and associations, deplored in "young Theodore" the

tendencies which he thought he saw toward jingo-
ism and "practical politics"; above all, he could not
tolerate Roosevelt's perfectly open and frank conferences with "Boss" Platt of New York State.
On the other hand, Roosevelt regarded Godkin as
the archetype of the uncompromising mugwump
and unpractical idealist who thought that the seven
or eight million citizens of New York could be
governed exactly as he governed the subscribers to
his newspapers, that is by admirably written messages and semi-satirical essays composed in the
seclusion of a private sanctum. I am a little dubious, therefore, as to what Theodore Roosevelt's
comment would be if he could hear me say, as I
now proceed to, that I think Mr. Godkin, without
knowing it of course, defined Theodore Roosevelt's
philosophy as well as it could possibly be defined in
so brief a compass. In an essay entitled "Criminal Politics," first printed in 1890 in the *North
American Review*, Mr. Godkin says:

Politics is a practical art. It deals with men as they are,
and not as we wish them to be. There is hardly one of us
who, if he had the power of peopling New York anew, would
not make an immense number of changes among its present
inhabitants. But the problem before the wise and good is
simply how to give the present inhabitants, such as they
are, with all their imperfections on their heads, the best attainable government.

Theodore Roosevelt never made any claim to be either wise or good—although the universal testimony of his fellow citizens, now that he is gone, is that he was both. But he did profoundly believe in dealing with men as they are and he strove for the best attainable government that imperfect mankind is capable of organizing in a democracy where the good, the bad, and the indifferent must somehow manage to work together.

This was the constant political background—steadily growing more distinct as his life developed—of his statesmanship. Only in the reflection and perspective of that background may the achievements of his genius as a statesman be intelligently measured and estimated.

What were some of those achievements? I shall try to interpret the most important in the following categorical fashion.

NATIONALISM.—The basic doctrine of Roosevelt's philosophy of statesmanship, the doctrine that ran like an always-visible golden thread through the entire fabric of his words and acts as a citizen and publicist, was Nationalism. His belief in a strong and virile development of national character and national action will be found in his very earliest utterances. It is sometimes thought that his urgency of what, during the last four years of his life, he called "one hundred-per-cent Americanism" was suggested to him by the dangers that threatened the unity if not the very existence of the American people during the dark days of the European war. But he had given expression to the same creed in almost the same words in the first book he ever published. When he was twenty-two years old he wrote his "Naval History of the War of 1812." It is so sound and fair a piece of historical writing that it has been adopted, I believe, by the British Admiralty as a standard authority on the naval battles of the first struggle of the English-speaking people to establish freedom of the seas. Take the following passage for example from that naval history:

They [certain aspects of the War of 1812] teach nothing new; it is the old, old lesson, that a miserly economy in preparation may in the end involve a lavish outlay of men and money, which, after all, comes too late to more than offset partially the evils produced by the original short-sighted parsimony. . . . The necessity for an efficient navy is so evident that only our almost incredible short-sightedness prevents our at once preparing one.

Does this not sound as if Roosevelt had written it in 1915 when, as a man nearly sixty years of age, he was laboriously endeavouring to arouse his fellow countrymen to the paramount duty and necessity of national preparedness?

This same doctrine was expressed to me in a letter which he wrote from the White House in January, 1903. It was in reply to one I had written about the judicial settlement of international disputes, saying that I believed that, in the last analysis, they must rest on the physical power of the court to make them effective. He wrote as follows:

Good for you! Important though it is that we should get the Hague Tribunal to act in this case, where it can properly act, it is very much more important that we have a first-class navy and an efficient, though small, army. No Hague Court will save us if we come short in these respects.

While I was talking over the war situation with Roosevelt one evening in the summer of 1917 in the north room at Sagamore Hill he said two things which seemed to me worth jotting down at the time as typical expressions of his belief in the necessity of a strong physical basis for both the individual and the nation.

The first was a reply which he said he once made to a boy who expressed the fear that he might be taken for a "goody-goody" if he followed a certain course that seemed to be called for by ethical principles. "Be always ready to fight if necessary. If you are ready to fight, you can be as good as you please and nobody is likely to complain."

The second was this succinct statement with regard to national vigour: "A race must do something else besides work, fight, and breathe; but if it does not do these three it will never live to do anything else."

It was this conviction of the righteousness of national vigour and of national self-defense that led him, when Assistant Secretary of the Navy— in opposition to the wishes and almost in violation of the definite orders of his chief, Secretary Long— to prepare the American Navy for the hostilities with Spain which he foresaw more clearly than most of his superiors in office. He did this by framing an important Personnel Bill, by accumulating ammunition, by encouraging the Navy in gunnery practice, and by distributing ships and supplies in such a way that the decisive victories of Admirals Dewey and Sampson were assured. It was this conviction that led him, when President, to send the Battle Fleet around the world in 1907, a feat of naval seamanship unparalleled before or since. The foreign experts said that it could not be done; that to send a Battle Fleet across the high seas, with all the attendant ships necessary for its maintenance, and to manœuvre it through distant straits and into unaccustomed harbours, would inevitably end in disaster. The dramatic and complete success of this unprecedented adventure did more to convince the European nations of the possibilities of efficiency in a self-governing democracy than untold volumes of blue books and state papers.

I speak with some confidence of Roosevelt's purpose in sending the Battle Fleet round the world because he talked somewhat fully to me about it—as will be seen from a passage in a letter which he wrote to me from Oyster Bay on August 29, 1907. It is proper, by the way, to interpolate the fact that the New York *Sun*, in those days, was under a different proprietorship and policy from those under which it is published to-day. Its present proprietor is Frank Munsey, a friend and supporter of Roosevelt, who bought the paper several years after the following letter was written:

There has been one extraordinary development during the last few days. I had not supposed that the *Sun* could surprise me. I know that there was no form of attack upon me which it would hesitate to make, and I also know that there was no type of corruption which would cause it even to turn a hair. But even corrupt men sometimes have other virtues and I had supposed that the *Sun* would remain loyal to its past in supporting the Navy and in refusing to sanction an attack upon the Administration which would cause the country discredit in foreign eyes. But the Wall Street campaign (I hate the term but I do not know what other to use) is so violent that it really looks as if they would go to almost any length. Upon my word I have never seen labour leaders go to greater extremes. They have actually taken to assailing the plan for sending the Battleship Fleet to the Pacific. Would it be of sufficient interest to have your brother and you come out here for lunch any day that suits you so that I can put before you in full all the reasons for the step? They have developed very rapidly.

It is hardly necessary to say that this invitation was promptly accepted. The reasons that Roosevelt gave me for his great naval venture were three in number:

First: As has already been intimated, he believed that the Navy is our first line of defence. He wished to have it not only powerful but maintained in a constant state of the highest efficiency. He wished both officers and men to have as nearly as possible the experience which they would undergo in fighting and manœuvring on the high seas. He felt that such a voyage would produce a spirit of confidence and of practical skill such as could be developed in no other way.

Second: He wanted to impress the country with the virtues and the capacities of a great navy. He knew that the best way to get American public opinion to support his policies for a strong navy was to arrest the attention and arouse the enthusiasm of the country in a dramatic fashion.

Third, and perhaps most important of all: He profoundly desired to maintain peace between

President Roosevelt reviewing the Battle Fleet at the time
of its world cruise

Japan and the United States whose relations at that time were strained, owing to the situation in California. He had insisted that the real rights of the Japanese in California should be respected, but he was equally determined to insist that the Japanese should respect the United States. "It is," he said, "rightly considered a great compliment for a naval fleet to visit a foreign country. For that reason, as a token of American friendliness for the Japanese people, I have directed the fleet to make its first important call upon Japan. I hope in this way to give the Japanese a visible sign of our friendship. At the same time, I want to impress upon them the fact that if the United States should ever be compelled to fight at sea its naval power is one to be respected."

This visit of the Fleet to Japan was not in the slightest degree a threat, nor did Roosevelt so regard it. It was a visit of friendship—but made under such conditions as to strengthen the dignity of the United States and Japan's respect for the power and determination of the American people. In a word, it put into visible form the doctrine which he expressed in one of those aphorisms that have become inseparably connected with his name: "Speak softly, but carry a big stick."

At the same time he was somewhat anxious about

the Japanese situation. There was and is a chauvinist or jingo party in Japan just as there is a chauvinist or jingo faction in the United States. If Japan intended to make war, Roosevelt intended to be prepared for it and he told me that his instructions were that the Fleet was always to be prepared for action no matter where it was. He did not propose to have anybody "pull a gun" on him and tell him to throw up his hands. He said that in an official speech privately addressed to a group of higher officers of the Fleet he had told them if war came and any commander lost a ship because he was surprised or unprepared he might just as well never come home himself.

What the effect of this voyage was upon the Japanese Government I do not of my own knowledge know, but I can testify that the Germans were particularly impressed. In 1910, during Roosevelt's memorable tour through Europe, I was present at a reception given to him jointly by our naval and our military attachés in Berlin. The guests, with three or four exceptions, were distinguished officers of the Kaiser's army and navy. The naval men in particular did not conceal their eagerness to meet the man who had performed a military deed at sea which they had regarded, when it was undertaken, as the foolhardy venture of an inexperienced braggart. More than one of them said to me that such an achievement was a stroke of genius and they literally crowded about Roosevelt eager to shake his hand as if he had been a kind of modern Neptune. It was perfectly manifest that their respect for him, and for the country which he represented, had been enormously increased by the fact that he had done what they, confident in their own skill as seamen, had predicted that neither he nor they nor any one else could do. It is no detraction from the heroic and splendid performance of the American Navy in the European war to believe, as I do, that if Mr. Roosevelt had been President in 1914, and had notified the Kaiser—as he certainly would have done—that he would throw the American Navy into the struggle the moment the foot of an invading German soldier was set upon the soil of Belgium the world would have been spared much of the bloodshed of the past four years and much of the chaos of the present day.

But Theodore Roosevelt's nationalism was not exclusive of internationalism; it was, rather, complementary to it. He believed that the nations of the earth could not and should not live together as members of one family like a gigantic Brook Farm or a Oneida Community but as independent and strongly developed families in a well-organized neighbourhood. He used to say that a man who professes to love all other families as much as he loves his own is likely not only to be a failure as a husband and father but also to be an undesirable neighbour. "Keep your eye on such a man," he once remarked to me; "he is not only foolish but he is liable to be dangerous." Roosevelt had no patience with the communistic vagaries of the French revolutionary philosophers. While socially and economically he was much more democratic than Hamilton or even, I venture to think, than Washington, he liked them better and trusted them more than Jefferson because of Jefferson's flirtations with the unpractical and closet idealists of the First French Republic.

In trying to interpret Mr. Roosevelt's nationalism I do not know how I can do better than to quote a passage from his "Life of Gouverneur Morris," in the American Statesmen Series. It was written when he was twenty-nine years old:

Jefferson led the Democrats to victory only when he had learned to acquiesce thoroughly in some of the fundamental principles of Federalism, and the government of himself and his successors was good chiefly in so far as it followed out the theories of the Hamiltonians; while Hamilton and the Federalists fell from power because they could not learn the one great truth taught by Jefferson—that in America a statesman should trust the people, and should endeavour to secure to each man all possible individual liberty, confident that he will use it aright. The old-school Jeffersonian theorists believed in a "strong people and a weak government." Lincoln was the first who showed how a strong people might have a strong government and yet remain the freest on earth. He seized—half unwittingly—all that was best and wisest in the traditions of Federalism; he was the true successor of the Federalist leaders; but he grafted on their system a profound belief that the great heart of the nation beat for truth, honour, and liberty.

This estimate of Lincoln, made before Roosevelt was thirty years old, became stronger and stronger during his life. He had a kind of divine reverence for Lincoln. He once told me that whenever he was facing a puzzling problem of action he would ask himself: "What would Lincoln have done in such a case?"—and would then try to shape his course according to what he believed would have been Lincoln's example.

During the Progressive campaign in 1912 Roosevelt made a speech entitled "The New Nationalism" which he later expounded by other speeches afterward collected and published in a fairly good-sized volume. These pronouncements at once attracted the attention of the country and created almost a furore of public discussion. It was said by his opponents that the theories and proposals in these speeches were subversive of the Constitution, that Roosevelt wished to alter the very structure of our government. His proposals, however, except in some minor details, were not at all new or radical when measured by his utterances and acts over a long period of years. They were simply a restatement, in more elaborate form, of the thought expressed in the foregoing quotation from the Life of Morris. He wished to show that a strong centralized government is not only compatible with but necessary to the protection of popular rights and even-handed justice in a representative democracy. Provided that the people have the free and untrammelled right to select their representatives at the ballot box, their best protection, he believed, lies not in the diffusion but in the concentration of power coupled with direct responsibility to the people for the exercise of that power.

This brings me logically to what I believe was the next most important article in his creed of statesmanship:

POLITICAL, INDUSTRIAL, AND SOCIAL REFORM.—While he was an ardent Nationalist and believed in a centralized government in which the ablest men were given great responsibilities and held to strict accountability, he recognized that as efficiency is a greater power for good so corruption is a greater power for evil in a strongly centralized government. He therefore endeavoured not only to improve the standards and personnel of government officials but, by what was literally preaching and exhorting, to arouse a sense of civic responsibility among the great body of citizens. No President, probably, has issued more or longer Messages to Congress, but while these papers were technically addressed to Congress they were really addressed to the whole country. He often spoke of his public and official speeches as "preaching," and he more than once said that he put what he had to say in the form of sermons because he had such a "bully pulpit." The result was that he attracted to his side and surrounded himself with official colleagues and associates who had the same enthusiasm and the same high standards that he himself had.

Political service in office took on a different meaning under the inspiration of his theory and practice. I think it not unfair to say that forty years ago a man in public office, particularly of a subordinate character, was generally regarded with some suspicion by the so-called "better citizens" until he had proved himself innocent. It was not an uncommon assumption that every man in public office took the position because he could get his hands and feet in the public trough. This at least is my recollection of the political atmosphere in 1880 when I cast my first presidential vote for Garfield. It was at this date that Roosevelt was elected to the New York Legislature. Roosevelt did more than any other American, in my judgment, to modify this attitude completely. At the close of his administration the public began to feel, as it ought always to feel, that the badge of public office is a badge of respect; it began to regard Federal officials as well as Federal clerks as it regards the officers and enlisted men in the Army and the Navy.

Certainly this was what Mr. Roosevelt wanted to accomplish. He believed that a man or a woman who works for the Government in any civil capacity ought to be actuated by the same patriotic motives and regard the service with the same patriotic respect that prevail in the Army and the Navy. No President has done more than did Roosevelt to discredit and put out of joint the old Jacksonian theory of party government that "To the victors belong the spoils."

Along with this work of political reform he undertook, in the face of the most overwhelming difficulties, the reform of the industrial corporations. He did not believe, to quote the words of

Theodore Roosevelt as President. Taken at his desk in the White House during his second term

The last meeting of the Roosevelt Cabinet

President Wilson, that "the American people are living a life of economic serfdom," but he was convinced that there was altogether too much secret and corrupt meddling with politics by the corporations for their own selfish benefit. He was a believer in the corporation as an instrument of industry. He did not at all think that badness is an essential element of bigness. He had not the slightest objection to the corporations doing a business on a gigantic scale, provided that these operations were honest, above-board, visible, subject to proper government control, and based on a just, fair, and civilized treatment both of employees and of the small investor. As a matter of fact, he cordially disliked the attitude of the extremists who seemed to feel that the corporations were enemies of society with whom there could be no possible basis of association.

In February, 1903, while he was struggling to obtain Federal legislation to put an end to railway rebates, he wrote me a long letter from the White House which contained the following paragraph:

No respectable railroad or respectable shipping business can openly object to the Rebate Bill; and the Nelson amendment and the bill to expedite legislation, to both of which there has been most violent opposition, have now been rather sullenly acquiesced in. But as soon as the business interests showed any symptoms of acquiescence, certain individuals at once asserted that the legislation was bad, because they did not want it unless it frightened the corporations.

He was not trying to destroy the corporations; he was not even trying to frighten them; he was trying to coöperate with them in making them real servants of society. His differentiation between "good" trusts and "bad" trusts was ridiculed at the time, but the European war has demonstrated the soundness of the principle. Tremendous organization is needed to accomplish tremendous tasks. The organization is to be judged by its spirit, its aims, and its accomplishments—not by its size.

His successful attacks upon the Standard Oil Company and the Sugar Trust were not made because these organizations were big, but because of certain pernicious practices. He could not tolerate what one of his colleagues, Senator Beveridge, has defined as "invisible government"—that secret partnership between "big business" and pliable politicians which grew to such huge proportions after the Civil War and reached its climax just about the time that Mr. Roosevelt became President. Under his administration the Federal Department of Commerce and Labour was established and the policy of government regulation of railways was greatly strengthened. He was one

of the first public men in this country to espouse
the doctrine of industrial democracy, that is to say,
the doctrine that the workers and toilers shall not
only have their proper share of the profits of industry but also some voice in the management of
industry.   In this connection it may not be out of
place for me to quote from a letter that Mr. Roosevelt wrote to me in the summer of 1907:

I continually get points from the *Outlook*. If you do not object, I am going to work into one of my speeches your admirable little thesis on adding democracy in industry to
democracy in political rights, education, and religion. You
have exactly hit upon my purpose, but you phrase my purpose better than I have ever phrased it myself.

What the *Outlook* had said, eliciting this comment, was that as the Reformation and the
emigration of the Puritans to the Western Hemi-
sphere had established the equal rights or freedom
of men in their religious activities; as the American Revolution and the Civil War had established
the equal rights or freedom of men in politics; and
as the establishment of the American public school
system had established equal rights or freedom in
education; so the American people, perhaps halt-
ingly but with evident purpose, were entering
upon a moment to establish equal rights or freedom
in industry.   Equal rights in religion of course

does not mean that every man shall be a bishop; in politics, that every man shall be a United States senator; or in education, that every man shall be a college president. But it does mean that every man shall have some kind of a voice in choosing his bishop, his senator, or the head of his educational system. So the workers who constitute what is called labour are not merely to be paid their real share of the total product of labour, but they are to have some opportunity to determine and regulate the conditions under which they shall work. It should never be forgotten, I think, that Mr. Roosevelt was one of the foremost pioneers in the movement, now rapidly accelerating, to establish Industrial Democracy, where all men shall have equal rights under the law and where there shall be no privileged or special interests exempt from the operations of the law.

CONSERVATION OF NATIONAL RESOURCES.—The old theory with regard to the natural wealth of the United States was that the forests and lumber, the water power, the oil wells, the coal, and other minerals belong to the private owner of the land to exploit and sell as he pleases for private profit. Along with this theory ran the policy of the Government, undoubtedly desirable and beneficial within proper limits, of giving away vast tracts of public land to the pioneer who would develop the natural wealth and so contribute to the general welfare of the country.

This system led not only to the concentration of riches in private hands but to the rapid exhaustion of certain forms of national wealth, especially lumber-bearing forests. The natural desire for quick profits was proving to be more powerful than the cautionary motive of preserving our capital resources for future generations. If Mr. Roosevelt did not invent the term "Conservation of National Resources," he was the first great leader in this country to espouse and establish the new theory with regard to our national wealth. This theory is that the Government—acting for the people, who are the real owners of public property—shall permanently retain the fee in public lands, leaving their products to be developed by private capital under leases, which are limited in their duration and which give the Government complete power to regulate the industrial operations of the lessees.

On June 8, 1908, Mr. Roosevelt, then President, appointed a National Conservation Commission. This commission made an inventory of our national wealth, which was published in 1909. It was the first inventory of its kind in history. Gifford Pinchot, an intimate personal friend and official colleague of President Roosevelt's, was chairman of the Commission and Mr. Pinchot, with the approval and support of Roosevelt, rapidly became the public representative of the Conservation movement. The country has by no means yet succeeded in putting an end to the extraordinary waste of its public wealth. In the *Atlantic Monthly* for March, 1919, Mr. Arthur D. Little, an accomplished and able chemical engineer of Boston, writes as follows:

The wastes in lumbering are proverbial, and, as Mark Twain said about the weather, we all talk about it, but nothing is done. With a total annual cut of forty billion feet, board-measure, of merchantable lumber, another seventy billion feet are wasted in the field and at the mill. In the yellow-pine belt the values in rosin, turpentine, ethyl alcohol, pine oil, tar, charcoal, and paper-stock lost in the waste are three or four times the value of the lumber produced. Enough yellow-pine pulp-wood is consumed in burners, or left to rot, to make double the total tonnage of paper produced in the United States. Meanwhile, our paper-makers memorialize the community on the scarcity of paper-stock, and pay $18 a cord for pulp-wood which they might buy for $3. It takes many years to produce a crop of wood, and wood-waste, which now constitutes from one-half to two-thirds of the entire tree, is too valuable a raw material to be longer regarded merely as an encumbrance, except by an improvident management.

But the wastes in lumbering, colossal though they are in

absolute amount, are trivial compared to the losses which our estate has suffered, and still endures, from forest fires. The French properly regard as a national calamity the destruction of perhaps a thousand square miles of their fine forests by German shells. And yet the photographs that they show of this wreck and utter demolition may be reproduced indefinitely on ten million acres of our forest lands, swept each year by equally devastating fire for which our own people are responsible. You have doubtless already forgotten that forest fire which last autumn, in Minnesota, burned over an area half as large again as Massachusetts, destroying more than twenty-five towns, killing four hundred people, and leaving thirteen thousand homeless.

Mr. Little is somewhat beside the mark in saying: "We all talk about it but nothing is done." Something has been done. The most important work of President Roosevelt in domestic statesmanship, next to his injection of moral ideas and moral impetus into administrative politics, was his inauguration and fostering of Conservation. I have space only to state that opinion here. The reader who is interested will find in the New International Encyclopædia under the title "Conservation" the best brief account, which has come under my eye, of the results and purposes of the Conservation movement inaugurated by Roosevelt with the aid of Gifford Pinchot.

Roosevelt was never greatly interested in mere questions of finance, nor in economics on its merely statistical side. But the moment that he perceived the human relationships of an economic question he threw himself into the problem with his fullest energies. It was the human aspect of Conservation that aroused his championship. Some other things that he did, as President, were so much more spectacular that there is danger of his leadership in Conservation being lost sight of. On the contrary, it deserves the fullest study of future historians.

The abject pacifism and the wasteful folly of the Chinese with regard to their natural resources stirred him about equally and he often referred to the lack of patriotic nationalism on the one hand, and to private greed in exploiting our national resources on the other as tendencies which, if persisted in, would "Chinafy" the United States. He believed that the incentives of private profit and of brave and virile pioneering are important factors in developing American character and American citizenship. But he also believed that they should be directed not by the whims of individuals but by the common and united determination of all the people.

COLONIAL POLICY.—By determining, at the close of the Spanish War, that Cuba should not be taken over by the United States—as all Europe

President Roosevelt with the members of the Conservation Commission

expected, and as an influential section of his party
hoped that it would be—but should be given every
opportunity to govern itself, he established the
precedent for the colonial policy which the Peace
Conference of Paris has now embodied in the so-
called "mandatory" principle, namely, that colonies
should be administered as a trust for the benefit of
the inhabitants.   It is true that Cuba was set on
her own feet during the Presidency of McKinley,
but when under the Platt Amendment the United
States intervened in Cuba during the Roosevelt
Administration there would have been every political and many moral justifications for our annexa-
tion of the island.   This Roosevelt would not consent to.   In his autobiography he refers to his
Cuban policy as follows:

We made the promise to give Cuba independence; and
we kept the promise.   Leonard Wood was left in as governor
for two or three years, and evolved order out of chaos, raising the administration of the island to a level, moral and material, which it had never before achieved.   We also, by
treaty, gave the Cubans substantial advantages in our mar-
kets.   Then we left the island, turning the government
over to its own people.   After four or five years a revolution
broke out, during my administration, and we again had to
intervene to restore order.   We promptly sent thither a small
army of pacification.   Under General Barry, order was re-
stored and kept, and absolute justice was done.   The American troops were then withdrawn and the Cubans reëstablished in complete possession of their own beautiful island,

and they are in possession of it now. There are plenty of occasions in our history when we have shown weakness or inefficiency, and some occasions when we have not been as scrupulous as we should have been as regards the rights of others. But I know of no action by any other government in relation to a weaker power which showed such disinterested efficiency in rendering service as was true in connection with our intervention in Cuba.

In numerous speeches and addresses he expressed his belief in a strong and efficient colonial government, but a government which should be administered for the benefit of the colonial people and not for the profit of the people at home. It is worth while to quote on this subject from a speech which Mr. Roosevelt made in Christiania, Norway, on May 5, 1910. The occasion was a public dinner given in his honour on the evening of the day when the celebration was held in recognition of the award to him of the Nobel Peace Prize. He had made his set and carefully prepared speech in the afternoon. At this dinner he spoke unexpectedly and wholly extemporaneously, but the address was taken down stenographically. In the course of it he said:

I was particularly pleased by what you said about our course, the course of the American people, in connection with the Philippines and Cuba. I believe that we have the Cuban Minister here with us to-night? [A voice: "Yes."] Well, then, we have a friend who can check off what I am going to say. At the close of the war of '98 we found our army in possession of Cuba, and man after man among the European diplomats of the old school said to me: "Oh, you will never go out of Cuba. You said you would, of course, but that is quite understood; nations don't expect promises like that to be kept."

As soon as I became President, I said: "Now you will see that the promise will be kept." We appointed a day when we would leave Cuba. On that day Cuba began its existence as an independent republic.

Later there came a disaster, there came a revolution, and we were obliged to land troops again, while I was President, and then the same gentlemen with whom I had conversed before said: "Now you are relieved from your promise; your promise has been kept, and now you will stay in Cuba." I answered: "No, we shall not. We will keep the promise not only in the letter but in the spirit. We will stay in Cuba to help it on its feet, and then we will leave the island in better shape to maintain its permanent independent existence." And before I left the Presidency Cuba resumed its career as a separate republic, holding its head erect as a sovereign state among the other nations of the earth.

All that our people want is just exactly what the Cuban people themselves want—that is, a continuance of order within the island, and peace and prosperity, so that there shall be no shadow of an excuse for any outside intervention.

.   .   .   .

We have in the Philippines a people mainly Asiatic in blood, but with a streak of European blood and with the traditions of European culture, so that their ideals are largely the ideals of Europe. At the moment when we entered the islands the people were hopelessly unable to stand alone. If we had abandoned the islands, we should have left them a prey to anarchy for some months, and then they would have been seized by some other Power ready to perform the task that we had not been able to perform.

Now I hold that it is not worth while being a big nation if you cannot do a big task; I care not whether that task is digging the Panama Canal or handling the Philippines. In the Philippines I feel that the day will ultimately come when the Philippine people must settle for themselves whether they wish to be entirely independent, or in some shape to keep up a connection with us. The day has not yet come; it may not come for a generation or two.

One of the greatest friends that liberty has ever had, the great British statesman, Burke, said on one occasion that there must always be government, and that if there is not government from within, then it must be supplied from without. A child has to be governed from without, because it has not yet grown to a point when it can govern itself from within; and a people that shows itself totally unable to govern itself from within must expect to submit to more or less of government from without, because it cannot continue to exist on other terms—indeed, it cannot be permitted permanently to exist as a source of danger to other nations.

Our aim in the Philippines is to train the people so that they may govern themselves from within. Until they have reached this point they cannot have self-government. I will never advocate self-government for a people so long as their self-government means crime, violence, and extortion, corruption within, lawlessness among themselves and toward others. If that is what self-government means to any people, then they ought to be governed by others until they can do better.

In respect to the facts that I have stated and the views that I have quoted from Mr. Roosevelt himself, is it not a reasonable conclusion to say that for the seven years of his administration as President he developed a policy of statesmanship quite new in the history of the United States?

THE RUSSO-JAPANESE PEACE.—The Nobel Peace Prize was awarded to Theodore Roosevelt for his acts as a mediator between Russia and Japan, which resulted in the Treaty of Portsmouth and the ending of the Russo-Japanese War in 1905. The prize consisted of a gold medal and forty thousand dollars. He acknowledged this award in the formal address in 1910 at Christiania already referred to. Officially it was delivered before the Nobel Prize Committee, but actually, it was a public oration spoken in the National Theatre of Christiania before an audience of two or three thousand people. His subject was: "International Peace." At the outset he said:

The gold medal which formed part of the prize I shall always keep, and I shall hand it on to my children as a precious heirloom. The sum of money provided as part of the prize, by the wise generosity of the illustrious founder of this world-famous prize system, I did not, under the peculiar circumstances of the case, feel at liberty to keep. I think it eminently just and proper that in most cases the recipient of the prize should keep, for his own use, the prize in its entirety. But in this case, while I did not act officially as President of the United States, it was nevertheless only because I was President that I was enabled to act at all; and I felt that the money must be considered as having been given me in trust for the United States. I therefore used it as a nucleus for a foundation to forward the cause of industrial peace, as being well within the general purpose of your committee; for, in our complex industrial civilization of to-day, the peace of righteousness and justice, the only kind of peace worth having, is at least as necessary in the industrial world as it is among nations.

Like most of Mr. Roosevelt's acts of statesmanship his course in the settlement of the Russo-Japanese War was widely, and sometimes acrimoniously, discussed at the time. As a matter of fact, what he did was a great and, in some respects, a complicated achievement, but the principles that he followed were simple, natural, and based upon common sense.

In September, 1908, I wrote an editorial of more than ordinary length which endeavoured to interpret the genesis and results of the Russo-Japanese peace treaty. This editorial was questioned at the time. As a matter of fact, it was based upon personal statements made to me by President Roosevelt, and I think it had his entire approval. The Springfield *Republican*, an avowed opponent of President Roosevelt's foreign policy, had published an article in which it said that skilful Russian diplomacy had cunningly manipulated Roosevelt so that he had become "Russia's strongest ally in forcing the Japanese to accept what were virtually the Russian terms of peace." In the course of my own editorial comment the following phrases were employed:

Our version of President Roosevelt's intervention in behalf of peace is exactly contrary to the Kovalevsky-*Republican*

version.   The desire for peace was not imposed upon Japan,
it came from Japan; Russia did not at once see an opportunity
of employing a conference for the purpose of turning military
disaster into a diplomatic and financial victory; on the contrary, the idea that peace was essential to Russia's future welfare was driven into the minds of an obstinate bureaucracy
only by the patient arguments of the President.   This view
of the Portsmouth Treaty, in our judgment, has been established by public records and by the processes of simple logic;
it will be confirmed, we believe, when the time comes for the
publication of the diplomatic correspondence and state
papers.   By the intervention of the President not only did
Japan receive what it was wholly wise for her to accept and
what she really desired to obtain, but Russia was protected
from the further disaster into which the folly of her bureau-
crats and the double dealing of her diplomacy would have
plunged her.

On October first, the President, having read my
editorial, wrote me a letter from the White House
in which he said:

Properly speaking, there are no "state papers" about the
Portsmouth Treaty on this side of the water.   It was done
on my private initiative, but there is no reason why you
should not specifically say that you had access to all the
original documents with which the President had any connection, and that you speak with full knowledge.

In talking with me, afterward, Roosevelt said:
"As a matter of fact, in spite of their great naval
and military victories, the Japanese statesmen—
not the Japanese people—were sagacious and far-
seeing enough to know that they were approaching

the end of their resources of both men and material
while Russia's resources were unlimited. The
Japanese came to me privately and, with some reluctance, expressed this point of view and asked
me if I could not do something. I said I would try.
I went to the Russians and pointed out the economic and political folly of continuing the war and
asked if they would not join in a peace conference
with the Japanese if I arranged it. They finally
said: 'Yes, if the Japanese will consent, but we do
not believe they will. We will come, however, if
you can persuade them.' I replied that I would
see what I could do, and [this with his characteristic
chuckle] all the time I had the Japanese request in
my breeches' pocket!"

A characteristic incident happened at the first
meeting of the Russo-Japanese conference in this
country. At the luncheon, to which President
Roosevelt invited the representatives of both nations, on board the presidential yacht *Mayflower*,
at Oyster Bay, Mr. Roosevelt told me that he was
somewhat puzzled what to do about the delicate
question of precedence. "If I took in Count
Witte," he said, "the Japanese would be offended;
on the other hand, if I took in Baron Komura it
would displease the Russians, so when luncheon
was announced I simply said 'Gentlemen, shall

Peace envoys on board *Mayflower*, August, 1905. Count Witte, Baron Rosen, President Roosevelt, Minister Takahira and Baron Komura

President Roosevelt at Panama inspecting the Canal which "he took"

we go into luncheon?'; and we all walked in together, pell-mell. I dare say both Russians and Japanese were somewhat astounded at this informality, but they probably put it down to my American inexperience in social matters!"

The Russo-Japanese Peace, which was effected almost solely by the strength of Roosevelt's influence and personality, was a boon to the two contestants, for it saved Russia from the inevitable consequences that continued persistence in stupidity and folly must have entailed while it strengthened Japan in her determination to preserve for herself the real fruits both of military victory and of a humane and sagacious statesmanship. Moreover, it put Roosevelt himself on record as an advocate of justice instead of belligerency in international relationships. In his address before the Nobel Prize Committee in Christiania on May 5, 1910, he said on this subject:

It is earnestly to be hoped that the various governments of Europe, working with those of America and Asia, shall set themselves seriously to the task of devising some method which will accomplish this result. [The establishment of an international supreme court of the world.] If I may venture the suggestion, it would be well for the statesmen of the world, in planning for the erection of this world court, to study what has been done in the United States by the Supreme Court. I cannot help thinking that the Constitution of the United States, notably in the establishment of the Supreme

Court and in the methods adopted for securing peace and good
relations among and between the different states, offers certain valuable analogies to what should be striven for in order
to secure, through the Hague courts and conferences, a
species of world federation for international peace and justice. . . .

Something should be done as soon as possible to check the
growth of armaments, especially naval armaments, by international agreement. No one Power could or should act by
itself; for it is eminently undesirable, from the standpoint of
the peace of righteousness, that a Power which really does
believe in peace should place itself at the mercy of some rival
which may, at bottom, have no such belief and no intention
of acting on it. But, granted sincerity of purpose, the Great
Powers of the world should find no insurmountable difficulty
in reaching an agreement which would put an end to the present costly and growing expenditure on naval armaments. . . .

It would be a master stroke if those Great Powers, honestly
bent on peace, should form a League of Peace, not only to
keep the peace among themselves, but to prevent, by force if
necessary, its being broken by others. . . .

In new and wild communities, where there is violence, an
honest man must protect himself; and until other means of
securing his safety are devised, it is both foolish and wicked
to persuade him to surrender his arms while the men who are
dangerous to the community retain theirs. He should not
renounce the right to protect himself by his own efforts until
the community is so organized that it can effectively relieve
the individual of the duty of putting down violence. So it
is with nations. Each nation must keep well prepared to
defend itself until the establishment of some form of international police power, competent and willing to prevent
violence as between nations. . . .

The combination might at first be only to secure peace
within certain definite limits and certain definite conditions;
but the ruler or statesman who should bring about such a

combination would have earned his place in history for all time, and his title to the gratitude of all mankind.

In this statement, made nine years ago, Roosevelt was the prophet and advocate of the international state of mind that has been produced by the World War.

THE PANAMA CANAL.—The greatest material contribution that Theodore Roosevelt made to his country, to his time, and to the world, was the Panama Canal. That canal will be his enduring monument, and its name, as has been suggested, might well be changed to "The Roosevelt Canal." It is not necessary here to enter into the details of its history. For five hundred years the project had been discussed. For one hundred years England had thought of—some time—undertaking it. The French did undertake it—and failed. If it had not been for Roosevelt, the world would have gone on debating and arguing about it for years to come.

In a previous chapter I have quoted his phrase, now known around the world: "I took Panama." In those three laconic words he means that he acted where others for years had failed to act. What he did was simply to seize with courage and vigour an opportunity that presented itself. The inhabitants of the State of Panama wanted the canal, and they seceded from the Republic of Colombia in order to give the United States an opportunity to build it. Everybody is satisfied, except the people of Colombia, who suffered from the greedy proclivities of some of their corrupt politicians. I must also except from the category of satisfied persons some members of the Wilson Administration who cannot bear to have the name of Roosevelt go down in history, in connection with the Panama Canal, unblotted and undimmed.

Roosevelt, I think, felt two great resentments against President Wilson. The first and most important was a patriotic one, arising from the fact that Mr. Wilson opposed by word and act the policy of preparedness which Roosevelt felt was essential to the safety of our national life during the first two years of the European war. The other resentment was personal. Mr. Wilson had proposed that the United States should pay the Republic of Colombia $25,000,000 as a reparation for the wrong which she alleged had been done her in the building of the Panama Canal. Mr. Roosevelt felt that such a payment would be nothing but blackmail; that either his course and that of his administration was just and right—in which case Colombia deserved nothing; or that Colombia had been robbed—and that the only just reparation, in logic, would be the entire cession of the canal to Colombia. Moreover, if the United States paid Colombia $25,000,000, it would be an acknowledgment of crime, and a petty and contemptible compounding of a felony. Of course, he did not for a moment believe that any crime had been committed. He never was more strenuous than when he was explaining and defending the action he took with regard to Colombia and the secession of Panama. He profoundly believed that he had performed not only an act of service to the world but an act of public justice.

In spite of his deep feeling, his irrepressible and buoyant humour enabled him often to see the comic side of the controversy. He once said to me that, in a Cabinet meeting, when he was reporting his executive action—which he describes briefly as "the taking of Panama"—and appealing for an endorsement of its legal and constitutional character, one of the secretaries—I think it was Attorney-General Knox—exclaimed ironically:"Oh, Mr. President, do not let so great an achievement suffer from any taint of legality!"

In 1914 I happened to be returning from Europe with a group of friends on the *Imperator*—the steamer in which Colonel Roosevelt was crossing after having been to Spain, to attend the wedding of his son Kermit, and to London, to deliver a lecture before the Royal Geographical Society on his South American explorations. The United States Minister to Colombia under the Taft Administration was on the steamer and he asked me to arrange that he might meet Mr. Roosevelt whom he (the Minister), with an incredible optimism, hoped to persuade to take a favourable view of the proposed 25,000,000-dollar payment to Colombia. Mr. Roosevelt consented to see the Minister. The interview, at which I was present, was a thoroughly lively one. The next day, in describing it to one of my steamer companions— Mr. William Hamlin Childs, later intimately associated with him in Liberal Republican politics— Roosevelt remarked: "You know, Childs, it is said that I started a revolution in Panama. The fact is there had been fifty revolutions in Panama from time to time, but while I was President I kept my foot on these revolutions; so that, when the Panama Canal situation arose, it was entirely unnecessary for me to start a revolution. I simply lifted my foot!"

In this chapter I have not tried to give a chronological history of Roosevelt's statesmanship nor to interpret it in the terms of the diplomatist or economist. I have simply attempted to show what I fully believe, that both the aims and the achievements of his statesmanship—some of them immortal so far as world history goes— had their source in his intense humanity. ' Pomposity, artificiality, cunning, secretiveness, and selfishness were totally foreign to him. He believed that statesmen and nations should meet and conduct their affairs on exactly the same plane as that upon which neighbours in a community stand in their relationship. He talked to ambassadors and kings as one man talks to another. That was the real secret of his power.

CHAPTER V

FOREIGN AFFAIRS

IN HIS autobiography Colonel Roosevelt says: "By far the most important action I took in foreign affairs during the time I was President related to the Panama Canal."

With the qualification: "during the time I was President" this is doubtless true, although there are three things that he did—one while he was President, and two after his retirement from that office—which had a moral influence or reaction upon foreign affairs that entitled them to be ranked very close to the Panama achievement. It is probable that if Roosevelt could read this statement he would question it. At any rate, he did not consider as important enough to mention in his autobiography the actions which I have in mind. He performed them in the ordinary course of the day's work. Nevertheless, I have always thought they made a permanent—an almost incalculable—impression upon our foreign relations.

The first of these achievements was the remission of the Chinese indemnity; the second was the speech he made at the Guildhall in London in 1910; and the third was his stimulating address to the French people at the Sorbonne in Paris in the same year.

THE CHINESE INDEMNITY.—As a result of the Boxer Rebellion in 1900 the United States received from China an indemnity of about twenty-five million dollars for the damage and dangers to American lives and property. The payments were being regularly made by China, she having accepted the indemnity as a just execution of international law.

In 1906, Dr. Arthur H. Smith—long an American missionary, resident in China—made a visit to this country. He knew and liked the Chinese, and few Europeans or Americans have become more familiar with their life, literature, customs, and manners. He is the author of two admirable books on modern China: "Chinese Characteristics" and "Village Life in China." As an old-time reader of the *Outlook* he came to our office to enlist our interest in a plan, regarding the Chinese indemnity, which he wished to bring to President Roosevelt's attention.

His plan, which he had carefully worked out in detail, was that one half of the Boxer indemnity, say about twelve million dollars, should be given back to China on the understanding that she use the money, or its income, for sending Chinese young men to American collegiate institutions, and for educating certain other young Chinese in American institutions in China.

His point of view was not that of the conventional missionary. It was really that of the statesman. He said that when he first went to China the American flag was seen on vessels in every harbour, but that now it was rarely visible; that America ought to do something to renew her intimate economic, industrial, and commercial relations and so cement the political friendship which had been fostered by Secretary Hay. He believed that with a body of young Chinese being graduated annually from American institutions, we should finally have a great company of influential men in China who understood American ways and sympathized with the American spirit; that no other way could China and the United States be brought together so effectively in their economic and political relationship.

The plan made a strong impression upon my father and myself, and my father wrote to the President asking whether he would see Dr. Smith. Mr. Roosevelt replied appointing a day for the meeting. It was early in March, 1906—I think the sixth. My father was unable to go to Washington, so, at Roosevelt's suggestion, I accompanied Dr. Smith and was present at the interview which took place in the Red Room. My recollection is that we first lunched with the President and afterward returned for a longer conference in the evening. At all events, Roosevelt showed his interest by giving Dr. Smith and myself a personal interview of much more than ordinary length, and the plan, in complete detail, was laid before the President by Dr. Smith. The result of that conference was that, the following year, the remission of the unpaid portion of the indemnity was authorized and the money that would have gone to the United States was devoted by China to educational purposes. (The complete record may be found in House Document No. 1275 of the second session of the Sixtieth Congress.)

Ten years after this visit of Dr. Smith to the White House I happened to be seated at a Princeton Faculty Club luncheon beside Dr. Robert McNutt McElroy, who had just been selected as the first American exchange professor to China, and he and I fell into conversation about Dr. Smith's part in the indemnity remission. Dr. McElroy was so much interested that he expressed a desire to relate the story in his lectures in China. I asked him not to do so until I had verified my recollection of the incident that had occurred ten years before. I accordingly wrote to Mr. Roosevelt at Oyster Bay recalling the White House interview which I have just described and Mr. Roosevelt replied under date of January 24, 1916, as follows:

My memory agrees with yours about Dr. Arthur H. Smith. I had forgotten his name; but I know that it was through your father that I first became interested in using that indemnity for educational purposes. The idea was suggested to me as you describe it; and then I asked Root to take it up and put it in operation.

Of course the remission of the Boxer indemnity established Chinese friendship for the American people on the firmest kind of basis. But this was not the only effect of this action on foreign affairs. There is another aspect of the achievement which seems worth bearing in mind.

It is said by many publicists that governments cannot have altruistic qualities and motives. In two cases, at least, the history of the United States shows that governments can, in practice, be altruistic. We were empowered to take $25,-000,000 from China in accordance with the best standards of international action and we voluntarily gave up half that sum in order to promote a moral idea. We took Cuba, a rich possession, in the course of a war which, at the very least, was a war carried on in accordance with common international procedure. Europe, especially Germany, said it was cant to assert that we made war for the benefit of the Cubans, and that our chief motive was to gain the splendid prize of Cuba. But we gave Cuba back to the Cubans, only asking that they keep it in order.

If there are in history any other two similar instances of national altruism, I do not know of them. These two historical facts, it seems to me, should be kept before the coming generations in their studies of the structure of government, not in order that we may plume ourselves upon our virtue, but in order to show that the moral law may be made to work in international practice just as it works in the individual practice of the citizens of a community.

These two acts of national morals are in a very real sense the acts of President Roosevelt and a product of his philosophy of statesmanship. He did not merely preach about national morals but somehow or other he got national things done on a distinctly moral basis; and he was not a mollycoddle, either!

His satisfaction in practical altruism appears in the following exchange of notes which I find

among my papers. On February 10, 1917, I wrote
Roosevelt as follows:

Everett P. Wheeler, who, as you know, is an old-line Democrat—and therefore, I suppose, naturally one of your critics—
has just published a book called "Sixty Years of American
Life." In looking it over, at the head of Chapter XII, which
deals with New York City politics, I find the following quotation ascribed to you: "Aggressive fighting for the right is
the noblest sport the world knows." Do you remember
where and when you said it? It is delightful to think of doing
good as a high-class sport.

To this query Roosevelt replied:

I remember perfectly using that sentence, but I cannot tell
you the exact date. It was when I was Police Commissioner
and, I think, in connection with an address to some college
boys.

THE GUILDHALL SPEECH.—Roosevelt took
a sporting chance in making his Guildhall speech,
which had a more far-reaching, if less direct, effect
on foreign affairs than the remission of the Chinese
indemnity.

Of all the public addresses that Roosevelt made
during his tour through Egypt and Europe in the
summer of 1910—a trip which I shall describe more
fully in the next chapter—the Guildhall speech
was, in my judgment, the most striking and notable. The occasion was the ceremony in the ancient
and noble Guildhall, one of the most perfect Gothic

interiors in England, which has historical associations of more than five centuries, when he was presented by the Corporation of the City of London (the oldest corporation in the world) with the freedom of the city. In this speech he praised the colonial administration of Great Britain in Africa and frankly criticized the course of the British Government then in power in its conduct of the protectorate of Egypt. In order to appreciate the furore that this speech aroused, his criticism must be read in its entirety:

Now as to Egypt. It would not be worth my while to speak to you at all, nor would it be worth your while to listen, unless on condition that I say what I deeply feel ought to be said. I speak as an outsider, but in one way this is an advantage, for I speak without national prejudice. I would not talk to you about your own internal affairs here at home, but you are so very busy at home that I am not sure whether you realize just how things are, in some places at least, abroad. At any rate, it can do you no harm to hear the view of one who has actually been on the ground, and has information at first hand; of one, moreover, who, it is true, is a sincere well-wisher of the British Empire, but who is not English by blood, and who is impelled to speak mainly because of his deep concern in the welfare of mankind and in the future of civilization. Remember also that I who address you am not only an American, but a Radical, a real—not a mock—democrat, and that what I have to say is spoken chiefly because I am a democrat, a man who feels that his first thought is bound to be the welfare of the masses of mankind, and his first duty to war against violence and injustice and wrong-doing, wherever found; and I advise you only in accordance with the principles on which I have myself acted as American President in dealing with the Philippines.

In Egypt you are not only the guardians of your own interests; you are also the guardians of the interests of civilization; and the present condition of affairs in Egypt is a grave menace to both your empire and the entire civilized world. You have given Egypt the best government it has had for at least two thousand years—probably a better government than it has ever had before; for never in history has the poor man in Egypt—the tiller of the soil, the ordinary labourer—been treated with as much justice and mercy, under a rule as free from corruption and brutality, as during the last twenty-eight years. Yet recent events, and especially what has happened in connection with and following on the assassination of Boutros Pasha three months ago, have shown that, in certain vital points, you have erred; and it is for you to make good your error. It has been an error proceeding from the effort to do too much and not too little in the interests of the Egyptians themselves; but unfortunately it is necessary for all of us who have to do with uncivilized peoples, and especially with fanatical peoples, to remember that in such a situation as yours in Egypt weakness, timidity, and sentimentality may cause even more far-reaching harm than violence and injustice. Of all broken reeds, sentimentality is the most broken reed on which righteousness can lean.

In Egypt you have been treating all religions with studied fairness and impartiality; and instead of gratefully acknowledging this, a noisy section of the native population takes advantage of what your good treatment has done to bring about an anti-foreign movement, a movement in which, as events have shown, murder on a large or a small scale is expected to play a leading part. Boutros Pasha was the best and most competent Egyptian official, a steadfast upholder of English rule, and an earnest worker for the welfare of his countrymen; and he was murdered simply and solely

Colonel Roosevelt crossing a part of the desert near Khartum

Colonel Roosevelt reviewing native Nubian and African troops of the British Army of the Sudan at Khartum

because of these facts, and because he did his duty wisely, fearlessly, and uprightly. The attitude of the so-called Egyptian Nationalist party in connection with this murder has shown that they were neither desirous nor capable of guaranteeing even that primary justice, the failure to supply which makes self-government not merely an empty but a noxious farce. Such are the conditions; and where the effort made by your officials to help the Egyptians toward self-government is taken advantage of by them, not to make things better, not to help their country, but to try to bring murderous chaos upon the land, then it becomes the primary duty of whoever is responsible for the government in Egypt to establish order, and to take whatever measures are necessary to that end.

It was with this primary object of establishing order that you went into Egypt twenty-eight years ago; and the chief and ample justification for your presence in Egypt was this absolute necessity of order being established from without, coupled with your ability and willingness to establish it. Now, either you have the right to be in Egypt or you have not; either it is or it is not your duty to establish and keep order. If you feel that you have not the right to be in Egypt, if you do not wish to establish and to keep order there, why, then, by all means get out of Egypt. If, as I hope, you feel that your duty to civilized mankind and your fealty to your own great traditions alike bid you to stay, then make the fact and the name agree and show that you are ready to meet in very deed the responsibility which is yours. It is the thing, not the form, which is vital; if the present forms of government in Egypt, established by you in the hope that they would help the Egyptians upward, merely serve to provoke and permit disorder, then it is for you to alter the forms; for if you stay in Egypt it is your first duty to keep order, and, above all things, also to punish murder and to bring to justice all who directly or indirectly incite others to commit murder or condone the crime when it is committed. When a people treat assassination as the corner-stone of self-government, it forfeits all right to be treated as worthy of self-government. You are in Egypt for several purposes, and among them one of the greatest is the benefit of the Egyptian people. You saved them from ruin by coming in, and at the present moment, if they are not governed from outside, they will again sink into a welter of chaos. Some nation must govern Egypt. I hope and believe that you will decide that it is your duty to be that nation.

These frank words aroused more opposition in the United States than they did in England. His political antagonists at home attacked him severely. In effect they said: "This is just like the impetuous, impulsive Roosevelt. On an occasion when the British have arranged to do him honour he 'butts in' and presumes to tell them how to run their own government!"

Whatever else the speech may have been, it was not impetuous and impulsive. It was the premeditated result of careful, considerate, and painstaking preparation. The story is an interesting one and throws as much light as any incident in his career that I know of upon his methods of thought and action, and I shall therefore relate it in some detail.

Just before Roosevelt arrived at Khartum in March, 1910, Boutros Pasha, the Prime Minister— a Copt, that is an Egyptian Christian, and one of

the best native officials that Egypt has ever produced—was openly and foully assassinated by an
agent of the so-called Egyptian Nationalist party.
That party consisted of extreme Radicals, mostly
young, who professed to wish to free Egypt from
British rule and to establish an independent republic. They were the "Sinn Feiners" of the Near East.
Perhaps "Bolshevists" of the Near East would be
a better term to apply to them, although the word
"Bolshevik" had not yet been invented. They
were both dangerous and foolish; dangerous, because they proposed to establish liberty on violence
and assassination, and foolish, because they did
not seem to realize that if the British were driven
out of Egypt that unhappy country would immediately fall back into the hands of the Turk
who did not care a fig about the vague and gran-
diloquent aspirations of the half-baked young
Nationalists.

The assassination of Boutros Pasha caused
almost a panic among the civil and military representatives of Great Britain in Egypt, a panic
which was augmented by the fact that the Liberal
Government in London appeared to be shilly-
shallying about the matter as the Gladstonian
Government in the eighties shillyshallied over the
Gordon Relief Expedition which resulted in the

death of that heroic soldier and the plunging of the Sudan into twelve years of savagery. Lord Cromer, one of the greatest colonial administrators in British history, had only recently retired from the position of British diplomatic agent in Egypt and had been succeeded by Sir Eldon Gorst who proved to be wholly incapable of dealing with the crisis.

By a curious coincidence I arrived at Khartum on the very day, March fourteenth, when Roosevelt came into that remarkable tropical city from the upper reaches of the Nile. Khartum is a veritable British capital, a beautifully appointed modern city in the midst of the desert. That evening, or possibly the following evening, a dinner was given in Roosevelt's honour at the palace of the Governor-General, Sir Reginald Wingate. Sir Reginald was absent in Cairo, owing to a temporary illness, and his place, both as Governor-General and as host, was filled by Slatin Pasha, the famous author of "Fire and Sword in the Sudan," who knew as well as any man living the horrors of the period when Gordon was assassinated and Khartum fell.

The subject of general discussion at the dinner, for it was uppermost in everyone's mind, was the murder of Boutros Pasha. Roosevelt was asked what he would do. He said: "It is very simple.

I would try the murderer at drumhead court
martial.   As there is no question about the facts,
for his own faction do not deny the assassination,
he would be found guilty.   I would sentence him to
be taken out and shot; and then if the home government cabled me, in one of their moments of vacil-
lation, to wait a little while, I would cable in reply:
'Can't wait; the assassin has been tried and shot.'
The home government might recall me or impeach
me if they wanted to, but *that* assassin would have
received his just deserts."

I happened to be sitting next to Colonel Asser,
a British officer who held a very high and important post under the Governor-General.   He was a
tall, blond, red-cheeked Englishman, a type of those
splendid men who in the awful first weeks of the
Great War made the British Expeditionary Force
in Flanders—the immortal "Contemptibles"—the
most heroic force that the world has known since
the days of Thermopylæ.   When Colonel Roosevelt
finished speaking Colonel Asser turned to me, and,
bringing his fist down on the palm of his hand,
said, with very deep feeling: "By heaven! I
wish that man were my boss!"   Similar sentiments were expressed by others at the table and
Roosevelt was actually implored to state his
views of the necessity of strong action in Egypt

to the people at home; home, being, of course, London.   All the way down the Nile civil and military officers urged him to support their cause when he reached London.   At Cairo he was asked to make a public address before the University of Cairo.

By this time Egypt was literally aflame with the threatening controversy excited by the murder of Boutros Pasha.   A few of the more timid felt that the affair should be allowed to "blow over"— if possible.   Their feelings were like those of a man who has an ulcerated tooth and who is about equally reluctant either to let the tooth stay in or to go to the dentist and have it out.   Some of these reluctant ones urged Roosevelt to omit all reference to the murder of Boutros Pasha in his speech at the University.   He replied: "Gentlemen, I am perfectly willing not to speak at all, if you so prefer, but if I do speak I assure you I shall speak frankly and openly about this assassination which seems to me to strike at the very roots of law, order, and justice in Egypt."

He spoke; and in the course of his address he said·

All good men, all the men of every nation whose respect is worth having, have been inexpressibly shocked by the recent assassination of Boutros Pasha.   It was an even greater calamity for Egypt than it was a wrong to the individual himself. The type of man which turns out an assassin is a type possessing all the qualities most alien to good citizenship—the type which produces poor soldiers in time of war and worse citizens in time of peace. Such a man stands on a pinnacle of evil infamy; and those who apologize for or condone his act; those who, by word or deed, directly or indirectly, encourage such an act in advance, or defend it afterward, occupy the same bad eminence.

The result was electrical. He was cheered to the echo by his audience. His fearlessness strengthened the hands of those officials who wanted to be backed up in maintaining law and order, and he was again urged by influential and important men to carry this message of upholding the moral law, by force if necessary, to the home government in London. Thanked on every hand for the help he had given to the force of strong and good government in Egypt and implored on every hand to present the needs of the British representatives in Egypt to the English people, he consented to do so. He wrote his Guildhall speech during his journey of six or eight weeks through Europe. He literally brooded over it. He consulted personal friends and British statesmen about it, and before it was delivered, men like Lord Cromer, Sir Edward Grey, Mr. Asquith, and, I think, Lord Kitchener, knew what he was going to say. He sought and accepted suggestions as to form and phraseology. This I know, because at Roosevelt's request I read the speech two weeks before it was delivered and ventured some minor suggestions of my own.

The stage setting of the Guildhall speech was a brilliant one. On the dais at one end of the hall sat the Lord Mayor and the Lady Mayoress. The special guests of the occasion were conducted by ushers, in robes and carrying maces, down a long aisle, flanked with spectators on either side, and up the steps of the dais where they were presented. Their names were called out at the beginning of the aisle and the audience applauded little or much, as the ushers or guests moved along, according to the popularity of the newcomer. Thus John Burns and A. J. Balfour were greeted with enthusiastic hand-clapping and cheers, although they belonged of course to opposite parties. The Bishop of London; Lord Cromer, who deserved to be called the maker of modern Egypt; Sargent, the painter; and Sir Edward Grey, Secretary of State for Foreign Affairs, were among those greeted in this way. In the front row on one side of the dais were seated the Aldermen of the City, in their red robes; and various officials, in wigs and gowns, lent to the scene an aspect curiously antique to the American eye.

My seat was on the dais, from which I could easily observe the great audience. At the outset of Mr. Roosevelt's address it was obvious that the frankness of his utterance, his characteristic attitude and gestures, and the pungent quality of his oratory startled his audience, accustomed to the more conventional methods of public speaking, but he soon captured and carried his hearers with him, as was indicated by the marks of approval printed in the verbatim report of the speech in the London *Times*. It is no exaggeration to say that the speech for a week or more was the talk of England—in clubs, in homes, and in the newspapers. There was some criticism, especially in the papers supporting the Liberal party then in power. But the best and most influential public opinion, while recognizing the unconventionality of Roosevelt's course, heartily approved of both the matter and the manner of the speech.

The London *Times* said:

Mr. Roosevelt has reminded us in the most friendly way of what we are at least in danger of forgetting, and no impatience of outside criticism ought to be allowed to divert us from considering the substantial truth of his words.

The *Daily Telegraph* (after referring to Mr. Roosevelt as "a practical statesman who combines with all his serious force a famous sense of humour") expressed the opinion that:

His candour is a tonic which not only makes plain our immediate duty but helps us to do it. In Egypt as in India there is no doubt as to the alternative he has stated so effectively: we must govern or go; and we have no intention of going.

The *Pall Mall Gazette's* view was that:

Mr. Roosevelt delivered a great and memorable speech—a speech that will be read and pondered over throughout the world.

The London *Spectator*, calling the speech the chief event of the week, remarked:

Timid, fussy, and pedantic people have charged Mr. Roosevelt with all sorts of crimes because he had the courage to speak out, and had even accused him of unfriendliness to this country because of his criticism. Happily the British people as a whole are not so foolish. Instinctively they have recognized and thoroughly appreciated the good feeling of Mr. Roosevelt's speech. . . . His speech is one of the greatest compliments ever paid to a people by a statesman of another country. . . . He has told us something useful and practical and has not lost himself in abstraction and platitude. . . . We thank Mr. Roosevelt once again for giving us so useful a reminder of our duty.

These sentiments of approval were repeated in a great number of letters which Mr. Roosevelt received from men and women in all walks of life. As I was in charge of his affairs at the time this correspondence came under my eye. There were some abusive letters, chiefly anonymous, but the predominating tone of the correspondence is fairly illustrated by the following:

Allow me, an old colonist in his eighty-fourth year, to thank you most heartily for your manly address at the Guildhall and for your life work in the cause of humanity. If I ever come to the great republic I shall do myself the honour of seeking an audience of your excellency. I may do so on my 100th birthday! With best wishes and profound respect.

The envelope of this letter was addressed: "His Excellency Govern-or-Go Roosevelt." That the *Daily Telegraph* and "the man in the street" should independently seize upon this salient point of the address—the "govern-or-go" theory—is significant.

The effect of the Guildhall speech upon the Government was quite as marked as upon the people at large. The Asquith Government then in power was inclined to be anti-imperialistic, but in 1911, as a direct result of the public sentiment aroused by Roosevelt's Guildhall speech, the Government sent Lord Kitchener to Egypt as Consul-General, and with his well-known vigour of action he suppressed the bolshevist tendencies of the young Nationalist party and reëstablished

Great Britain's authority and prestige. If some such man as Kitchener had not accomplished this during the years 1911-14 it is highly probable that, taking advantage of Egypt's disorganization, the Turks and Germans might have captured the Suez Canal thus cutting off one of the main arteries of British military existence in the war. It may, therefore, be said that Roosevelt, by his Guildhall speech, made a great contribution to the final success of the Allies.

THE SORBONNE SPEECH.—On his way to London, from Egypt, Mr. Roosevelt passed through Paris, where on April 23, 1910, he gave a lecture at the Sorbonne, by invitation of the officials of the University of Paris. It was an appeal for the highest type of citizenship based upon the simple but eternal and universally recognized laws of individual and social morality. Said Mr. Roosevelt:

The success of republics like yours and like ours means the glory, and our failure the despair, of mankind; and for you and for us the question of the quality of the individual citizen is supreme. . . . I speak to a brilliant assemblage; I speak in a great university; which represents the flower of the highest intellectual development; I pay all homage to intellect, and to elaborate and specialized training of the intellect; and yet I know I shall have the assent of all of you present when I add that more important still are the commonplace, every-day qualities and virtues.

With his characteristic frankness, Mr. Roosevelt attacked race suicide, in speaking to a nation whose birth-rate was decreasing:

Even more important than ability to work, even more important than ability to fight at need, is it to remember that the chief of blessings for any nation is that it shall leave its seed to inherit the land. It was the crown of blessings in Biblical times; and it is the crown of blessings now. The greatest of all curses is the curse of sterility, and the severest of all condemnations should be that visited upon wilful sterility. The first essential in any civilization is that the man and the woman shall be father and mother of healthy children, so that the race shall increase and not decrease.

In this address he also stated succinctly his position with regard to the relations of labour and capital:

My position as regards the moneyed interests can be put in a few words. In every civilized society property rights must be carefully safeguarded. Ordinarily, and in the great majority of cases, human rights and property rights are fundamentally and in the long run identical; but when it clearly appears that there is a real conflict between them, human rights must have the upper hand, for property belongs to man and not man to property.

A passage which elicited enthusiastic applause was the following in which he paid his

tribute to the man who strenuously struggles on
against all obstacles:

It is not the critic who counts; not the man who points out
how the strong man stumbles or where the doer of deeds
could have done them better. The credit belongs to the
man who is actually in the arena, whose face is marred by dust
and sweat and blood; who strives valiantly; who errs, and
comes short again and again—because there is no effort without error and shortcoming—but who does actually strive to
do the deeds; who knows the great enthusiasms, the great
devotions; who spends himself in a worthy cause; who, at the
best, knows in the end the triumph of high achievement, and
who at the worst, if he fails, at least fails while daring greatly,
so that his place shall never be with those cold and timid
souls who know neither victory nor defeat.

But the most significant passage of the address,
the truth of which has been more than substanti-
ated by the chaos of Russian bolshevism, was what
he had to say about the danger of extreme social-
ism based on class war:

I am a strong individualist by personal habit, inheritance'
and conviction; but it is a mere matter of common sense to
recognize that the State, the community, the citizens acting
together, can do a number of things better than if they were
left to individual action. The individualism which finds its
expression in the abuse of physical force is checked very early
in the growth of civilization, and we of to-day should, in our
turn, strive to shackle or destroy that individualism which
triumphs by greed and cunning, which exploits the weak by
craft instead of ruling them by brutality. We ought to go

with any man in the effort to bring about justice and the
equality of opportunity; to turn the tool user more and more
into the tool owner; to shift burdens so that they can be more
equitably borne. The deadening effect on any race of the
adoption of a logical and extreme socialistic system could
not be overstated; it would spell sheer destruction; it would
produce grosser wrong and outrage, fouler immorality, than
any existing system. But this does not mean that we may
not with great advantage adopt certain of the principles professed by some given set of men who happen to call themselves Socialists; to be afraid to do so would be to make a
mark of weakness on our part.

The effect of this address on French public
opinion was remarkable. Not long after its delivery I received from a friend, an American
military officer stationed in Paris, a letter from
which I quote the following passage:

I find that Paris is still everywhere talking of Mr. Roosevelt. It was a thing almost without precedent that this
blasé city kept up its interest in him without abatement for
eight days; but that a week after his departure should still
find him the main topic of conversation is a fact which has
undoubtedly entered into Paris history. The Temps, one
of the foremost daily newspapers of Paris, has had fifty-seven
thousand copies of his Sorbonne address printed and distributed free to every school-teacher in France and to many
other persons. The socialist or revolutionary groups and
press had made preparations for a monster demonstration on
May first. Walls were placarded with incendiary appeals
and their press was full of calls to arms. M. Briand [the
Prime Minister] flatly refused to allow the demonstration,

and gave orders accordingly to M. Lepine [the Chief of Police]. For the first time since present influences have governed France—certainly the first time in fifteen years—the police and the troops were authorized *to use their arms in self-defence.*

The result of this firmness was that the leaders countermanded the demonstration, and there can be no doubt that many lives were saved and a new point gained in the possibility of governing Paris as a free city, yet one where order must be preserved—votes or no votes.

Now this stiff attitude of M. Briand and the Conseil is freely attributed, in intelligent quarters, to Mr. Roosevelt. French people say it is a repercussion of his visit—of his Sorbonne lecture—and that, going away, he left in the minds of these people some of that intangible spirit of his; in other words, they felt what, in a similar emergency, he would have felt, and, for the first time in their lives, showed a disregard of voters when they were bent upon mischief. It is rather an extraordinary verdict, but it has seized the Parisian imagination, and I, for one, believe it is correct.

If the international socialists had got control of Paris in 1910 they might have wielded the influence which they sought to exert in the early days of the war in behalf of a "Brest-Litovsk" peace between France and Germany. Such a peace would have meant the extinction of France, and so it has always seemed to me that Roosevelt contributed personally something to the vigour of the French people.

While Roosevelt was lying ill in the Roosevelt Hospital in the city of New York in November,

1918, with what at the time was supposed to be a
severe attack of sciatica—an illness which was
followed by his death in the following January—
I wrote him this letter:

Please accept this word of sympathy and best wishes.
Some years ago I had a severe attack of sciatica which
kept me in bed a good many days; in fact, it ·kept me
in an armchair night and day some of the time because
I could not lie down, so I know what the discomfort and
pain are.

I want to take this opportunity also of sending you my
congratulations. For I think your leadership has had very
much to do with the unconditional surrender of Germany.
Last Friday night I was asked to speak at the Men's Club of
the Church of the Messiah in this city and they requested me
to make you the subject of my talk. I told them something
about your experience in Egypt and Europe in 1910 and said
what I most strongly believe, that your address at the Sorbonne—in strengthening the supporters of law and order
against red Bolshevism—and your address in Guildhall—
urging the British to govern or go—contributed directly
to the success of those two governments in this war. If
Great Britain had allowed Egypt to get out of hand instead
of, as an actual result of your Guildhall speech, sending Kitchener to strengthen the feebleness of Sir Eldon Gorst, the
Turks and Germans might have succeeded in their invasion
and have cut off the Suez Canal. So you laid the ground for
preparedness not only in this country but in France and
England.

I know it was a disappointment to you not to have
an actual share in the fighting but I think you did a greater
piece of work in preparing the battleground and the battle
spirit.

In reply he sent me this note:

That's a dear letter of yours, Lawrence.   I thank you for it and I appreciate it to the full.

This was the last exchange of letters I had with him.

CHAPTER VI

A MAN OF LETTERS

THE first thing that strikes the ordinary observer about Roosevelt's work as a man of letters is its prodigious volume. The list of books which he published—exclusive of pamphlets, occasional addresses, and uncollected magazine articles—numbers at least thirty separate titles. His "Life of Gouverneur Morris" is about fifty or sixty thousand words in length; his "African Game Trails" about two hundred thousand words. It is, to be sure, a very rough estimate, but let us suppose that his books average seventy-five thousand words. This means that he wrote two million and a half words in permanent literary form.

One of his official secretaries has said that, during his governorship and Presidency, Roosevelt wrote one hundred and fifty thousand letters. Suppose they averaged one hundred words each—I myself have received scores from him that were very much longer than that; this amounts to fifteen million words more and this volume of material covers only the epistolary side, a comparatively brief part of his active career, and on the literary side only that portion of his writing which he himself felt might be put into permanent form.

A man who does two thousand words of creative work day in and day out for every working day of the year is performing a portentous job from the brain-worker's point of view. If the estimate that Roosevelt produced eighteen millions of written words in his lifetime is at all reasonable, that alone would represent the work of thirty years of the lifetime of a literary man. Roosevelt had about forty years of active work, assuming that he began his productive activity when he published "The Naval War of 1812" not long after he had passed his twentieth year. Thus, in his forty working years he produced as a writer what in amount, at least, would have been a creditable fruitage of thirty years' labour by a professional man of letters who did nothing else but write. Writing, however, was merely one of Roosevelt's avocations. While all this production of written words was going on he was also soldiering, exploring, travelling, governing, speaking, studying, and reading. What he did, therefore, as a man of letters is, in the first place, an astounding feat of physical endurance.

I am not competent—nor have I the space—
to undertake here a literary criticism of his standing
as a man of letters.   The very fact that he was so
profuse in his writing makes some of it diffuse.
It varies very much in merit, but it must be remembered that he did not have the leisure for incubation,
consideration, and revision which the professional
man of letters requires.   Most of his writing was
done at high pressure or in extraordinary circumstances.   Father Zahm, the well-known scientist
and man of letters in the Catholic Church—who
accompanied Roosevelt on a large part of his South
American explorations, and who originally proposed that trip—thus describes his two methods
of work, in an article published in the *Outlook* not
long after Roosevelt's death:

The articles intended for one of the magazines of which he
was a contributor were dictated to his secretary, and dictated
for the most part immediately after the occurrence of the
events described, while all of the facts were still fresh in his
memory.   Descriptions of scenery were rarely delayed more
than one day, usually not more than a few hours.   As soon
as he returned from a visit to a museum, a cattle ranch, or a
public gathering of any kind he called his secretary, and we
soon heard the clicking of the keys of the typewriter.   And
it mattered not where he happened to be at the time—on a
railway train, or on a steamer, or in a hotel—it was all the
same.   The work had to be done, and it was accomplished
at the earliest possible moment.   .   .   .
The articles which appeared in another magazine describ-

ing his hunting experiences in Matto Grosso, unlike those recounting incidents of his triumphal march through other parts of South America, were written by his own hand, and often with the expenditure of great labour. Most people have come to believe that because Roosevelt wrote so much— and that often under the most unfavourable conditions—he must therefore have dashed off his articles for the press with little or no effort. Nothing is further from the truth. No one was more painstaking or conscientious than Roosevelt was in his literary work. I had frequent evidence of this, especially in the upper Paraguay. Here it often happened that he received different and contradictory reports regarding the habits of certain animals, but he would not put in writing his own opinions about the disputed questions until he had thoroughly investigated the subject and had satisfied himself that he had arrived at the truth. . . .

Sometimes his observations were penned after he had returned from a long and tiresome hunt in the jungle. Any other man would have thrown himself into his hammock and taken a rest. But not so our Nimrod. He would refresh himself by a plunge into a stream, if there was one near by, or by a copious ablution in his portable bath, and then he would forthwith seat himself at a folding writing table, which he always carried with him, and set down the experiences of the day while they were still vividly before his mind. He would thus continue to write for an hour or two, or even several hours, according to the time at his disposal. . . .

He wrote with indelible pencil, and, by means of carbon paper, three copies were made of each article. This was as a precaution against loss of the manuscript in the mails. He did not aim at stylistic effects, and never made any attempt at meretricious adornment of his thoughts. Like Cardinal Newman, his chief effort was to be clear and to express himself in such wise that no one could mistake the meaning he desired to convey. It is for this reason that the style of his hunting articles is so graphic and pellucid, and that he was able to make his readers see the marvels of tropical scenery as he saw them himself.

Robert Bridges, the editor of *Scribner's Magazine* —in which Roosevelt's records of his African journey were first published—also describes his method of work as a writer:

When he promised a manuscript for a certain date, that promise was kept absolutely, no matter what intervened.

When he returned from the Spanish-American War and landed at Montauk, he sent word to the magazine that he wanted to talk about his proposed story of "The Rough Riders." Just before he started on that expedition he had said in a brief interview: "If I come back, you shall have the first chance at anything I write."

It was, therefore, on the first afternoon after he returned to his home at Oyster Bay that, on the lawn at Sagamore Hill, we talked over the book which developed into "The Rough Riders." It was all perfectly clear in the Colonel's mind. He knew the grand divisions of his story, although he had not written a line. There were to be six articles, and the date was set for the delivery of the first one so that the serial could begin in the magazine promptly.

Very soon he was nominated for Governor of New York. I said to him one day: "I suppose this will interfere with your dates for 'The Rough Riders'?"

"Not at all," he replied; "you shall have the various chapters at the time promised."

As everybody knows, he made a vigorous campaign for Governor of New York, and was elected, and inaugurated in the following January. Notwithstanding this arduous and exciting time, he fulfilled every promise and the book was delivered on time.

It was the same way with his "Oliver Cromwell," which

was written while he was Governor of New York. He was a busy man, but his literary work was just as complete as though he had devoted his whole time to it.

When he was President he sent for me, and, taking me into his library, opened a drawer in his desk, lifted out a complete manuscript, put it on the desk, and said in effect:

"It isn't customary for Presidents to publish a book during office, but I am going to publish this one."

We then went over together the complete manuscript of "Outdoor Pastimes of an American Hunter." Some of these papers had been written before. Other chapters were the product of his hunting trips in Colorado and Louisiana while President. The book was ready for the printer, title-page and all. . . .

To him the making of a book was a delight. He knew all the machinery of it, and he read his proofs with the accuracy and industry of an expert.

But the literary work that he best enjoyed was writing his "African Game Trails." The whole book, even the preface, was written by his own hand, word for word, in triplicate, in the very heart of Africa. One of the men who was with him said that no matter how arduous the day in the hunting-field, night after night he would see the Colonel seated on a camp-stool, with a feeble light on the table, writing the narrative of his adventures. Chapter by chapter this narrative was sent by runners from the heart of Africa. Two copies were despatched at different times. When he got to the headwaters of the Nile one of the chapters was sent from Nairobi and the duplicate was sent down the Nile to Cairo. These blue canvas envelopes often arrived much battered and stained, but never did a single chapter miss.

Brander Matthews, one of the very best of American contemporary critics of literature, in

an article in *Munsey's Magazine* on "Theodore
Roosevelt as a Man of Letters," has said that:

> Roosevelt's style is firm and succulent; and its excellence
> is due to his having learned the lesson of the masters of Eng-
> lish. He wrote well because he had read widely and deeply,
> because he had absorbed good literature for the sheer delight
> he took in it. Consciously or unconsciously he enriched his
> vocabulary, accumulating a store of strong words which he
> made flexible, bending them to do his bidding. But he was
> never bookish in his diction; he never went in quest of recon-
> dite vocables, because his taste was refined, and because he
> was ever seeking to be "understanded of the people."

Of Roosevelt's autobiography, Brander Matthews adds that, while it has a lasting character
as a human document, it is open to the criticism
that it sounds like "an improvisation." It was an
improvisation—at least in part. It came about in
this way. After the turmoil of the Progressive
campaign—in which the partisan passions of the
country were deeply stirred and which resulted in
Roosevelt's defeat—it seemed to us desirable, both
for him and for the *Outlook*, that if possible his pen
should take a vacation, for a time at least, from
controversial political topics. We cast about to see
what suggestion we could make to him that might
turn his attention to other subjects and at the same
time give him the opportunity to furnish our
readers with that which they had come to look

for from him; that is to say, contributions on political, social, and industrial questions. It was my brother, I think, who suggested that if we could get him to write some of his reminiscences both objects would be accomplished. I went to him, therefore, and asked him if he would not give us some chapters of autobiographical reminiscences. He demurred at first very decidedly. "I do not want to write about myself," he said. "Moreover, I am sure Mrs. Roosevelt would not like it." But I urged him to let me come down to Oyster Bay and interview him with a stenographer. "When the result is put in shape," I said, "you can look it over and if you and Mrs. Roosevelt do not like it we can 'kill' it—to use the technical phrase of a newspaper office—and no harm is done. If, however, the result is satisfactory we can try another interview and continue them as long as you have the patience and inclination to do so."

This plan struck him as feasible, and I met him at Sagamore Hill by appointment. The stenographer was Frank Harper a young Englishman whom we had engaged to be Mr. Roosevelt's private secretary and who had travelled with us in that capacity during the European trip. I warned Harper to efface himself as much as possible so that Roosevelt would be as little conscious as we could make him that his words were being taken down; and I also instructed him to make a record of everything—questions, answers, interpolations, comments, etc.—without any regard to whether his notes made a coherent whole or not.   Roosevelt sat down with me in his study.

"Now, Mr. Roosevelt," I said, "I am not going to ask you to dictate anything to Harper to-day. I am simply going to ask you some questions, get you to tell me some of the stories you have told me from time to time about your early life, and Harper will take the notes which I will give you later as memoranda which you can use later in writing your recollections. You have told me you were a sickly boy and yet from the time I first knew you you have been an extraordinarily vigorous and athletic man.   What kind of a boyhood and education did you have that could have produced such a striking result out of such an inauspicious beginning?" (I have said elsewhere, I think, that Roosevelt was one of the most delightful table talkers and *raconteurs* that I ever listened to.)

My question interested him, and he began to tell something about his boyhood, his father, his mother, his bringing up in the Twentieth Street home, his narrative, fresh and extemporaneous, being full of humour and anecdote. Suddenly, catching sight of Harper, he straightened up and began to dictate in a more formal and literary vein. I did not interrupt, but waited until he said something, in the course of what had now become a somewhat formal essay, that gave me a chance to ask him a question or two, reminding him, perhaps, of some anecdote that he had told me previously. Thus diverting him from what had quite apparently become a self-conscious and awkward feeling that he was writing a formal paper about himself, I started him off again, forgetful of the stenographer, on a current of reminiscential talk.

In this way the afternoon was spent. When Harper's voluminous notes were written I took them to my own home and worked a day or two upon them, striking out the questions and irrelevant remarks. By cutting up the typewritten pages and pasting them together again I adjusted the sequence and chronology of the story (for we had skipped in our conversation from boyhood to Harvard and from Harvard back to boyhood again as my questions had suggested ideas and recollections to Roosevelt). This was done, of course, without adding a single word to anything he had said or changing a single sentence. I had a fair copy made of this re-arrangement, which formed a consecutive narrative and composed the first chapter of his autobiography, and submitted it to him. He was satisfied with the result and needed no further intervention on my part. With his usual quickness of perception he caught the idea which I was very desirous of getting before him, and completed the autobiography himself largely on the lines laid down in the first chapter. He occasionally fell into the argumentative and essay style later on in the volume and I think somewhat overloaded it with appendices and documentary evidence. It has always seemed to me, however, that in those chapters where he adhered to what Brander Matthews called the method of "improvisation" he recorded recollections of a peculiar charm, both from a personal and a literary point of view.

It is hard to say whether that portion of his literary work which was dictated or that which was written with his own hand was done with the greater care. The danger of dictation always is that one is apt to be verbose, but all his dictated work he always went over very carefully—after it was typed—correcting, deleting, and interlining with his pen. This was true even of his letters. To the latter he often added postscripts in his own hand which not infrequently proved to be the flavouring kernel of the entire letter.

As an illustration of the variety of Roosevelt's work and of the appeal which he made to his fellows, it may be recorded that Brander Matthews intimates that Roosevelt ought to have chosen the writing of history as his profession for "his ultimate reputation as a man of letters will most securely rest upon his stern labours as a historian"; while Father Zahm thinks that a great scientist was lost when he entered upon a political career. Father Zahm says:

Those who have read any of the Colonel's books bearing on natural history—especially his recent works: "Life Histories of African Game Animals" and "Through the Brazilian Wilderness"—know what a keen and trained observer he was, and how not even the most trifling peculiarities of form and colour escaped his quick and practised eye. But the general reader is not aware that Colonel Roosevelt's first love was natural history and not politics, and that it was only an untoward combination of circumstances that prevented him from embracing the career of a naturalist.

I am not sure but that Father Zahm has the weight of evidence for his claim. It does not seem to me that Roosevelt's historical essays, such as those which form the basis of his addresses at the University of Berlin and Oxford, are comparable in style or charm, or even in originality, with some of his more human and spontaneous writing. I do not know where, for example, one can find a more simple and yet a more vivid picture of sunset on the desert than is found in the account he wrote, in three articles, of a western trip which he took in 1913. His articles were written for the *Outlook* and, so far as I know, have not been republished. The sunset passage is as follows:

During the afternoon we shogged steadily across the plain. At one place, far off to one side, we saw a band of buffalo, and between them and us a herd of wild donkeys. Otherwise the only living things were snakes and lizards. On the other side of the plain, two or three miles from a high wall of vermilion cliffs, we stopped for the night at a little stone resthouse, built as a station by a cow outfit. Here there were big corrals, and a pool of water piped down by the cowmen from a spring many miles distant. On the sand grew the usual desert plants, and on some of the ridges a sparse growth of grass, sufficient for the night feed of the hardy horses. The little stone house and the corrals stood out, bare and desolate, on the empty plain.

Soon after we reached there a sand-storm rose and blew so violently that we took refuge inside the house. Then the wind died down; and as the sun sank toward the horizon we sauntered off through the hot, still evening. There were many sidewinder rattlesnakes. We killed several of the gray, flat-headed, venomous things; as we slept on the ground, we were glad to kill as many as possible. Except this baleful life there was little save the sand and the harsh, scanty vegetation.

Across the lonely wastes the sun went down. The sharply channelled cliffs turned crimson in the dying light; all the heavens flamed ruby red, and faded to a hundred dim hues of opal, beryl, and amber, pale turquoise, and delicate emerald; and then night fell and darkness shrouded the desert.

His "Winning of The West," as Brander Matthews says, is probably "an abiding contribution to American historical literature." On the political side, however, I think his "Naval War of 1812" and his "Life of Gouverneur Morris" ought not to be—and will not be—forgotten. He himself had, for some reason, a peculiar interest in a volume: "Hero Tales from American History" which he wrote in collaboration with Henry Cabot Lodge. In 1916 I was preparing a list, for a correspondent, of books on American history which could be read by a young layman with the kind of interest which such readers take in narrative rather than in technical studies. I wrote to Roosevelt telling him what I was doing and saying that I had put in Rhodes's "Oxford Lectures on the Civil War" (a great favourite of mine) and his own "Naval War of 1812." In reply he said:

> I would certainly put in Rhodes' Oxford Lectures on the Civil War. If you want anything from me, don't take the "War of 1812," but take "Hero Tales from American History," which Lodge and I wrote together.

The chapter in the "Hero Tales" on the Death of Stonewall Jackson affords a good example of Roosevelt's strong admiration for the type of man who is an upright and righteous and yet hard-fighting soldier.

He was a voracious and omnivorous reader. It is impossible to estimate the amount of Roosevelt's reading but it must have been phenomenally large for he read all sorts of books, modern and ancient, at all sorts of times and with almost unbelievable rapidity. In the life of Robert Houdin, the famous French conjuror and magician of the early nineteenth century it is related that he had the gift, developed and augmented by constant practice, of being able to pass through an elaborately furnished room and then to describe in minute detail the various articles of furniture and ornament which it contained. His eye received and his mind grasped in a moment or two impressions which it would take the ordinary man half an hour to tabulate.

Roosevelt had this gift in reading. The child laboriously reads syllable by syllable or word by word; the practised adult reads line by line; Roosevelt read almost page by page and yet remembered what he read. Mr. Neil, United States Commissioner of Labour, during Roosevelt's administration once described to me how he took a report to the President on which he had spent a laborious month of preparation. It consisted of a number of typewritten pages. Roosevelt took the report, fixed his eyes upon it—or rather his eye, for one had been so damaged in boxing that for many years he saw only dimly with it—turned over the sheets about as steadily and rapidly as an old-fashioned Grandfather's clock ticks, finished the document and handed it back to the Commissioner with comments and suggestions so fresh and pertinent that it was quite clear that he had not only read the words of the report but had clearly understood its scope and significance. "It had taken him less than thirty minutes," said Mr. Neil, "to understand, and to improve by adding new facts and arguments, the treatment of a subject to which I had devoted hours of study."

It was not only because he read with extraordinary speed but because he used spare minutes for reading that his range was so wide.

He read while waiting for trains and for people to keep appointments and when driving in his automobile to the city. I have seen him pick up a book surrounded by a roomful of talking and laughing friends and in a moment become so absorbed in it that he had no more knowledge of what was going on about him than if he had been in a cloister cell. During the railway journey from Khartum to Cairo on the tour of 1910, described more fully in a later chapter, a special dinner was to be served one evening in the private saloon dining car placed at Roosevelt's disposal by the Governor-General of the Sudan. This dinner was to be attended by some important officials and other guests, who had taken the train at one of the stations we' passed through and were to leave it at another specified stopping-place. It was therefore essential that the company should assemble at the table promptly, but when dinner was announced Mr. Roosevelt was nowhere to be found. I searched the train for him and finally discovered him in one of the white enamelled lavatories with its door half open where, standing under an electric light, he was busily engaged in reading, while he braced himself in the angle of the two walls against the swaying motion of the train, oblivious to time and surroundings. The book in which he was absorbed was Lecky's "History of Rationalism in Europe." He had chosen this peculiar reading room both because the white enamel reflected a brilliant light and he was pretty sure of uninterrupted quiet. This was typical of the way in which he seized spare moments for the information or entertainment that books afford.

The fact, however, that it was Lecky, instead of Mark Twain or O. Henry, was purely fortuitous, for he was no pedant. He liked novels and stories of adventure and books of humour, but he wanted

them to be written by men of intelligence and skilful workmanship. Books of travel and exploration especially appealed to him although he was not
interested, as he once told me, in mere biography.

At the Mohammedan University in Cairo which
we visited, an ancient and medieval seat of learning, established in a spacious building, where the
chief subject of study appeared to be the Koran
taught to classes of boys and men squatting upon
their haunches on the floor in Oriental fashion,
Roosevelt was especially interested in the library.
The language of the University was Arabic, but
we had with us a Syrian interpreter who, having
been educated at the American College at Beirut,
spoke English fluently. Roosevelt was surrounded
by an interested group of Mohammedan teachers
and officials, both young and old. He had not
been long in this library of ancient literature when
he asked through the interpreter if they had in
their collection the travels of Ibn Batuta. When
that name was mentioned there was a great light-
ing up of faces and a great scurrying of willing
messengers, who presently came back with a volume printed in Arabic which Roosevelt took in his
hands with almost devout interest. "Read that,"
said he to the interpreter, pointing to the first page,
which the interpreter proceeded to do, with a dozen

heads bent over the hieroglyphics. "Yes," said
Roosevelt, as the reading finished, "that's it. Now
doesn't he say so-and-so further on?" Whereupon the interpreter turned over the pages and,
sure enough, Ibn did say so-and-so at the beginning
of the next chapter, to the delighted surprise of the
Arab group surrounding us who were literally over-
joyed to find that the famous visitor from the West
knew one of their great authors. When we went
out Roosevelt explained to me that Ibn Batuta
was the Arabian Marco Polo who made a voyage
around Africa in the fourteenth century and left
an account of his great adventure in the volume
we had just been looking at. Roosevelt had read
it many years before in a French translation and
had remembered it with such accuracy that he
could point out a specific passage not, of course, in
the Arabic text, but from the context as translated
by the interpreter.

He had a human interest in universities although
he was not in the slightest degree academic, in
spite of the fact that he had received as many
academic honours as any man of his time, including
the greatest one that can be conferred upon a
modern—that of being created a D. C. L. by
Oxford. But when universities did things that
seemed to him contrary to social morals he had little

use for them. He once wrote me a letter of outraged
protest when Columbia and Yale had paid marked
distinction to two American journalists who, he
thought, had exercised a sinister influence upon
American life. But after he had let off his steam
of vigorous criticism, he cheered himself, as he
often did, by a quizzical comment: "Universities
are middling queer creatures, aren't they!" was
his conclusion of the matter.

Unless the literature was the fiction of adventure
or of humour Roosevelt chiefly got either social
or industrial suggestions and inspirations out of his
reading. This aspect of his work as a man of
letters is shown in a communication I received from
him while he was in Africa in 1909-1910. It was
one of the letters written in his own hand with
indelible pencil.

Naivasha, October 21st.
If President Eliot's "List of Best Books" is complete, will
you send it to me? If I am able I'd like to write something
on it; I don't believe in a list of "100" or "25" "best" books,
because there are many thousands which may be "best" according to the country, the time, the condition, the reader;
but I do believe in "a" 25 to 100 or any other number of
"good" books, each such list being merely complementary
to and not a substitute for many other similar lists. The
books in my pigskin library on this hunt are good; they are
no better than any one of the totally different sets I took on
each of my last three hunting trips, except that I have a
longer list for the longer trip.

I liked Kennan's article on what I said about Tolstoi—I like everything that he writes!—and am in fundamental agreement with what he says, especially in his unsparing condemnation of the cruel, ruthless, bureaucratic tyranny under which Russia lies in festering misery. But there are one or two points on which I should like to give reasons for what I said; if you care to you can send this to him.

First as to Tolstoi's immorality. Have you ever read his "Kreutzer Sonata" (if that's the way to spell it)? I read it, or rather as much of it as was necessary to a pathological diagnosis. The man who wrote that was a sexual and a moral pervert. It is as unhealthy a book, as vicious in its teaching to the young, as Elinor Glyn's "Three Weeks" or any other piece of pornographic literature—for I need hardly say that the worst pornographic literature is that which, with conscious or only half-conscious hypocrisy, calls itself by some other name; some of the very vilest of such books are often written under the pretense of being in the interests of social or hygienic reform. In your father's delightful Vesper Sermons was one the other day on the Song of Solomon, which dealt with the love of married lovers in a spirit which I believe to be as true as it is lofty. I think that the love of the really happy husband and wife—*not* purged of passion, but with passion heatened to a white heat of intensity and purity and tenderness and consideration, and with many another feeling added thereto—is the loftiest and most ennobling influence that comes into the life of any man or woman, even loftier and more ennobling than wise and tender love for children. The cheapest, most degrading, and most repulsive cynicism is that which laughs at, or describes as degraded, this relation. Now the "Kreutzer Sonata" has, as its theme, that this relation is bestial and repellent, and its whole purpose is to paint the love of husband and wife as loving exactly the same as the squalid and loathsome intimacy between a rake and a prostitute. When that book appeared it seemed to me to reveal, as by a flash, the strange hidden perversion of morals which has made Tolstoi in his professedly moral writings, as distinguished from his really far more moral novels, inveigh against all the relations of man and woman as if the highest and most ennobling and the lowest and most depraved stood on the same plane. No greater wrong can be done humanity than to inculcate such doctrine; at its best it makes the wife feel that she ought to regard herself as on a par with a prostitute; at its worst it enables the "man swine" to say that, after all, he is not a bit worse than his most upright neighbour. How can there be more revolting and monstrous teaching?

Now about hypocrisy. If there is one thing upon which we should insist in writer and talker, but above all in professed prophet and reformer, it is that he shall make his words *measurably* good (it is not in human nature completely to realize an ideal) by his deeds. I believe that the root-vice in our political life is the demand by part of the public that a candidate shall make impossible promises, and the grin of cynical amusement and contempt with which another portion of the public regards his breaking even the promises he could keep; and one attitude is as bad as the other. As it is with politicians, so it is with philosophers. I think Rousseau did much good by some of the principles he advocated; and more harm because he taught people by his actions to regard the enunciation of lofty aspirations as a substitute for lofty deeds and indeed as an atonement for a life that gave the lie to the aspirations. Mr. Kennan quotes Tolstoi's words as proofs of repentance. Repentance must be shown by deeds, not words. One lapse is quite pardonable; but persistence in doing one thing while preaching another is not pardonable. It seems to me that Tolstoi is one of those men, by no means uncommon, *of perverted moral type* who at bottom consider the luxury of frantic repentance—and the luxury of professing adherence to an impossible and undesirable ideal—as full atonement for, and as really permitting, persistence in a line of conduct which gives the lie to their professions. Tolstoi preaching against those relations of man and woman, without which there would either be no humanity, or a humanity perpetuated by those of its members who stand closest to beasts, is a contemptible figure in my eyes; but he is made more contemptible when we know that all the time he is having sons and daughters.

I saw X——(once a man of high and fine promise) ruined, and rendered a worse than worthless citizen, by falling under Tolstoi's baleful influence; and Y——has, because of the same influence, sunk from being a most useful citizen to the position of a well-meaning agitator who latterly has done rather more harm than good, by sheer folly, committed in the name of philanthropy.

About the Douma. I agree absolutely with Kennan as to the cause of the Douma's inefficiency. But I think harm comes to the cause of morality and reform in Russia if, because of our sympathy with its advocates, and our abhorrence of what it seeks to overthrow, we are betrayed into acquiescence in either wickedness or folly. Bryan, for instance, favours a section of the Douma which, if its doctrines were put into practice, would within a year make men hail any tyranny or despotism as a relief from a system in which folly raised to the Nth power would inevitably produce a grade of wickedness proportionately high. Think of the Douma passing a proposed law to do away with capital punishment and at the same time refusing to pass a resolution condemning the murder of officials! We all warmly sympathize with the overthrow of the *Ancien Régime* in France; but when the so-called friends of liberty brought about the Red Terror they did France a wrong so hideous that the nation has not yet wrought out its atonement. There! You'll never want to hear from me again.

Does not this comment on Russia, written nearly ten years ago, take on the aspect of prophecy in the light of the present results of Russian Bolshevism?

I find that naturally I come back to the political and social aspect of Roosevelt's work as a man of letters. In October, 1912, he published a short paper in the *Outlook* entitled "How I Became a Progressive." I print it here because it has not been dug out of the pages of that periodical by anybody else so far as I know and it deserves a permanent form both as an autobiographical document and as a specimen of Roosevelt's simple, direct, and popular style.

I suppose I had a natural tendency to become a Progressive, anyhow. That is, I was naturally a democrat, in believing in fair play for everybody. But I grew toward my present position, not so much as the result of study in the library or the reading of books—although I have been very much helped by such study and by such reading—as by actually living and working with men under many different conditions and seeing their needs from many different points of view.

The first set of our people with whom I associated so intimately as to get on thoroughly sympathetic terms with them were cow-punchers, then on the ranges in the West. I was so impressed with them that in doing them justice I did injustice to equally good citizens elsewhere whom I did not know; and it was a number of years before I grew to understand—first by association with railway men, then with farmers, then with mechanics, and so on—that the things that I specially liked about my cow-puncher friends were, after all, to be found fundamentally in railway men, in farmers, in blacksmiths, carpenters—in fact, generally among my fellow American citizens.

Before I began to go with the cow-punchers, I had already, as the result of experience in the Legislature at Albany, begun rather timidly to strive for social and industrial justice. But at that time my attitude was that of giving justice from above. It was the experience on the range that first taught me to try to get justice for all of us by working on the same level with the rest of my fellow citizens.

It was the conviction that there was much social and industrial injustice and the effort to secure social and industrial justice that first led me to taking so keen an interest in popular rule.

For years I accepted the theory, as most of the rest of us then accepted it, that we already had popular government; that this was a government by the people. I believed the power of the boss was due only to the indifference and short-sightedness of the average decent citizen. Gradually it came over me that while this was half the truth, it was only half the truth, and that while the boss owed part of his power to the fact that the average man did not do his duty, yet that there was the further fact to be considered, that for the average man it had already been made very difficult instead of very easy for him to do his duty. I grew to feel a keen interest in the machinery for getting adequate and genuine popular rule, chiefly because I found that we could not get social and industrial justice without popular rule, and that it was immensely easier to get such popular rule by the means of machinery of the type of direct nominations at primaries, the short ballot, the initiative, referendum, and the like.

I usually found that my interest in any given side of a question of justice was aroused by some concrete case. It was the examination I made into the miseries attendant upon the manufacture of cigars in tenement-houses that first opened my eyes to the need of legislation on such subjects. My friends come from many walks of life. The need for a workmen's compensation act was driven home to me by my knowing a brakeman who had lost his legs in an accident, and whose family was thereby at once reduced from self-respecting comfort to conditions that at one time became very dreadful. Of course, after coming across various concrete instances of this kind, I would begin to read up on the subject, and then I would get in touch with social workers and others who were experts and could acquaint me with what was vital in the matter. Looking back, it seems to me that I made my greatest strides forward while I was Police Commissioner, and this largely through my intimacy with Jacob Riis, for he opened all kinds of windows into the matter for me.

The Conservation movement I approached from slightly different lines. I have always been fond of history and of science, and what has occurred to Spain, to Palestine, to China, and to North Africa from the destruction of natural resources is familiar to me. I have always been deeply impressed with Liebig's statement that it was the decrease of soil fertility, and not either peace or war, which was fundamental in bringing about the decadence of nations. While unquestionably nations have been destroyed by other causes, I have become convinced that it was the destruction of the soil itself which was perhaps the most fatal of all causes. But when, at the beginning of my term of service as President, under the influence of Mr. Pinchot and Mr. Newell, I took up the cause of Conservation, I was already fairly well awake to the need of social and industrial justice; and from the outset we had in view, not only the preservation of natural resources, but the prevention of monopoly in natural resources, so that they should inhere in the people as a whole. There were plenty of newspapers—the New York *Times*, *Sun*, and *Evening Post*, for instance—which cordially supported our policy of Conservation as long as we did not try to combine it with a movement against monopolization of resources, and which promptly abandoned us when it became evident that we wished to conserve the resources not for a part of the people but for all of the people.

The country-life movement was simply another side of this movement for a better and juster life. From Mary E. Wilkins to Sarah Orne Jewett, in story after story which I would read for mere enjoyment, I would come upon things that not merely pleased me but gave me instruction—(I have always thought that a good novel or a good story could teach quite as much as a more solemnly pretentious work, if it was written in the right way and read in the right way)—and then my experience on farms, my knowledge of farmers, the way I followed what happened to the sons and daughters of the farmers I knew, all joined to make me feel the need of arousing the public interest and the public conscience as regards the conditions of life in the country.

Here again I have been fortunate enough to live with my own people, and not to live as an outsider, but as a man doing his share of the work. I know what the work and what the loneliness of a farmer's life too often are. I do not want to help the farmer or to help his wife in ways that will soften either, but I do want to join with both, and try to help them and help myself and help all of us, not by doing away with the need of work, but by trying to create a situation in which work will be more fruitful, and in which the work shall produce and go hand in hand with opportunities for self-development.

Very early I learned through my reading of history, and I found through my association with reformers, that one of the prime difficulties was to get the man who wished reform within a nation also to pay heed to the needs of the nation from the international standpoint. Every little city or republic of antiquity was continually torn between factions which wished to do justice at home but were weak abroad, and other factions which secured justice abroad by the loss of personal liberty at home. So here at home I too often found that men who were ardent for social and industrial reform would be ignorant of the needs of this Nation as a nation, would be ignorant of what the Navy meant to the Nation, of what it meant to the Nation to have and to fortify and protect the Panama Canal, of what it meant to the Nation to get from the other nations of mankind the respect which comes only to the just, and which is denied to the weaker nation far more quickly than it is denied to the stronger.

It ought not to be necessary to insist upon a point like this, with China before our very eyes offering the most woeful example of the ruin that comes to a nation which cannot defend itself against aggression—and China, by the way, offers the further proof that centuries of complete absence of militarism may yet result in the development of all the worst vices and all the deepest misery that grow up in nations that suffer from over-much militarism. Here again I learn from books, I learn from study, and I learn most by dealing with men.

I feel that the Progressive party owes no small part of its strength to the fact that it not only stands for the most far-reaching measures of social and industrial reform, but in sane and temperate fashion stands also for the right and duty of this Nation to take a position of self-respecting strength among the nations of the world, to take such a position as will do injustice to no foreign power, strong or weak, and yet will show that it has both the spirit and the strength to repel injustice from abroad.

It would be a pity to leave the impression, as perhaps would be the case if Roosevelt's Progressive creed were made the conclusion of this chapter, that his interests were exclusively—or even primarily—social and political. The fact is that he was so varied and had so many facets to his personality that I am confused myself to determine what he was most interested in. He had a deep love for pure beauty in literature. Keats's "Ode on a Grecian Urn" was, for example, one of his favourite poems. Its appeal to him was, I think, not merely because of its music and the artistry of its form, but because it takes its reader completely out of material life and puts him into the quieting and problemless universe of pure imagination.

The day before he left London, on his return from his African and European tour in 1910, Roosevelt disappeared. It was known that he had gone off with Sir Edward (now Viscount) Grey, but where he went nobody knew—and the newspapers could not find out. This, in his own language, was what happened:

Like most Americans interested in birds and books, I know a good deal about English birds as they appear in books. I know the lark of Shakespeare and Shelley and the Ettrick Shepherd; I know the nightingale of Milton and Keats; I know Wordsworth's cuckoo; I know mavis and merle singing in the merry green wood of the old ballads; I know Jenny Wren and Cock Robin of the nursery books. Therefore I have always much desired to hear the birds in real life; and the opportunity offered last June. As I could snatch but a few hours from a very exacting round of pleasure and duties, it was necessary for me to be with some companion who could identify both song and singer. In Sir Edward Grey, a keen lover of outdoor life in all its phases, and a delightful companion, who knows the songs and ways of English birds as very few do know them, I found the best possible guide.

We left London on the morning of June 9, twenty-four hours before I sailed from Southampton. Getting off the train at Basingstoke, we drove to the pretty, smiling valley of the Itchen. Here we tramped for three or four hours, then again drove, this time to the edge of the New Forest, where we first took tea at an inn, and then tramped through the forest to an inn on its other side, at Brockenhurst. At the conclusion of our walk my companion made a list of the birds we had seen, putting an asterisk opposite those which we had heard sing. There were forty-one of the former and twenty-three of the latter, as follows:

*Thrush, *Blackbird, *Lark, *Yellow Hammer, *Robin, *Wren, *Golden-Crested Wren, *Goldfinch, *Chaffinch, *Greenfinch, Pied Wagtail, Sparrow, *Dunnock (Hedge Accentor), Missel Thrush, Starling, Rook, Jackdaw, *Black Cap, *Garden Warbler, *Willow Warbler, *Chiff Chaff, *Wood Warbler, *Tree Creeper, *Reed Bunting, *Sedge Warbler, Coot, Water Hen, Little Grebe (Dabchick), Tufted Duck, Wood Pigeon, Stock Dove, *Turtle Dove, Peewit, Tit (?Coal Tit), *Cuckoo, *Nightjar, *Swallow, Martin, Swift, Pheasant, Partridge.

The foregoing account is taken from an article on English Song Birds which he wrote for the *Outlook* on his return. When he got back he went out at Sagamore Hill to compare what he saw of the home birds with "the notes and actions of the birds I had seen in England." He ends the article in this way:

I sent the companion of my English walk John Burroughs's "Birds and Poets." John Burroughs's life-work is beginning to have its full effect in many different lines. When he first wrote there were few men of letters in our country who knew nature at first hand. Now there are many who delight in our birds, who know their songs, who keenly love all that belongs to out-of-door life. For instance, Madison Cawein

Roosevelt as Lieutenant-Colonel of the Rough Riders

Colonel Roosevelt with the Rough Riders

and Ernest McGaffey have for a number of years written of
our woods and fields, of the birds and the flowers, as only
those can write who join to love of Nature the gift of observation and the gift of description.   Mr. Cawein is a Kentuckian;
and another Kentuckian, Miss Julia Stockton Dinsmore,
in the little volume of poems which she has just published,
includes many which describe with beauty and charm the
sights and sounds so dear to all of us who know American
country life.   Miss Dinsmore knows Kentucky, and the Gulf
Coast of Louisiana, and the great plains of North Dakota;
and she knows also the regions that lie outside of what can be
seen with material vision.   For years in our family we have
had some of her poems in the scrap-book cut from newspapers
when we knew nothing about her except the initials signed
to the verses.   Only one who sees with the eyes of the spirit
as well as the eyes of the body could have written the "Thre-
nody," curiously attractive in its simplicity and pathos, with
which the little book opens.   It contains many poems that
make a similar appeal.   The writer knows bluebird and robin,
redbird and field lark and whippoorwill, just as she knows
Southern rivers and Western plains; she knows rushing winds
and running waters and the sights and sounds of lonely
places; and, moreover, she knows, and almost tells, those
hidden things of the heart which never find complete utterance.

I wonder whether birds and children and home
did not have a deeper interest for Roosevelt than
soldiering or pioneering or statesmanship?   After
all is said and done, should not the final estimate
be that he was, not a literary man, not a political
man, not a military man, but a homely man?

CHAPTER VII

AFRICAN AND EUROPEAN TOUR

WHEN Roosevelt made his plans in the autumn of 1908 and the early winter of 1909 to explore the African jungle as a hunter-naturalist, to use his own phrase, I arranged, with his approval, to accompany him as far as Mombasa, on the western shore of the Red Sea, whence he was to enter the wilderness. He was to sail on Tuesday, March 23rd, on the North German Lloyd steamship *Hamburg*, bound for Naples. I had arranged my passage and bought my tickets when he wrote me as follows from the White House on February first:

After considerable thought I told the Associated Press people that I did not wish even you to go with me on my trip. I don't want any people able to say that I am responsible for any newspaper man or magazine writer accompanying me on my trip. I want to be able to say that I have done my best to keep every representative of the press from accompanying me or from advertising the trip in any way and that beyond the formal exchange of courtesies I have had no communication with any newspaper man while on the trip.

Of course I cheerfully, but regretfully, cancelled my passage and stayed behind.

When Roosevelt left New York he had arranged to make three formal public speeches during his return home through Europe in 1910—the address at the Sorbonne (referred to in the preceding chapter), an address at the University of Berlin, and the Romanes Lecture at Oxford University. The three addresses, which were to be not political but academic in character, had been written before he left America. I was anxious to hear them because I believed that the occasions of their delivery would prove to be university events of the first importance. So during the autumn of 1909 I wrote and asked him whether he had any objection to my joining him in France the following spring, in order to hear these three addresses.

There lies before me, as I write, an autograph letter from Roosevelt—dated "On Safari, December 2, 1909"—which was chiefly devoted to the controversy about the record of the Rough Riders at San Juan Hill. It may be of interest to quote here what he said of this controversy:

About B——'s letter concerning the Rough Riders at San Juan Hill my own idea is that a public controversy on the subject would be unwise. You can write B——- what I now say:

Mr. B——, by his own letter, shows that I stated the facts exactly in the volume I wrote. ["The Rough Riders."] There is no misapprehension in the matter at all, except in minds like Mr. B——'s. The San Juan Block House was simply one of the points of attack; the rest of the San Juan Ridge, and the hills near by, like Kettle Hill, form other points of attack. The cavalry charged at "San Juan Hill" just as much as the infantry; to deny this is merely to quibble—and to quibble untruthfully at that; and they charged "over the hill at San Juan." The titles of the pictures to which Mr. B—— objects are absolutely accurate. Let him for a moment think of the Battle of Gettysburg. This took its name from the village of Gettysburg, where there was much hard fighting. But there was also hard fighting at Culp's Hill, at Round Top, and at the stone wall facing Pickett's charge. To say, as Mr. B——does, that the Rough Riders and the regular cavalry "had no hand in the matter" of the San Juan charge is as foolish and untruthful as to say that Pickett's Virginians and all the men who fought at Round Top and Culp's Hill "had no hand in the fight at Gettysburg."

The infantry brigades which went up the Blockhouse Hill at San Juan did admirably; they deserve no less, and no more, credit than the cavalry brigades who at the same time did their share in the charge, that is the battle, of San Juan (it was all a charge and then holding the ground we had taken). Only one of the five or six regiments in the two infantry brigades which charged at the Blockhouse Hill suffered as heavy a percentage of loss in the Santiago fighting as the Rough Riders did. The first position captured on the "San Juan Heights"—that is the hills, loosely so-called, which defended the town—was Kettle Hill, by the cavalry. To try to start a quarrel over the relative credit of the regiments who fought in this fight is foolish and wrong; "the famous charge up San Juan" as Mr. B—— calls it, was made by both cavalry and infantry, at different points, and Mr. B——'s position is merely a disingenuous quibble.

The special interest about this letter is that it was written in the jungle, under circumstances that make some of the handwriting very hard to decipher and, like the article on the Pigskin Library, referred to later, without access to any maps or books of reference. It is one of many evidences that Roosevelt's mind was stored with facts of all kinds—historical, geographical, and scientific—and that he could take these facts out, often with literal and accurate quotations, from their various mental pigeon-holes.

In a postscript to this letter he added: "I hope you will meet me at Khartum on March fifteenth." So on February 10, 1910, I took passage for Naples, whence I proceeded via Alexandria, Cairo, and the upper reaches of the Nile, to Khartum. I found that Mrs. Roosevelt and Ethel Roosevelt, now Mrs. Derby, were going on the same steamer; I was therefore, happily for myself, able to act as their escort.

It was typical of Mr. Roosevelt's exactness in planning and carrying out his engagements that he should have arrived at Khartum on March 14th, the day before that which, in the previous December, he had appointed as the date of our meeting. On reaching Khartum I learned that through the considerate thoughtfulness of either

Mr. or Mrs. Roosevelt—perhaps of both—I was to be their fellow guest at the Governor-General's palace, a really beautiful and delightful establishment built in the custom of tropical countries round three sides of a patio or courtyard filled with flowers and shrubs.

The Roosevelt party consisted of Mr. and Mrs. Roosevelt, their daughter and son, Ethel and Kermit. I found that Mr. Roosevelt proposed to buy the tickets, check the trunks, write his own letters, and keep track of his own engagements. In a word, he expected to make the journey from Khartum through Europe like any American tourist.

I was with him only three or four hours when I foresaw that fulfillment of this programme would be absolutely impossible. It was apparent that he was going to be treated like a royal ambassador, and that it would be necessary for him to have some kind of secretarial assistance. I volunteered to help him and I think he was glad to get my help, for almost every one of his waking hours was fully occupied from the very moment of his arrival within the precincts of civilization. Indeed he said in accepting my offer, and employing a characteristic exclamation associated with him in the mind of every contemporary American

A page from Roosevelt's Ms. of "The Pigskin Library"

newspaper writer and cartoonist, that he was "delighted!"

One of the first of my self-imposed duties was to copy in my own hand the draft of his article on "The Pigskin Library" which was written in indelible pencil in the jungle, originally published in the *Outlook*, and afterward incorporated in an appendix of his book "African Game Trails." The accompanying photographic reproduction of a page of this manuscript will indicate to the reader that the job was not altogether a simple one. I remember that I sat up until about two or three o'clock on the night of my arrival in Khartum making this transcript.

Finally I found that I could not perform my voluntary task without assistance and I told Mr. Roosevelt that I proposed to cable to my office in New York for a stenographic secretary. He demurred at first on the ground that he did not wish to put the office to what he was afraid would be a large and unprofitable expense, but I persuaded him to consent, telling him that I was thinking more of my own comfort than I was of his. I cabled; and Mr. Harper jumped on the first steamer and joined us at Rome. Even Harper was unable to keep up with all the work, so at Berlin I was compelled to engage another stenographic assistant

Photo by Carl E. Akeley

Colonel Roosevelt in Africa photographing a jackal who is eating his fill inside the carcass of an elephant

and, in London, two others. As a matter of fact in London Mr. Roosevelt's old friend of Spanish War days, Captain (now Sir Arthur) Lee, placed at our disposal the office in his hospitable house where he transacted much of his business as a Member of Parliament. This office, with desks, telephone, two stenographic secretaries (some of the time three), was busy all day long during Mr. Roosevelt's stay in London of ten days or so, transacting his correspondence, planning his engagements, and attending to other matters connected with his visit. There was, for example, the complicated work of exchanging visiting cards. This necessary but very uninteresting side of diplomatic usage reached its climax in Rome. There, I recall, I had to spend a day with Captain Long—formerly of the presidential yacht *Mayflower* but at that time our Naval Attaché at Rome and Vienna—going over a basket full of visiting cards, culling out those that needed Mr. or Mrs. Roosevelt's, or Mr. and Mrs. Roosevelt's card left in exchange, and the following day a clerk of Captain Long's office spent most of his time in a taxi-cab, with a carefully mapped out itinerary in his hand, going about Rome leaving the right cards at the right places.

But to revert to Khartum. I soon found that,

in writing letters or seeing people on Mr. Roosevelt's behalf, it was necessary to have some sort of official authority. At Cairo all sorts of distinguished people were calling at the hotel at which Mr. Roosevelt was staying. If Prince X——called, in Mr. Roosevelt's absence, and I went down to receive him, my name would mean nothing to him; but if I said that I was Mr. Roosevelt's secretary, while he undoubtedly would be disappointed he would at least have transacted his business with me as he would have with the secretary of an embassy or a legation. I suggested this to Mr. Roosevelt and he approved. Thereafter I saw people officially, and signed all letters—except the few that were signed by Mr. Roosevelt himself —as "Secretary to Mr. Roosevelt." The result was that as we went through Europe I received cards to important functions and met important personages, which made my trip a peculiarly interesting one and enabled me to get an impression—that I could not have otherwise received—of the way in which both the great and the plain people of Europe were affected by Roosevelt's personality. It is impossible here to draw a detailed picture of this unique journey. I can only give sketches of what seemed to me to have been interesting and significant incidents here and there. Nor shall I pursue diarial methods.   I shall simply put down what my recollection suggests while I write.

The first thing that I recall is my grateful relief at having the vexed question of tipping settled for me at the very beginning.   I must explain that within twenty-four hours of meeting Mr. Roosevelt at Khartum I had charge of all his money, checks, letters of credit, etc., and undertook to pay all the bills.   I bought a single-entry ledger and kept a careful account.   Mr. Roosevelt would occasionally come to me and ask for a little pocket money, say twenty francs.   I would reply: "I will see if I can get it through the Committee on Appropriations"!   This became a standing joke between us.

I may say, running ahead a little, that when we sailed for New York from Southampton in June, I reported to Mr. Roosevelt that I had, as I recollect, the sum of about three thousand dollars to his credit.   He answered with some surprise: "That's good!   That will help me to pay the duties on my baggage at the custom house."   For he had declined to avail himself of the ambassadorial privilege which had been offered to him of entering the port of New York without an examination of his baggage.   I really think that if I had told him that he owed me three thousand dollars he would have said: "That's good! I supposed it was much more."

The fact is that he had less interest in money, as mere money, than almost any man that I have ever known. He was very much more interested in work and service. In 1908, on visiting Sagamore Hill to conclude the final arrangements about his joining the staff of the *Outlook*, when I mentioned the amount which we were prepared to pay him—a fairly large sum, it is true, for us, but a really small amount in comparison with offers that had been eagerly made him for journalistic and literary work—he put his arm around my shoulder and said: "Now, that is very good of you, Lawrence; but do you really think you can afford it? I should be very sorry if my connection with the *Outlook* did not prove to be the advantage to you which you say you anticipate." And on September 10, 1909, he wrote me from the African jungle:

The *Outlook* keeps me in touch with things just as I desire to be kept. I am exceedingly pleased at what you write as to being satisfied with the effect of my editorials; I have been a little uncomfortable lest you should feel that you weren't getting much good out of my connection with the magazine.

So long as his family was well taken care of and he had reasonably good food, reasonably appropriate clothing, and a reasonable opportunity to be hospitable to his friends, money meant nothing to him. His brother-in-law, the late Douglas Robinson, who was himself an eminently successful and systematic man of affairs, once told me that when Roosevelt was about leaving home to go into the Spanish War as Lieutenant-Colonel of the Rough Riders he, Douglas Robinson, could not by hook or crook persuade the Colonel to come down town in order to go over his investments and securities which were in Mr. Robinson's charge. Mr. Robinson finally got him to visit his office by saying: "Theodore, if you don't come down and go over these papers and valuables with me I shall have to get Edith [Mrs. Roosevelt] to do it." Whereupon Mr. Roosevelt instantly consented, for he was not willing to impose a burden on his wife which he should assume himself.

But I have strayed too soon from Africa. As we were leaving Khartum after a delightful stay of several days at the palace, Roosevelt asked me to be sure that the servants—both outdoors and in—were given suitable tips with an expression of his thanks for their services to him. Now most of these servants were Nubians, black as to face and white as to garments and turbans. It was as impossible to tell one from another as it is to identify individual sheep feeding in

a flock on a Western plain. In my puzzlement
I went to Slatin Pasha's personal aide, a most
kindly and agreeable young British officer, Captain
Clayton. (If he has survived the European war
and should ever happen to see these words I hope
he will accept them as an expression of very real
gratitude for all his courtesies.) I stated the
situation frankly to Captain Clayton and asked
him whether he could help me. He replied that
if I would leave a sum of money with him he would
see that it was properly distributed, and suggested
that we both go in to Slatin Pasha and consult
with him as to the proper amount.

We did so. I found that both these gentlemen
were more anxious to protect Roosevelt financially
than I was. They named a sum, which I thought
was not sufficient, and accepted as generous the
amount I left on Roosevelt's behalf. Captain
Clayton gave me an official receipt for this sum.
This started me on my career, as a courier, re-
joicing, and at every hotel I left a lump sum
with the manager to be distributed among the
domestics. I pursued the same method, which
it seems was the method of royal and ambassadorial personages, at two or three of the palaces
where Mr. Roosevelt was a guest. In each case I
had from an official a receipt like the following,

which lies before me, written on paper bearing an embossed coat of arms:

X——Castle

I acknowledge that I have received from Mr. Abbott the sum of one hundred dollars as a gratification to the servants of the Royal Palace from Mr. Roosevelt.

Y. Z——,

Master of the Royal Household

X——, May 6, 1910.

Such an experience as this was perhaps one of the least important, but certainly not one of the least interesting, of the journey—to an American at any rate.

It was not until we began to approach Rome that the social and political atmosphere began to be impregnated with some of the electricity that I had seen so often play about the figure of Roosevelt at home. I refer, of course, to what is now known as the Vatican controversy. I can best tell the story by transcribing here the following memorandum which I wrote on board the steamship *Prinz Heinrich* on April 1, 1910, during the voyage from Alexandria to Naples:

Mr. Roosevelt wrote from Gondokoro to Ambassador Leishman at Rome saying that he would be glad of the honour of a presentation to His Holiness, the Pope. At Cairo he received the following cable message from Mr. Leishman, dated Rome, March 23rd:

"The Rector of the American Catholic College [Monsignor

Kennedy] in reply to the enquiry which I caused to be made, requests that the following communication be transmitted to you: 'The Holy Father will be delighted to grant audience to Mr. Roosevelt on April 5th and hopes that nothing will arise to prevent it such as the much regretted incident which made the reception of Mr. Fairbanks impossible.—THOMAS KENNEDY, Rector'. I merely transmit communication without having committed you in any way to accept the conditions imposed as the form appears objectionable, clearly indicating that the audience would be cancelled in case you should take any action while here that might be construed as countenancing the Methodist Mission work—LEISHMAN.''

To this despatch Mr. Roosevelt replied by cable on March 25th as follows:

"Please present the following through Monsignor Kennedy: 'It would be a real pleasure to me to be presented to the Holy Father, for whom I entertain a high respect both personally and as the head of a great Church. I fully recognize his entire right to receive or not to receive whomsoever he chooses for any reason that seems good to him, and if he does not receive me I shall not for a moment question the propriety of his action. On the other hand I, in my turn, must decline to make any stipulations or to submit to any conditions which in any way limit my freedom of conduct. I trust that on April 5th he will find it convenient to receive me.'—ROOSEVELT.''

It should be here stated that, while this correspondence was pending, Mr. Roosevelt had persistently declined, either directly or indirectly, to make any public engagements of any kind whatsoever in Rome, except his visit to the King. In order to go as far as he could with propriety in meeting the wishes of the Vatican he deferred his own decision as to any possible public engagements until his arrival in Rome. This had been his answer to all invitations; he felt that he would be obliged first to find out from the Ambassador the exact situation.

Answering Mr. Roosevelt's despatch of March 25th, above quoted, Monsignor Kennedy on March 28th transmitted the following reply through Ambassador Leishman:

"His Holiness would be much honoured to grant an audience to Mr. Roosevelt for whom he entertains high esteem both personally and as the former President of the United States. His Holiness quite recognizes Mr. Roosevelt's entire right to freedom of conduct. On the other hand, in view of circumstances, for which neither His Holiness nor Mr. Roosevelt is responsible, the audience could not take place except on the understanding expressed in former message."

In response Mr. Roosevelt sent the following despatch to Ambassador Leishman:

"Proposed presentation is of course now impossible. Please be scrupulously careful that not one word on matter is said until I see you in Rome.—ROOSEVELT."

In some further cable correspondence the Ambassador suggested the desirability of Mr. Roosevelt's issuing a formal statement in order to prevent his attitude being misunderstood or his exchange of notes with the Vatican being garbled by the press or other interested parties. In order, however, to give his personal friend and associate John Callan O'Laughlin—a Roman Catholic but a loyal supporter of Mr. Roosevelt's principles and position in the matter—a last chance to see whether the Vatican could not be persuaded, for the sake of the American Catholic Church, to change its stand, Mr. Roosevelt, very generously I think, deferred any personal statement or comment until Mr. O'Laughlin could go to Monsignor Kennedy himself. At this writing (April 1st) Mr. O'Laughlin has, through his wife, cabled a message to Archbishop Falconio, the Papal legate at Washington, urging him to advise the Vatican that its action, if persisted in, would injure the Catholic Church in America. Mr. O'Laughlin goes by first train to Rome to-morrow morning, on our arrival in Naples, to see Monsignor Kennedy personally. I need hardly add that this is done on Mr. O'Laughlin's own initiative and is consented to by Mr. Roosevelt only on the explicit understanding that the consent is given out of a feeling of regard for his Catholic friends at home and not because he himself has the slightest desire or inclination to urge his presentation to the Pope. It was explicitly understood by both Mr. O'Laughlin and myself that, under no consideration, would Mr. Roosevelt recede from the position taken by him in his cable message, above quoted, of the date of March 25th.

The result, of course, was that Mr. Roosevelt did not meet the Pope. Nor did he visit the Methodist mission; he declined to receive the head of that mission, at the official reception which was given to him at the American Embassy, after it was definitely settled that he was not to go to the Vatican. From the beginning he had no intention of taking sides in the conflict between the Methodists and the Roman Church, a conflict which had arisen over the previous visit of Vice-President Fairbanks. His contention was solely that he must reserve the right to exercise his own judgment as to what his course should be without accepting conditions imposed by others. He cabled to New York the following statement with regard to the controversy:

Through the *Outlook* I wish to make a statement to my fellow-Americans regarding what has occurred in connection with the Vatican. I am sure that the great majority of my fellow-citizens, Catholics quite as much as Protestants, will feel that I acted in the only way possible for an American to act, and because of this very fact I most earnestly hope that the incident will be treated in a matter-of-course way, as merely personal, and, above all, as not warranting the slightest exhibition of rancour or bitterness.   Among my best and closest friends are many Catholics.   The respect and regard of those of my fellow-Americans who are Catholics are as dear to me as the respect and regard of those who are Protestants. On my journey through Africa I visited many Catholic as well as many Protestant missions, and I look forward to telling the people at home all that has been done by Protestants and Catholics alike, as I saw it, in the field of missionary endeavour.   It would cause me a real pang to have anything said or done that would hurt or give pain to my friends, whatever their religious belief, but any merely personal considerations are of no consequence in this matter.   The important consideration is the avoidance of harsh and bitter comment such as may excite mistrust and anger between and among good men.   The more an American sees of other countries the more profound must be his feelings of gratitude that in his own land there is not merely complete toleration but the heartiest good will and sympathy between sincere and honest men of different faiths—good will and sympathy so complete that in the inevitable daily relations of our American life Catholics and Protestants meet together and work together without the thought of difference of creed being even present in their minds.   This is a condition so vital to our National well-being that nothing should be permitted to jeopard it.   Bitter comment and criticism, acrimonious attack and defense, are not only profitless but harmful, and to seize upon such an incident as this as an occasion for controversy would be wholly indefensible and should be frowned upon by Catholics and Protestants alike.   I very earnestly hope that what I say will appeal to all good Americans.

Mr. John Callan O'Laughlin at the same time cabled the following statement to the New York *Times:*

> Familiar as I am with all the facts, and looking at his action from the viewpoint of an American Catholic, I personally feel that any other action Colonel Roosevelt might have taken would have resulted in the humiliation not only of himself but of the American people, Catholic as well as Protestant, and would have established an unwise precedent of serious consequences in the future.

The controversy was clearly understood by ecclesiastics, in Italy and other parts of Europe, to be one not between Mr. Roosevelt and the Pope but between Mr. Roosevelt and Cardinal Merry del Val, the Papal Secretary of State. Merry del Val was not only a prelate but an astute and able politician. I have always felt that he drew swords with Mr. Roosevelt in order to make a test of the question whether he was not more skilful than the American who had come to Europe with such a reputation as a political manager. The test was a complete one and showed that the Cardinal was out-generaled.

In Vienna, the capital of the most ultramontane country in Europe, only a comparatively few days after the Vatican episode, the Papal Nuncio at that capital appeared at a reception given in honour of

Mr. Roosevelt, and made this appearance in his official ecclesiastical robes. This was recognized in Vienna and elsewhere as a semi-official intimation that the high priests of the Church believed that Mr. Roosevelt was right and Merry del Val wrong. Immediately after this reception Roosevelt called officially on the Papal Nuncio who had returned to his palace. This exchange of courtesies created considerable discussion and comment in the newspapers. By many it was expected that the Nuncio would be visited with some sort of discipline from the Vatican. He was not, however; and those who knew the inside of church politics said that it was the method which the Pope took to indicate that he did not wholly approve of Merry del Val's management of the affair.

There were certain echoes of the controversy during the rest of the journey through Europe. At Porto Maurizio the distinguished novelist and poet, Antonio Fogazzaro, who died the following year, called upon Mr. Roosevelt and had a long and quiet personal interview with him. Fogazzaro, a devout Roman Catholic, had two or three years earlier published his novel, "The Saint"—which dealt with the question of Modernism and was read around the world. This book was distinctly religious in spirit but also distinctly liberal in its theology. Because of its support of the Modernist movement it had been placed upon the *Index Expurgatorius* and the author disciplined by the Church. At the time of Mr. Roosevelt's visit Fogazzaro had made his submission and had been taken back into full communion. After Fogazzaro's call I walked back with him to the town—Mr. and Mrs. Roosevelt were staying with Mrs. Roosevelt's sister at her villa on an outlying hillside— and he told me that because of his own somewhat delicate position in the Church and because of Mr. Roosevelt's controversy with the Vatican he had felt it necessary to ask his bishop whether he might make this personal call on the ex-President, and his bishop had told him to go by all means. Later on in the journey two or three Philippine friars had private interviews with Mr. Roosevelt with episcopal permission. These incidents confirm the opinion which I have already expressed that the sympathies of many of the influential dignitaries of the Church were with Mr. Roosevelt rather than with the pontifical Secretary of State.

Although Mr. Roosevelt was not received at the Vatican he was received with great cordiality at the Quirinal. The King of Italy, Victor Emanuel III, was the first of a considerable company of European monarchs that Mr. Roosevelt met on this tour. It was quite apparent that the kings liked him. At all events, after the formal and punctilious hospitalities had been fulfilled they all, without exception, went out of their way to show him personal attention. There was something about his personality that attracted them. European kings have not always had an entirely happy time even in days of peace. Their relations with their fellowmen are necessarily circumscribed and often artificial. With Roosevelt it was as though they said to themselves: "Here is a real man that we can meet, talk to, and associate with as men, not kings. He won't kowtow to us and he won't embarrass us." There was really an element of pathos in it.

When Mr. Roosevelt came home he was accused, during the Progressive campaign, by some of his silliest opponents, of an ambition to become king of America. His comment on these foolish critics was: "I know kings and they don't. A king is a kind of cross between a vice-president and a leader of the Four Hundred. I have been vice-president, and know how hollow the honour is, and I have never had any desire to be a leader of the Four Hundred!" There was nothing of personal criticism in Roosevelt's democratic estimate of kingship. Indeed, he was drawn to the King of

Italy because of the latter's democratic character, which later, during the European war, was respected and honoured by all the peoples of the Allies. After meeting Victor Emanuel somewhat informally Mr. Roosevelt came back to the hotel one night and said to me: "I like the King. He is a genuine man—the kind of man who could carry his own ward in an election!" That the feeling was reciprocated was disclosed by an amusing incident.

The King desired to have Mr. Roosevelt visit the famous Italian cavalry school in the neighbourhood of Rome, the Italian cavalry being among the most expert war horsemen in the world. An appointment was made, and on the day and the hour named I was awaiting in the lobby of our hotel for the automobile to come for Mr. Roosevelt. The hotel was a quiet and pleasant one, much frequented by certain diplomats and functionaries, but was not one of the ultra-fashionable caravansaries of the city. At the appointed hour a handsome limousine drove up with a liveried chauffeur and footman. The King with his aide, the latter in his military uniform, alighted and came into the lobby of the hotel. The effect was electrical. The *portier* or doorman, the liftman, the manager, and the head waiter almost prostrated themselves in their ecstasy of surprise and delight at the honour

Colonel Roosevelt and the author viewing the Roman Forum from a point on the Palatine Hill under the guidance of the late Jesse B. Carter, Director of the American School of Classical Studies in Rome

thus paid to their establishment. The King waited and drove Mr. Roosevelt off in great glee. I doubt if the King had ever visited a hotel in Rome in such fashion before. At all events, we learned afterward that the visit greatly enhanced the reputation of the hotel and were amused to hear that the proprietor had instituted a suit against the Paris *Herald* for saying that Mr. Roosevelt was a guest at some other hostelry, thus depriving him, the owner of the only genuine Roosevelt stopping place, of the important advertising benefit which he alleged that Mr. Roosevelt's visit conferred.

After a strenuous week in Rome—which had been preceded by a fortnight of exhausting sight-seeing and speech-making in Egypt—Mr. Roosevelt went to Porto Maurizio, as I have already said, for a visit to Mrs. Roosevelt's sister and to enjoy a well-earned vacation. Porto Maurizio is a small but ancient and picturesque Italian city on the shore of the Mediterranean not far from the French frontier. Behind it lie hills and valleys thick with olive trees and vineyards, and still farther back is a fine range of mountains, capped with snow at the season of the year when Roosevelt made his visit. Everywhere are roads and paths enticing to the walker and affording a constant succession of beautiful views of the characteristic Italian landscape.

The pleasant villa of Mrs. Roosevelt's sister, Miss Carow, stands in a flowery garden on a hillside overlooking the sea. It was an ideal place for a rest. But in the lexicon of the cable, the telegraph, and the post-offices there is no such word as "rest"; the eagerly anticipated vacation was broken into by a procession of messengers bringing communications—some, it is true, important, but most of them of the greatest unimportance—who trooped to the "Villa Magna Quies" (which by a curious irony of fate means "Villa of Great Quiet") at literally all hours of the day and night. Most of these communications were appeals for help in private cases or public affairs, or for political and personal advice, or to make engagements for lectures and speeches on Roosevelt's return to America.

Speaking of these letters Roosevelt said to me: "These good people have expectations as to what I can do that would not be justified if I were George Washington, Abraham Lincoln, and the Angel Gabriel all rolled into one." Indeed, during his entire European tour the number and character of the appeals that were made to him were almost incredible. It was half amusing and half exasperating to see how much of the time of an already over-driven man was taken up in answering epistolary demands and requests for interviews.

The letters ranged from applications for autographs, stamps, and picture postal cards to inquiries as to his views on the Bacon-Shakespeare controversy; or for his opinion on the Referendum as applied to the matter of municipal expenditure; or for a description of a special kind of African antelope because "the pupils in this school would find it interesting"; or for an article for an American college paper on "Politics as a Career for Young Men of Means"; or, from a Hungarian editor, for a paper about "Hungarian Emigration to the United States"; or for a review of a book of poems which was sent by the author; or for a "brief article" for a young men's lyceum on the question of "International Peace." I specify these because it happened that every one of these requests was contained in one morning's mail.

With regard to this aspect of the trip I find the following in my journal, written at Budapest in April, 1910:

Even while he was in Africa Mr. Roosevelt received requests that, without exaggeration, may be called appalling in their number and character. A favourite request was for tigers' claws, the writers being in beautiful ignorance of the fact that no tigers are found in Africa. Other unknown correspondents frequently asked for lions' claws, apparently not

understanding that to take off the claws of course ruins the
skin, so that each request was practically that Mr. Roosevelt
should go out and kill a lion exclusively for the benefit of a
correspondent of whose previous existence he had never
heard. He was appealed to for monkeys, parrots, and lion
cubs by other well-meaning people; one gentleman wanted a
pair of small elephants, another a pair of zebras, another a
250-pound snake—these requests evidently being made in
bland ignorance of the fact that to meet them would have
demanded a totally different type of expedition, especially
equipped at a cost of many thousands of dollars, to catch wild
animals for the purpose of distributing them gratis to unknown individuals. As for requests for horns and skins on
the part of men who apparently thought that the expedition
was conducted on a broad eleemosynary basis, they were
legion—one man standing out above his fellows because of
his modest request for "enough leopard skins to make an
overcoat"!

All sorts of things are sent for Roosevelt's inspection or
approval, or to reinforce a request for his special aid. Birth
certificates, university diplomas, and papers of this kind
which are of real value to the people who send them are forwarded to him by writers who apparently suppose that he has
nothing to do but to make parcels and packages and buy
postage stamps. In Austria one lady inclosed some well-
worn newspaper clippings evidently taken from her most
precious archives, one of them being an obituary notice of her
late husband and the other a description of the costume she
wore when she was presented some years ago at one of the
royal courts of Europe. Another lady, a Russian, mailed to
Mr. Roosevelt some papers connected with her son's university career, and because she did not get a personal reply by
return of mail called at the hotel at seven o'clock in the morning in a state of great agitation which was really pathetic to
behold. A Hungarian artist sent a registered package containing a pen-and-ink portrait of the Emperor Francis Joseph

which he had made with indescribable toil by shading the microscopic letters forming a biographical account in three thousand words of the Emperor's career. In the package was a large hand magnifying glass loaned for the purpose of examining the portrait, which the artist hoped would induce Mr. Roosevelt to give him a commission for a similar portrait of "the illustrious ex-President." Of course all these things have to be carefully sifted out, preserved, and returned, to do which involves an annoying expenditure of time and labour.

I suppose that the daily correspondence of any well-known public man would furnish similar displays of the curious workings of certain human minds.

While I was in the act of writing the words of the previous sentence a hall-boy of the hotel presented me with twelve visiting-cards, twelve letters, and four telegrams for Mr. Roosevelt, who at the moment is out inspecting the famous Agricultural Museum of Budapest. These communications constitute a sort of light afternoon supplement to the daily batch of letters, the majority of which arrive in the morning hours. Of the telegrams one is in French and one in Hungarian or in German. Of course the Hungarian correspondence has to be specially translated before it can be attended to, as none of Mr. Roosevelt's immediate party has had time between letters to learn what is perhaps the most difficult of all modern European languages. One letter, however, is from an entirely unknown correspondent in England. "I write to ask," she says, "if you would feel inclined to help me. I am the widow of a clergyman, and since his death I have had heavy expenses which I cannot meet on my small income, but if I could get clear of debt I think my daughter and I could manage. I am trying to get three hundred pounds to relieve me of my burden."

It is such correspondence as this that makes it impossible for a man of Mr. Roosevelt's public position to enjoy a real vacation unless he is absolutely cut off from the post-office, the telegraph, and the telephone.

When the University of Christiania conferred upon Mr. Roosevelt the honorary degree of Doctor of Philosophy—a degree which had never been conferred before upon any person by the University—Professor Broch, Dean of the Faculty of Philosophy, likened Mr. Roosevelt to a railway engine whose course is concealed from the near-by spectator by a cloud of dust and smoke, but which, nevertheless, pursues its course with rapidity and power toward a definite goal, leaving behind it a straight and shining track. This semi-humorous analogy was not inappropriate to Mr. Roosevelt's journey through Europe. In my journal at the time I wrote:

It is almost impossible for one who has been close to Mr. Roosevelt in this remarkable and unprecedented journey to appreciate its significance himself or to give any adequate idea to American readers of what it has meant to the people of Europe. If the reader will take a map and, with a pencil, trace the course of this journey, some faint notion may be obtained of what Mr. Roosevelt has done physically in his six weeks' tour between the dates of April 2d, when he landed in Naples, and May 15th, when he left Berlin for London. In miles alone the lineal distance which he has covered is prodigious—Naples to Rome, Rome to Genoa, Genoa to Porto Maurizio, Porto Maurizio back to Genoa, Genoa to Venice, Venice to Vienna, Vienna to Budapest, Budapest to Paris, Paris to Brussels, Brussels to The Hague, The Hague to Amsterdam, Amsterdam to Copenhagen, Copenhagen to Christiania, Christiania to Stockholm, and Stockholm to Berlin! When it is considered that in each of these chief stopping places there were dinners, receptions, official festivities, private and personal calls, academic celebrations—and in four cities great public addresses—besides an uncounted number of greetings from and extemporaneous speeches to people gathered at railway stations, in schoolhouses, and in the village streets, it is not surprising that it is difficult in the midst of it all to form an intelligent impression of the significance and importance of such a journey in their correct proportion.

The cumulative effect of the extraordinary pilgrimage was a very distinct impression that the people, the political leaders, and the rulers of Europe recognized in Roosevelt a personification of the moral power of human nature—the power not merely to appreciate high ideals but to put them into practical effect in every-day life. It is a painful thing to have to admit that so many good people are uninteresting and so many interesting people are not always good. Roosevelt was both thoroughly good and thoroughly interesting. In some respects his European tour may be said to have been a missionary journey in behalf of political and social morality; yet it was full of gayety and vivacity of life and he enjoyed its colour, its movement, its social festivities, and its good living with as much appreciation as a *bon vivant*. To quote again from my journal:

The common people as well as many of the most distinguished personages of Europe have not merely shown admira-

tion for Roosevelt's character but have found real fascination
in his personality. People not merely want to see him out
of curiosity, but when they have once seen him they want
to be with him and talk to him. Everywhere the most striking proofs have been given that he possesses in a very marked
degree what is somewhat tritely called "personal magnetism."

In Porto Maurizio, for instance, both the popular
and the official receptions of Mr. Roosevelt were
very remarkable in their recognition of his moral
leadership. The town was placarded with posters,
issued by the municipal authorities in the Italian
language, in which a welcome was expressed to Mr.
Roosevelt as "the promoter of international peace
and the champion of human fraternity and solida-
rity." When he appeared on the streets the citizens
—especially the working people and the peasants—
bombarded his carriage with flowers, so that it was
filled almost to overflowing. People leaned from
the third-story windows of what in New York
we should call tenement houses to throw down their
home-made floral tokens. One day when he drove
out into the country I saw an old peasant woman
standing by her cottage door eagerly waiting the
approach of the carriage, and when, with a trem-
bling hand, she tossed to him a bunch of flowers,
there was pinned to a large green leaf a scrap of
paper, and on it, written with painful effort, the
words: "*Viva, viva, viva Roosevelt!*" This old

woman had never seen him before, would never see him again; she received, in acknowledgment, only a smile and a lift of the hat; and yet it was pathetically evident that she had been eager to pay her slight tribute to the man who stood, in her mind, as "the champion of human fraternity."

An incident in Paris showed in a delightful way Roosevelt's hold upon the ordinary man—upon those whom Lincoln called "the plain people." A feature of the Paris programme was a review of some French troops at Vincennes. Mr. Roosevelt went out to the field with the American Ambassador, Mr. Bacon, and the French Ambassador to Washington, M. Jusserand. Each of the three was, of course, dressed in the conventional frock coat and high hat, but the general officer in command asked Mr. Roosevelt if he would not like to ride. He quickly responded by mounting a horse with no opportunity of changing his costume beyond the addition of a pair of leggings which an orderly took off and placed at Mr. Roosevelt's disposal. The review was a successful and picturesque one. Some days later, while in Holland, Mr. Roosevelt received from the enlisted men the following letter, which bore in the upper left-hand corner a picture of a horse of the French cavalry:

Vincennes, le 27 Avril, 1910.

Monsieur le Président Roosevelt:

Nous sommes les cavaliers du 2ᵉ Escadron du 23ᵉ Dragons, et c'est le cheval *Peppino* de chez nous que vous avez monté pour la manœuvre d'aujourd'hui. Nous en avons été très fiers et l'escadron ne l'oublira jamais. Nous respecterons ce cheval avec fidélité. Nous nous permettons de vous écrire pour que vous le sachiez. Nous n'oublierons jamais non plus que nous vous avons vu.

Nous sommes vos cavaliers respectueux et dévoués,

(Signé): LES CAVALIERS DU 2ᵉ ESCADRON,

QUI AIMENT L'AMÉRIQUE.

Or in English:

Mr. President:

We are the troopers of the 2nd Squadron of the 23rd Dragoons, and this is our horse Peppino which you rode to-day at the manœuvres. We were very proud of it, and the squadron will never forget it. We venture to write to you to assure you that we shall take care of this horse hereafter with the utmost respect. Nor shall we ever forget that we have seen you.

We are, respectfully and devotedly,

The Cavalrymen of the 2nd Squadron

Who Admire America.

These soldiers from the ranks, representing, as the phraseology of their letter shows, the modest homes of France, were not the less loyal to their own country because in so spontaneous and simple a fashion, with no personal axe to grind, they expressed their appreciation of the human qualities which Mr. Roosevelt represented.

There is no room in this impressionistic sketch

to give a detailed narrative of the visits to Belgium, to Holland, to Denmark, to Norway, and to Sweden. In each of these countries Mr. Roosevelt was received with the most friendly courtesy and attention by the rulers and by the people themselves. In Brussels he and his family dined with the King and Queen; in Holland they lunched with the Queen and her Consort; in Denmark they were the guests of the Crown Prince; in Christiania they were the guests of the King and the Queen at the Royal Palace; and in Stockholm, the guests of the Crown Prince and the Crown Princess at the Castle. The three great Scandinavian cities were beautifully decorated, and the hospitality both of the citizens and of the royal families was of the most generous character. Special "saloon carriages" (private cars, as we call them) and dining-cars, and in some cases special trains, were placed at the disposal of Mr. Roosevelt, his family, and his party by the government railways of France, Belgium, Holland, Denmark, Norway, Sweden, and Germany; in the three Scandinavian kingdoms, in addition to ambassadorial and royal dinners, splendid banquets were given in his honour by large bodies of citizens; and everywhere crowds of people lined the streets— eager to catch a glimpse of him and to cheer him as he passed. This rather bald account of what was really a beautiful, generous, spontaneous, and in many respects unprecedented hospitality is excusable only on the ground that American readers ought to know what friendliness was shown by the European peoples and governments to one whom they regarded as the representative of the best type of Americanism. Those Americans who had the pleasure of being near-at-hand spectators of these greetings learned that warm-hearted enthusiasm is not confined to races of southern blood; neither Italy nor France could have outdone the Viking cities of Scandinavia in either the public or private manifestations of approval of their distinguished guest.

Among my papers I find the following carefully-worked-out itinerary and time-table of the journey from Brussels to Copenhagen. It required, of course, much correspondence and many conferences with officials, and may give the reader an impression that such a tour as Roosevelt's was not altogether a pleasure jaunt.

THE HAGUE AND AMSTERDAM TRIP.

FROM BRUSSELS TAKE ONLY IN TRAIN THE LUGGAGE WHICH WILL BE REQUIRED FOR THE FIRST DAY, SEND THE OTHER LUGGAGE THROUGH, BUYING VALET'S TICKET RIGHT THROUGH TO THE HAGUE, AND CHECKING ALL THE BAGGAGE ON THIS TICKET.

Leave Brussels 7.53 A. M. Friday, April 29th, on private car attached to ordinary train. Meet special train coming from Holland at Roosendaal, at 9.53 A. M. and have carriage attached to it.   Reach Arnheim at 12.30.   Mr. Roosevelt and family then motor to Het Loo (the Palace) arriving at one o'clock, where they will lunch with the Queen at 1.30. Mr. Roosevelt will afterward leave Het Loo (Apeldoorn Station) at 3.40, on private car already arranged for, arriving Amsterdam at 5.05.   (Mrs. and Miss Ethel Roosevelt will go to Hotel des Indes, The Hague: Mr. Beaupré will arrange their passage there.)   Mr. Roosevelt will dine with the Bur-gomaster, and afterward a reception will be held at the house of Mr. A. J. Cremer.   Leave Amsterdam the same evening on a special coach attached to the ordinary train, or on a spe-cial train, arriving at The Hague (Hotel des Indes) the same (Friday) evening.   Mr. Beaupré is arranging the train from Amsterdam to The Hague.

Saturday, April 30th.   Received by Queen Mother at 12 o'clock.   Mr. Roosevelt and family lunch with Minister of Foreign Affairs.   Dine at Legation at 8 o'clock.   Reception at 10 o'clock.   Return to Hotel des Indes.

Monday, May 2nd.   Arrive Hamburg 6.33 A. M., leaving again at 7.05 A. M. and arriving Copenhagen 4.48 P. M.   Met at Station by Crown Prince.   He will take Mr. Roosevelt and family in carriages to Palace.   Messrs. Abbott and Har-per will stay at Hotel d'Angleterre.   Mr. Egan will come to Palace at which presentation has been held, and he will take Mr. Roosevelt to meet Prince Vlademir and Prince Hans. Afterward return to Palace and dine with King.   At 9.30 to 10.30, at the Legation, will be an American Reception. Mrs. Roosevelt will be provided with a bouquet, so that she will not be expected to shake hands.   Return to Palace to sleep.

May 3rd.   Tuesday: Leave by automobile at 8 A. M.   Visit a Model Dairy, a Model Farm, and a Model "Small-Holder." Then to Roskilde to see the Cathedral, with the Royal burial places.   From thence to Hollerd, to see the Castle of Fred-eriksburg, which contains the National Gallery, and from there, via Fredensborg, to Elsinore. Arrive at Elsinore about 12 o'clock, and go aboard the Scandinavian-American fast passenger boat, *Queen Maud*, to Copenhagen, which will enable Mr. Roosevelt to see the beautiful coast of Sjaelland. Arrive in Copenhagen at about 2 o'clock. At 5.45 Municipality dinner, at which no ladies will be present, in view of the early departure that evening. Depart from Copenhagen for Christiania at 9.05 P.M.

To this time-table I append the account which my friend Maurice Egan, American Minister to Denmark during Roosevelt's visit, has given me of some of the details and effects of the ex-President's visit to Scandinavia:

When it was finally settled that Colonel Roosevelt should come to Europe, the three Scandinavian consuls—at this time I happened to be American Minister in Denmark— showed the most ardent interest. Denmark was especially interested because to the Danes Mr. Roosevelt represented a tendency toward that revolt against plutocracy which many of the Danes believed to be a menace to the best institutions of our country. He was also, without doubt, the most picturesque figure in the world at that time. As the Minister I was besieged with all kinds of questions as to whether Mr. Roosevelt would come or not. He made it so plain in many public utterances that I was a friend of his, and everybody in Denmark knew that I had been appointed by him, so that the Danes felt it was my duty to induce him to visit their country.

One day, speaking to my friend and colleague, the Norwegian Minister, I was astonished to discover that he felt that Mr. Roosevelt had not been exactly polite to the Nobel Prize Committee when he had refused to give—or postponed giving—the customary address of the Nobel Prize men at

Christiania. Following this hint, which was very delicately given, I made some further investigations and discovered there there was a feeling among the Norwegians and the Swedes that no American ought to be offered the prize since the most distinguished of Americans had rather cavalierly refused to comply with the traditional condition. I said to a very influential member of the Committee: "If I had anything to do with the Nobel Prize I should certainly give it to either Mr. Elihu Root or Mr. Richard Watson Gilder." This was a feeler. "Oh," my friend said, "I do not think it would be worth while to name any American for that prize now."

Mr. Roosevelt I knew very well would suffer any inconvenience rather than stand in the way of any fellow American receiving this honour, so I wrote at once three letters to be forwarded to him in Africa by various people. One was, I think, to our Consul at Naples. In a reasonable time his reply came. He was willing to give me a day or so at Copenhagen. Of course, this was not enough. When I considered the presentation to the royalties, the ceremonies of the municipalities, the various courtesies which many of my Danish friends would feel it their duty to show them, I was in despair. Besides, I must secure him for Christiania first, where the great question of the Nobel Prize remained to be settled. I concealed the fact from my friends and the newspapers that he had promised to come to Copenhagen and in the meantime extorted a promise from him that he would go to Christiania as well. I communicated his determination to my colleague, Mr. Pierce, at Christiania who was delighted and who insisted in giving me credit for Mr. Roosevelt's consent at the Norwegian Court.

A short time after this came a note from Frederick VIII asking me to come to see him. I presented myself. "My dear Mr. Minister," he said, "my son Haakon tells me that you have induced your distinguished patriot to go to Christiania. Why cannot you induce him to come here?" And then I answered: "If your Majesty wants him to come here I shall communicate your wish to Colonel Roosevelt, and he will consider at once your request as a command." The King was evidently very much pleased and then it occurred to me that I might just as well make Mr. Roosevelt's stay in Copenhagen as splendid as possible. "I regret that my legation is not large enough for many guests——" "Ah," the King interposed, "I shall be so pleased to have Colonel Roosevelt here, that although I am obliged to go for my health to the Riviera at the end of the week I shall command my son, the Crown Prince, to act for me and to give him all the attention that I would give if I could be present here." Then he broke off. "When do you think he is going to Germany and where do you think his Imperial Majesty will lodge him?" "Ah, in the palace at Potsdam I am sure," I answered. "I can do no less, and I should like to do more," his Majesty remarked; "I shall offer him and his family the palace of Christian VII." This I knew was considered a great honour, as nobody but a crowned head was received as guest in this palace; King Edward and Queen Alexandra had been its last occupants. I at once telegraphed this to Colonel Roosevelt and asked him for more time. He replied, giving me a day or two more. After that it was my business to excite expectation, which the press was only too willing to do. The Crown Prince was most enthusiastic and, through the amiability of the Minister of Commerce I managed to secure all the properties, rugs, palms, etc., which were always used to adorn the station whenever royalty appeared.

The question of ranking Colonel Roosevelt was a serious one. The Court Marshal was very much perturbed; what rank had an ex-President of the United States in his own country? As a colonel he would hardly be visible in the galaxy of court officials who would certainly be present at any function given in his honour. Throwing aside all the prejudices of democracy I suggested that he should be ranked as the late Consort of Queen Victoria or the present Prince

Consort of the Queen of Holland, as a Royal Highness.   Mrs. Roosevelt, Ethel, and Kermit were equally ranked, and Mr. Lawrence Abbott, of whom Mr. Roosevelt had enthusiastically written, was put down as a visiting Minister Plenipotentiary.   This made things easy.   The station was quite as magnificent as it had been when the Czar of Russia or the Kaiser or King Edward came; our Consul-General, Mr. Bond, saw to that!

The great day came; Copenhagen was in a furore of expectation; the Crown Prince, accompanied by a brilliant suite, drove to the station; I followed at a reasonable distance with our best footmen on the box adorned with the largest red, white, and blue cockades we had ever used; my wife and daughter were too fine for words!   The Crown Prince occupied the centre of the circle and the dramatic effect, I said to myself, was going to be worthy of the occasion.   Suddenly, Colonel Roosevelt escaped from Mr. Lawrence Abbott's guiding hand, rushed through the train, and descended two cars below all this waiting magnificence.   The Crown Prince, the tallest man in Europe, with the longest legs, ran down the platform to meet him; and after that we all went helter skelter.   Colonel Roosevelt wore an army coat and an ancient sombrero.   He seemed pleased beyond words to see us all.   I presented him very formally, "Permit me, your Royal Highness, to present to you His Excellency the late President of the United States."   The Crown Prince bowed, shook Mr. Roosevelt warmly by the hand, and then Colonel Roosevelt said, "Now I have lost my baggage.   Let's go and look for it."   The Prince was very much amused and felt that here at last was a human being.   Mr. Lawrence Abbott was the only person at all perturbed by this incident of the missing trunks, for which he was in no wise responsible; so we left him, ranking as he did as a Minister Plenipotentiary, to look after the luggage!

It had been arranged that the Crown Prince should give a gala dinner at the Court to be followed at ten o'clock by a reception at the American Legation. Neither Colonel Roosevelt nor Mrs. Roosevelt seemed especially perturbed about the loss of their evening clothes and I think that Kermit and Ethel would have been glad of any accident that kept them away from ceremonies; they had their own plans which had nothing to do with court functions. Colonel Roosevelt had his Norfolk jacket brushed, Mrs. Roosevelt came in to dinner with the Crown Prince looking perfectly gracious and at ease in a travelling suit, and the dinner proceeded with unusual spirit and gayety. Royal people can safely be trusted, owing to their special education, to smoothe embarrassing situations and nobody seemed to remember whether Mr. Roosevelt wore a lounge coat or a uniform. Mademoiselle Wedel-Hainan who was one of the Ladies in Waiting to the old Queen, said: "It was worth while to see how simply Mrs. Roosevelt acted on this occasion; nobody but royalty could have made a situation of that kind go off so well; Queen Alexandra did it once and just in the same way." The Crown Princess said to my wife: "As Mrs. Roosevelt is a representative American woman nobody after this can ever say that they give too much attention to dress. How embarrassing it would have been for us all if she had not accepted the situation in such a perfectly charming manner." Of course all Denmark knew the circumstances the next day and the incident—trivial as it may seem—added a new ray to the star of glory of the visiting Americans. Before ten o'clock the missing trunks arrived and Mr. Lawrence Abbott, who was determined that everything should be technically correct, was happily relieved.

At the reception at our legation later in the evening Colonel and Mrs. Roosevelt were able to appear in the usual ceremonial garb. We managed to crowd over three hundred persons into the drawing room and the dining room and, with a little prompting as to what language you should speak to each person—Colonel Roosevelt's German was excellent and his French very fair—he had a most enjoyable time which was reflected in the faces of everybody he met. He said the appropriate thing, being very receptive to any hint from the Minister who stood near him and pleased even the tenors of the opera by repeating something that was both cordial and appropriate.

Altogether, no guest in Denmark ever left such an impression of strength, of sincerity, of power as Mr. Roosevelt left. On my leaving Denmark last year, King Christian, formerly the Crown Prince said, most pleasantly: "Assure Colonel Roosevelt of my affectionate esteem.   He is a man."

Until Minister Egan gave me the foregoing description, while I was preparing this chapter, I was unaware that I had any standing higher than that of Secretary of Legation while on this journey. If I had only known that he had conferred upon me the brevet and temporary honour of a plenipotentiary rank it would have saved me perhaps one very embarrassing experience!

On the day when we arrived in Christiania a luncheon, followed by a reception, was given at the house of the American Minister, Mr. Peirce. They were attended both by the King and by Mr. Roosevelt. King Haakon of Norway is a fine specimen of a man, six feet or a little over in height, of a well-shaped and athletic-looking figure; and his frank, open face bears the marks of strength, refinement, and good health. His Queen is the daughter of King Edward of Great Britain. Having served in the British Navy, King Haakon spoke English perfectly. I left the reception early and went up to the sitting room or *salon* in the suite assigned to Mr. Roosevelt in the palace and began to work with Harper on the mail and other matters connected with the journey. Before long the door opened and the King entered. I recognized him because I had just seen him at the reception; but he had taken off his frock coat, abandoned his high hat, and appeared in an ordinary suit of tweed —what we should call in this country a business suit. I rose, of course, and he began to talk to me about some details of Mr. Roosevelt's further journey to Stockholm for which the King wished his private saloon railway carriage to be employed. In his hand he had a letter about it which he gave me with some instructions.

Just then the door opened again and in blew Mr. Roosevelt—I do not know what other verb to use to describe the refreshing breeziness which was characteristic of his unexpected appearance on any occasion. He still had on his frock coat and carried his high hat in his hand, for he had to stay at the reception until it was all over.

The King was almost visibly embarrassed. It was as though he were saying to himself: "Now what shall I do to entertain this apostle of the strenuous life!" He remarked after a slight pause: "Colonel Roosevelt, wouldn't you like a cup of tea?" With real enthusiasm the Colonel answered: "By George, your Majesty, the very thing I should like!" While Roosevelt punctiliously observed all the proprieties in his royal visits, he was perfectly natural, and as I have already remarked, the kings apparently enjoyed for once having a free, natural, man-to-man relationship with a fellow-being. The King disappeared and in a few moments the folding doors were opened and there in an adjoining room was a pleasant tea-table, set in the English fashion, round which we all gathered.

Mr. Roosevelt—and he was one of the best table-talkers and *raconteurs* that I have ever listened to—told stories of his frontier life in the West. I remember that he gave an account of meeting his friend Seth Bullock over the dead body of a desperado whom they—as sheriff and deputy sheriff—were both pursuing during his ranching days. "Your Majesty," he said, "is sufficiently familiar with grouse shooting in England to realize that we met in the attitude of 'My bird, I believe'." He told other tales of Seth Bullock, whom he greatly liked and respected, and said that he wished the King could meet Bullock as a fine type of western American. I rather think the King did meet him, for—and perhaps this afternoon tea

suggested the idea to Roosevelt—he cabled to Seth
Bullock to join him in London. This Bullock did;
and there, with Roosevelt as friend and cicerone,
he met many of the distinguished people of the
day.

Now that night a splendid state dinner was given
in the palace in honour of Mr. Roosevelt. The
guests, one or two hundred in number, under the
direction of the Court Marshal, gathered at their
places in the great state dining room. It was a
fine company, for the Scandinavians are splendid
physical specimens. There were, of course, many
army and navy men in uniform and government
officials resplendent with orders.

At the high table, arranged like the speakers'
table at an American banquet, sat the royal party
consisting of the King with Mrs. Roosevelt and
the Queen with Mr. Roosevelt. This table was
on my right. We had reached the fish course,
I think, when a liveried footman came to my
left side, as was proper, and began to speak to
me in Norwegian. Of course I did not understand a single word, but I saw that the man
was labouring under some excitement. I wondered
whether he could be warning me not to put any
gold spoons into my pocket! I swung around—
the better to hear him—with my back almost

toward the royal table, when a gentleman down the table a little—my immediate companions not being able to speak English—leaned forward and said: "He is trying to tell you that the King wishes to drink a glass of wine with you." I thereupon hastily turned around toward the royal table and saw the King smiling, with his wine glass charged, prepared to go through the Scandinavian ceremony of drinking a health. Fortunately I had been in Scandinavia before and I knew what this ceremony was, but I did not know whether I ought to follow my instinct and rise from my seat. Such a procedure, I felt, would make me a marked man, and whatever I may be at home I certainly was shy on this occasion. I wondered whether one with so low a rank as that of Secretary was entitled to rise. Of course, all this flashed through my mind far more quickly than I can describe it, and I determined to rise only half way, so that I should be only half wrong, in any event. This with bended and quaking knees I did, and proceeded to bow and smile and say "*Skol*". When the ceremony was finished I fell back in my chair with embarrassment and did not eat much for a course or two.

Presently I saw another footman approach a gentleman in civilian dress, but with a brilliant order on his shirt front, at the opposite long table.

This gentleman rose, and it was apparent that he wished he had been eight feet high. He clicked his heels together and with perfect precision went through the health-drinking ritual. I realized my mistake. I should have stood erect like the Minister Plenipotentiary—which it now seems I really was, by the grace of Dr. Egan!

After dinner the company adjourned to one of the fine and spacious reception rooms where we were, or some of us were, presented to the King. As I had been standing almost shoulder to shoulder to him that afternoon, and am about six feet in height myself, I determined to apologize for my awkwardness at dinner, so I said: "Your Majesty, I appreciate the honour which you did me by drinking a glass of wine with me at dinner, and if you saw a rather short man rise when you expected to see a rather tall man I must explain that I have not been long enough in your hospitable country to know whether any one under the rank of an admiral or a general is entitled to rise on such an occasion; so, in my embarrassment of modesty, I rose only half way, and must have looked about as much out of place as a bent pin." Possibly the American frankness of it all amused the King. At all events, he laughed cordially and once or twice in later correspondence with Mr. Roosevelt sent some kind of a friendly message to "the bent pin"!

Perhaps the most notable incident of this European tour, at any rate in the light of subsequent history, was Roosevelt's meeting with the Kaiser in Berlin. His visit to the Prussian capital had been arranged before he left America, and was made for the purpose of delivering a lecture at the University of Berlin. This lecture did not particularly interest me. It was entitled: "The World Movement." I can't help feeling that Roosevelt subconsciously strove to impress the university pedants of Germany that an American democrat could be as scholarly and academic as they were and could deal in abstract ideas as ponderously as they could. The address—in my judgment—does not compare in style, in content, or in effectiveness with his speeches at the Sorbonne and the Guildhall or with the extemporaneous address to the undergraduates of Cambridge. Nor was the ceremony itself as human and interesting as that at the Sorbonne, although it was much more elaborate and formal. It is true that a chorus of students—dressed in the rather theatrical and bizarre costumes of their various "corps"—sang, as only Germans can sing, finely harmonized arrangements of "Hail Columbia" and "The Star-

Spangled Banner." But the professors in their academic gowns struck me as rather stodgy. The Kaiser, dressed in what I supposed to be a Hussar's uniform, was in the audience; and, much as I despise his course in the European war, I must admit that he had a very marked attractiveness of personality and manner.

On the day of his arrival in Berlin Roosevelt lunched with the Emperor at the palace in Potsdam and I had the good fortune to be one of the party. We went out from Berlin by special train and with a brilliant company of army and navy officers and government officials. Chancellor von Bethmann-Hollweg was of the party. Everything had been done by the Kaiser to make it evident that he wished to treat Roosevelt with special honour. For example, the day following the luncheon, the Kaiser invited Mr. Roosevelt to review with him some remarkable field manœuvres of the German troops and they spent in this operation five hours together on horseback.

Ex-Ambassador Henry White, who was the only civilian present except Kermit Roosevelt, described the scene to me that evening. The Emperor was dressed in the uniform of a general of his army, Mr. Roosevelt in a simple riding suit of khaki and a black slouch hat. As they sat side by side in the saddle, responding together to the salutes of the officers and troops who passed by in review, the scene must have been of dramatic interest—the only difference in their station being indicated by the fact that the Emperor was dressed in uniform while Mr. Roosevelt wore the dress in which he would ride across country at home, and by the manner of their salutes, the Emperor as commander-in-chief touching his visor, Mr. Roosevelt as private citizen raising his hat. During the review the Emperor, with his body-guard of officers in brilliant uniform gathered about him, raised his helmet and, turning to Roosevelt, said in German: "Roosevelt, *mein Freund*, I wish to welcome you in the presence of my guards; I ask you to remember that you are the only private citizen who ever reviewed the troops of Germany." Those who are familiar with the strict military procedure of the German Empire under Kaiser Wilhelm II and who understand the intimacy of the German expression "*mein Freund*," can understand the real intention of the Kaiser to impress his officers and the country with his desire to confer what he believed was a mark of distinction upon Roosevelt.

Roosevelt appreciated these courtesies but I think he rather felt the element of mediævalism and artificiality in them. At all events, they did not turn his head as similar flatteries turned the heads of some American exchange professors to Germany during the European war, for at the very outset he denounced the invasion of Belgium.

In its issue of September 23, 1914, the *Outlook* published an article by him, which had been written at least ten days previously, in which he said:

When once Belgium was invaded, every circumstance of national honour and interest forced England to act precisely as she did act. She could not have held up her head among nations had she acted otherwise. In particular, she is entitled to the praise of all true lovers of peace, for it is only by action such as she took that neutrality treaties and treaties guaranteeing the rights of small Powers will ever be given any value. . . . What action our Government can or will take, I know not. It has been announced that no action can be taken that will interfere with our entire neutrality. . . . Neutrality may be of prime necessity in order to preserve our own interests and maintain peace in so much of the world as is not affected by the war. . . But it is a grim comment on the professional pacifist theories as hitherto developed that our duty to preserve peace for ourselves may necessarily mean the abandonment of all effective effort to secure peace for other unoffending nations which through no fault of their own are dragged into the war.

When this article was being written I was endeavouring, although not a Wilson man, to give support to the President as the representative of the whole country in a time of crisis. At my request Roosevelt put into the article some *caveats*

as to Mr. Wilson's policy of neutrality in the
hope that Wilson might slowly come to see the
need of defending Belgium. These *caveats*, taken
from their context, some of his unscrupulous
political antagonists tried to employ later to show
that at the outbreak of the war he did not feel
about the rape of Belgium as he did later in the
struggle. For this error of judgment, which was
due to my desire to be loyal to the Government
as well as non-partisan, I am afraid Roosevelt
never forgave me, although he never alluded to it
in criticism or blame. From the very beginning
his own sentiments expressed in private conversation were those uttered in the following telegram,
sent on December 28, 1916, to Mr. W. J. Hand,
a lawyer and citizen of Scranton, Pennsylvania,
who was chairman of a Belgian Protest Meeting
held in the town hall of that city:

I wish all success to your meeting. Every American
worthy of the name should join in indignant and emphatic
protest against the hideous wrong-doing committed by Germany in Belgium. Righteousness comes before peace, and
neutrality between right and wrong is as immoral now as in
the days of Pontius Pilate.

This whole episode I have described fully in an
article which was published in the *Outlook* of
March 29, 1916. My interpretation was con-

firmed by an editorial in the Kansas City *Star* of March 31st:

The *Star* can add confirmatory evidence. Colonel Roosevelt spoke in Kansas City, Kansas, on September 21, 1914. To at least one member of the *Star* staff at that time he expressed forcibly his views regarding the duty of the United States toward Belgium, and added that he did not know how much longer he was going to be able to keep from speaking out on this subject. A few weeks later he made his first public declaration in criticism of the Administration's attitude.

But to go back for a moment to the luncheon at Potsdam. It was perfectly appointed and managed and the etiquette of precedence was scrupulously observed. It was served at small round tables in one of the state dining rooms to a company of, I should say, fifty or sixty ladies and gentlemen, including Mrs. Roosevelt, the Empress, and ladies of the Court. On leaving the table we adjourned to a great reception room known as the *Muschelsaal,* so called because the artist who built it in Frederick the Great's time stuck the yet-soft plaster full of iridescent mussel shells with the typically Prussian notion of æsthetics that this would form a decoration of beauty. It is hardly necessary to add that it does not. Colonel Roosevelt and the Kaiser withdrew to one corner of the great *Mussel Salon* and entered into a lively conversation. The rest of the party remained at the other end of the room chatting as a group of guests would do anywhere at a special luncheon.

After some time had elapsed I noticed the military commander in charge of the affair—I think it was General von Plessin—go up and whisper to Chancellor von Bethmann-Hollweg. The two pulled out their watches and then consulted Baron Schön, the Minister of the Interior. The three next went to the Empress and talked with her in low voices. Their agitation was so marked and so out of keeping with what had been the precision thus far observed that I turned to a young captain of infantry whose acquaintance I had made coming out on the train and who spoke English perfectly and knew my official relation to Roosevelt, and said: "May I ask if anything has gone wrong?" He replied: "Yes, the special train returns to Berlin at four o'clock. It is now twenty minutes to four and we are afraid that we shall not reach the station in time." Of course in those days if a German railway train, especially a royal railway train, was delayed the entire operation of the empire was apt, temporarily at least, to go to pieces. But the exacting and all-powerful domination of the Kaiser was such, and the officers of his Court had been so trained from their earliest youth, that there was not one person in that room—not even the Prime Minister of the Empire, not even the Empress herself—who dared step across the floor and remind the Kaiser of an important engagement. No one could leave the room until he gave the signal.

By and by he came out of the hypnotic influence which seemed to be exercised by the "Colonel of the Rough Riders" (as the Kaiser liked to call him) and gave the necessary intimation that we were to go. We were rushed to the station, piling into the vehicles with very little attention to the precedence which had been scrupulously observed when we came from Berlin in the morning, and barely got our train. This incident seemed amusing to me at the time, but I now think that it was much more than amusing, that it had an important significance. It was a symptom of that kind of idolatory which led the German people to follow the Kaiser and his Potsdam circle into the greatest national disaster of history.

But the Kaiser and his Court ought not to form the final recollection of the continent of Europe which this journey affords. And it shall not.

I return to Brussels for a moment to pay a tribute of respect and admiration to King Albert and Queen Elizabeth of Belgium. They entertained

Colonel Roosevelt and his party arriving in England from
Germany where they had been entertained by the Kaiser.
This was in 1910

Mr. Roosevelt and his party at a delightful dinner at the Palace of Laeken, which lies in a beautiful park in the suburbs of the capital. Their genuineness, simplicity, and cordiality were of a kind which has been proved to be characteristic of the three personages who, in the history of the European war, will stand out supremely, I think, for nobility of character and heroism of action. The third is the Belgian Cardinal, Mercier.

Queen Elizabeth is of a German royal family but she threw in her lot with her husband and adopted his people in a way that entitles her to an honour far higher than can be conferred by any coronet or hereditary rank. She is not only a woman of noble character but of high intelligence. She had studied medicine and I was told practised philanthropically not a little among the poor of Brussels by whom she was fairly idolized.

During the evening, after dinner, learning that I was Secretary to Mr. Roosevelt, she sought me out and engaged me for some time in a conversation about his personality and career. She was much interested in the political situation in the United States at the time, and I explained to her as well as I could some of the policies and movements which Roosevelt had espoused and led, and which on the one hand drew about him as great a company of devoted admirers, and on the other hand ranged against him as strong and vigorous an opposition, as the political history of the United States had ever displayed. Her grasp and understanding of such questions seemed to me to be quite extraordinary in a foreigner. But King Albert had visited the United States some years before in quite an informal way and made a study of our institutions. Both the King and the Queen, democratic and human by nature, looked with especial interest upon the development of democratic institutions in America.

From Berlin Roosevelt went to England. Many of his experiences there have been set forth in other chapters. The chief object of his visit when he left America was to give the Romanes lecture at Oxford and to receive from that celebrated university the honorary degree of Doctor of Civil Law. Regarding this occasion I may quote from an introduction which I contributed to the volume of his "African and European Addresses":

The Romanes lecture at Oxford University was the last of Mr. Roosevelt's transatlantic speeches. I can think of no greater intellectual honour that an English-speaking man can receive than to have conferred upon him by the queen of all universities the highest honorary degree in her power to give, and in addition, to be invited to address the dignitaries and dons and doctors of that university as a scholar speaking to scholars. There is no American university man who may not feel entirely satisfied with the way in which the American university graduate stood the Oxford test on that occasion. He took in good part the jokes and pleasantries pronounced in Latin by the Chancellor, Lord Curzon; but after the ceremonies of initiation were finished, after the beadles had, in response to the order of the Chancellor, conducted "*Doctorem Honorabilem ad Pulpitum*," and after the Chancellor had—this time in very direct and beautiful English—welcomed him to membership in the University, Mr. Roosevelt delivered an address the serious scholarship of which held the interest of those who heard it and arrested the attention of many thousands of others who received the lecture through the printed page.

As I have been writing these words I have also been looking over again this Oxford-Romanes lecture. I find in it a passage which strikes me with new force. It confirms, I think, the interpretation of his internationalism which will be found at the conclusion of the chapter on Statesmanship:

The foreign policy of a great and self-respecting country should be conducted on exactly the same plane of honour, of insistence upon one's own rights, and of respect for the rights of others, that marks the conduct of a brave and honourable man when dealing with his fellows. Permit me to support this statement out of my own experience. For nearly eight years I was the head of a great nation, and charged especially with the conduct of its foreign policy; and during those years I took no action with reference to any other people on the face of the earth that I would not have felt justified in taking as an individual in dealing with other individuals.

If I were to try to put in a single phrase the impression which Roosevelt made upon Europe I should say it was that of personal magnetism.

This magnetic quality of Roosevelt's, which acted as a kind of electrical stimulant upon those who came in contact with him, was remarked upon in a striking way by the physician who attended him in London. Unceasing private conversations and innumerable public and semi-public speeches during his journey tore his voice literally to pieces. In Berlin he was under the care of a throat specialist and for a day or two it was a question whether he himself would be able to read his address at the University of Berlin. In London, while he was staying at the house of his friend Sir Arthur Lee, one of the most distinguished throat surgeons in Great Britain gave him daily treatments to remove the hoarseness which had attacked his overstrained vocal chords. When this surgeon was leaving the house after his last professonal visit, just before our departure for America, it was my duty to pay his fee, and, having performed this formality, I walked out with him to his waiting automobile brougham. He kept me standing on the sidewalk for some moments while he talked about Roosevelt, expressing his admiration for him and his astonishment at his extraordinary personality. "In all my experience," he said, "I have never known anything like that man's vigour. Usually when I treat a patient as I have been treating Colonel Roosevelt I feel that some of my vital force has gone out of me into the patient and I come away slightly relaxed or exhausted. I suppose all physicians have the same feeling, in similar circumstances. But I have been treating Colonel Roosevelt now for several days; and each time, instead of coming away relaxed, I have come away invigourated, as though some kind of vital energy had passed from *him* into *me* instead of from *me* into *him!*

Readers of this volume will have surmised already that this vital energy of Roosevelt's—which not only enabled him to do an unprecedented amount of work but also inspired and toned up all his associates to efforts and desires that surprised them when they stopped to think about it—was the characteristic for which he will be longest remembered by his contemporaries. It is, however, a force of character very difficult to describe, in language which does not seem extravagant, to those who did not know him and did not come within range of his electric vitality.

There were all sorts of echoes in America of this Old World tour. One of the most interesting, to me, is that contained in a letter which I received in

1916 from Madame Le Braz, the American wife of Professor Anatole Le Braz of the University of Rennes in France. Madame Le Braz, who died not long after Mr. Roosevelt, was a Kentuckian of great cultivation and charm. She knew of and shared my admiration for Roosevelt, and her letter, while only a part of it deals with his African expedition, will perhaps make a not inappropriate conclusion to this chapter. She wrote:

It was in August of 1912. I was travelling with a dear friend, a schoolmate of my younger sister, from Paris to Montreux. When the train stopped at Lausanne, a man sitting opposite us in the railway carriage descended, taking occasion for exercise to walk up and down the platform during the fifteen minutes' wait at the station. During his absence I took the liberty of looking at an American magazine containing an article on Mr. Roosevelt and the political situation in America, which he had been reading. In European papers the space devoted to news of happenings and politics in America was so brief that I was hungry for fuller accounts of the intensely interesting turn of events over there in the New World—at once the melting pot and practical laboratory for the nations and ideas of Europe.

Mr. Roosevelt—representing in himself, in a singular and striking way, the union of radical and conservative ideas and of conservative and radical action—had already come to represent (for me) the most truly American of all America's distinctive spirit and genius. With a knowledge of the past, and a grasp and vision of the future, and a consequent characteristic fearlessness of speech and action, he so mystifies the slow-thinking heavy brains, that they call him inconsistent—just because they cannot keep pace with the brilliant, versatile mind which bares like a searchlight the truth of things. Never losing sight of the general view and meaning as a whole, he nevertheless has the faculty of attention to the details of events as they pass, which enables him to judge justly and generously of both people and things, while he turns from one to another—passing judgment in a way that at times seems harsh to those whose very fear of inconsistency acts as fear always acts—arresting, powers, whether of body or mind, of digestion or clear thinking. Another reason that he is capable of dealing with all, is because he cares to look all squarely in the face. His life both private and public is an open book, he is "gentleman unafraid." There certainly are many who, for personal or political reasons, or both, detest this great man. My friend was one of these; her mother had been a warm friend of "dear Maria"; she heartily disapproved, and could not see or acknowledge any good in Mr. Roosevelt. We agreed so entirely on many, indeed most, subjects and views of life, that when we wanted to enjoy the spice of a real argument, with our views wholly and diametrically opposed, we opened the subject of this great American.

Thus had we just been arguing when the owner of the magazine returned to his place in the carriage, and the train moved out of the station. He politely begged me to keep the article, if I was interested, and we began to speak of America. His speech was very English in intonation and when I asked if he was American he said "Yes"—but explained that he had been educated partly in England.

In course of conversation I mentioned the fact that my friend and I did not agree in any particular on the subject of Mr. Roosevelt. I added: "She denounces him as unfair, untruthful, unjust, and so on; she makes statements sometimes which I cannot refute with facts, though I feel sure they might be refuted. For instance, she declares that Mr. Roosevelt was not at San Juan Hill, but several miles distant."

To this our fellow passenger replied promptly: "Well,

he was *very much* there; I wasn't thirty feet away from him, and I tell you he put courage into the hearts of us all. I can truthfully say that his spirit and fearlessness inspired every mother's son. I don't approve of all he has done lately. I'm sorry he has broken with his party and taken the stand he has, but it is because I admire him so much that I regret his present attitude. He is a wonderful man: his ability to see and act quickly and calmly in the midst of confusion and excitement is amazing and was well proved. For instance, in the charge, when Hamilton Fish fell, Roosevelt took time to say to some of those near at hand: 'If there's a spark of life in Fish for God's sake get him to a hospital!'"

Our fellow passenger's actual name we did not learn. We left the train at Montreux, but he had told us that he was nephew or grandson of General Beauregard, and he had been one of the Rough Riders under Theodore Roosevelt. This incident answered very directly my friend's accusation as to the question of San Juan Hill. Later my arguments in Mr. Roosevelt's favour were to find further confirmation quite as unexpected and even more far-reaching.

We had taken passage for our return to America on the same ship that had carried us to England. On the list of passengers I noticed the name of Sir Percy Girouard. His brother had married a distant cousin of mine, and I was interested to meet this Canadian who had been Governor successively of two colonies of South Africa during an absence of thirteen years from Canada. The first day my friend and I amused ourselves guessing which might be Sir Percy. Our decision finally rested between two of the passengers; one of these wore a monocle—with perfect right and propriety, I may add, for he had only the sight of one eye, as he himself admitted to us later. This was Sir Percy. He was very agreeable and entertaining. We spoke of things foreign and American and naturally of Mr. Roosevelt.

I explained that my friend Miss X—— and I did not at

all agree as to Mr. Roosevelt, and then I could not help recounting the experience in the railway carriage on the way to Montreux. Whereat Sir Percy, growing more and more enthusiastic, continued the Rough Rider's eulogy of our great American by telling of his own experience. He said that, when Governor of the Protectorate of East Africa, it was his privilege to have Colonel Roosevelt as his guest (for three weeks I think he said but I am not sure that I recall just the time he stated). Both he and his wife, he told us, felt something of consternation at the prospect of a visit from this strenuous American, accounts of whose amazing energy in every line had given the impression that they would find it hard indeed to entertain him—endlessly fatiguing to say the least. "Well," said Sir Percy, "we were never more delightfully surprised, for a more charming guest in every way it would be impossible to imagine. Mr. Roosevelt was a constant wonder and delight to us all. I was amazed at the brilliancy, the versatility, the grasp and scope of his mind. Among the other guests were several men of note in their line, and when he spoke with a certain great scientist on that one's preferred subject, one would have thought he had studied that question by preference to all others. When he spoke with an eminent artist, one might judge that art had occupied his attention more especially than other things. He seemed strangely at home—if I may say so—on all subjects. I have never met any one who gave so quickly and decidedly this impression. One is staggered at the thought of all he must have read and studied and retained; and this with the very active life at all times that he has had—the very full life of a great public man. It is nothing short of astounding. I have served under five of the great men of England, of the world—under Kitchener, Lord Roberts, Lord Cromer. . . . [I have forgotten two of the five names that Sir Percy mentioned]; I knew Cecil Rhodes very well—I'll just throw him in for good measure; and I say to you your Mr. Roosevelt is far and away greater than them all.'"

CHAPTER VIII

PERSONAL QUALITIES

ONE of the greatest figures in the history of English literature is that of a man whose writings are little read to-day, except by academic students who are compelled to dig into abandoned literary dust heaps. Few moderns read "The Vanity of Human Wishes" or "Rasselas" for pleasure, but no English writer gives greater pleasure to a whole army of readers than the author of these nearly obsolete literary productions—Dr. Samuel Johnson. His writings are half forgotten, but he himself lives and moves and talks with us to-day as he did more than a century ago, with the group of cronies and friends in Grub Street—a group which has been made immortal by his association with it. Dr. Johnson was what we call a "character"—a man in whom the ordinary human qualities were developed and manifested in an extraordinary degree. His humour, his epigrammatic wit, his common-sense philosophy, his downright honesty and sincerity, his satire of all that was mean and shabby, his admiration for what was genuine and fine, his self-respect and self-reliance in the face of poverty and physical ills, his marvellous vitality, his sure-footed sympathy, which enabled him to find the real and detect the sham in human society, regardless of the distinction of poverty or wealth or past or class, have drawn men to him in a kind of affectionate attachment possessed by no other English writer. What Dr. Johnson gave to the world was not literature but personality.

So I believe that Theodore Roosevelt's greatest contribution to his country and his time was personality—was Theodore Roosevelt himself. Unlike Dr. Johnson, he made great and permanent contributions to the policies and the social life of his period. He showed more clearly than any other American statesman that international peace rests on justice and morals expressed through physical power; by his action in Cuba and in the Philippines he established the precedent for the colonial policy of the proposed League of Nations, namely, that colonies shall be administered as a trust for the benefit of the inhabitants; the Panama Canal is his creation as much as if he had digged it with his own hand. But it is as a living, breathing human person that he will be longest remembered. There doubtless have been greater states-

men, greater writers, greater explorers, greater
preachers, greater soldiers; but there never was
a greater patriot, nor has any one individual man
in modern times touched so many and so varied
fields of activity in human life with such zest and
vitality, or with such practical and successful
achievements in all of them. Among soldiers he
was greeted as a soldier; among statesmen, as a
statesman; among pioneers and woodsmen, as a
hunter and naturalist; among scientists, as a
scholar and explorer; among men of letters, as a
writer and historian; among preachers, as a teacher
of morals; among kings, as a man of royal preroga-
tives; among plain men and women, as a fellow
citizen and democrat; and—last, but far from
least—among children, as a protector and sympathetic companion. His personality was a unique
and unprecedented combination of many qualities,
any one of which, carried to a high development,
makes what we call a great man.

Personality is an illusive and mysterious force,
easy to perceive and feel but hard to define. I
know of no better a definition than that given in
one of his books on Japan by Percival Lowell, the
astronomer.

About certain people there exists a subtle something which
leaves its impress indelibly upon the consciousness of all who

come in contact with them. This something is a power, but a power of so indefinable description that we beg definition by calling it simply the personality of the man. It is not a matter of subsequent reasoning, but of direct perception. We feel it. Sometimes it charms us; sometimes it repels. But we can no more be oblivious to it than we can to the temperature of the air. Its possessor has but to enter the room and insensibly we are conscious of a presence. It is as if we had suddenly been placed in the field of a magnetic force.

Roosevelt had this magnetic force of personality in a very marked degree. It surrounded him as a kind of nimbus, imperceptible but irresistibly drawing to him everyone who came into his presence—even those who believed they were antagonistic or inimical to him. It is impossible in a sketch of this character to make a complete analysis of Roosevelt's magnetic personality or to achieve a full and rounded portrait with a careful and accurately studied perspective. I shall content myself with speaking of the four of his qualities which made the greatest impression upon me. The first was his CAUTION.

To speak of caution as a characteristic of Theodore Roosevelt will strike many readers who did not know him intimately as being amusing. He was popularly supposed to be rash, impetuous, impulsive; to act upon the spur of the moment; to follow the emotion that controlled him for the time being. Nothing could be further from the truth. He was not only a believer in preparedness in national life but in individual life as well. Very early in his career he found that he was hampered by certain physical defects and he set to work with care and deliberation to make himself vigorous and strong. He tells the story in his autobiography:

Having been a sickly boy, with no natural bodily prowess, and having lived much at home, I was at first quite unable to hold my own when thrown into contact with other boys of rougher antecedents. I was nervous and timid. Yet from reading of the people I admired—ranging from the soldiers of Valley Forge and Morgan's riflemen to the heroes of my favourite stories—and from hearing of the feats performed by my Southern forefathers and kinsfolk, and from knowing my father, I felt a great admiration for men who were fearless and who could hold their own in the world, and I had a great desire to be like them.

Until I was nearly fourteen I let this desire take no more definite shape than day-dreams. Then an incident happened that did me real good. Having an attack of asthma, I was sent off by myself to Moosehead Lake. On the stage-coach ride thither I encountered a couple of other boys who were about my own age, but very much more competent, and also much more mischievous. I have no doubt they were good-hearted boys, but they were boys. They found that I was a foreordained and predestined victim, and industriously proceeded to make life miserable for me. The worst feature was that when I finally tried to fight them, I discovered that either one singly could not only handle me with easy contempt, but handle me so as not to hurt me much and yet to prevent my doing any damage whatever in return.

The experience taught me what probably no amount of good advice could have taught me. I made up my mind that I must try to learn so that I would not again be put in such a helpless position; and having become quickly and bitterly conscious that I did not have the natural prowess to hold my own, I decided that I would try to supply its place by training. Accordingly, with my father's hearty approval, I started to learn to box. I was a painfully slow and awkward pupil, and certainly worked two or three years before I made any perceptible improvement whatever. . . .

There were all kinds of things of which I was afraid at first, ranging from grizzly bears to "mean" horses and gun-fighters; but by acting as if I was not afraid, I gradually ceased to be afraid. Most men can have the same experience if they choose. They will first learn to bear themselves well in trials which they anticipate, and which they school themselves in advance to meet. After a while the habit will grow on them, and they will behave well in sudden and unexpected emergencies which come upon them unawares.

It is, of course, much pleasanter if one is naturally fearless, and I envy and respect the men who are naturally fearless. But it is a good thing to remember that the man who does not enjoy this advantage can nevertheless stand beside the man who does, and can do his duty with the like efficiency, *if he chooses to*. Of course, he must not let his desire take the form merely of a day-dream. Let him dream about being a fearless man, and the more he dreams, the better he will be, always provided he does his best to realize the dream in practice. He can do his part honourably and well, provided only he sets fearlessness before himself as an ideal, schools himself to think of danger merely as something to be faced and overcome, and regards life itself as he should regard it—not as something to be thrown away, but as a pawn to be promptly hazarded whenever the hazard is warranted by the larger interests of the great game in which we are all engaged.

As a result of this precautionary care he became a man of great athletic powers, not only a skilful boxer, an accomplished horseman, and a first-rate shot, but an explorer who endured physical privations and struggles in mountains, wilderness, and jungle, that would have broken down many men endowed in the beginning with naturally stronger bodies. In my editorial association with him I found the same sense of precautionary preparation. He never wrote an article without verifying his statements of fact, and he invariably submitted the articles, when done, to one or more of his colleagues for criticism and suggestion. How painstaking he was in this respect is illustrated by this incident which occurred when he was preparing his autobiography and of which I am reminded by happening upon the correspondence about it, while going over my papers and letters in preparation for this chapter. In July, 1913, Roosevelt wrote me from Sagamore Hill:

Like the horse-leech's daughter, I come back! In either Chapter 10 or Chapter 15 will you insert in an appropriate place, the following:

"The American public rarely appreciates the high quality of the work done by some of our diplomats, work, usually entirely unnoticed and unrewarded, which redounds to the interest and the honour of all of us. The most useful man in the entire diplomatic service, during my Presidency and

Colonel Roosevelt and a group of distinguished citizens reviewing a parade — New York City's first drafted men

for many years before, was Harry White. When I left the Presidency he was Ambassador to France; he was removed shortly afterward by Mr. Taft, for reasons unconnected with the good of the service, and to the serious detriment of the service."

In reply I wrote suggesting that he say "*one* of the most useful men . . . was Harry White"; and that he omit the last phrase: "and to the serious detriment of the service." Referring to these suggested changes I said: "I make the first, because it will relieve you of the possibility of some stupid persons saying that it proves you did not find Robert Bacon useful, and the second, because I think the line stricken out is a little of an anti-climax."

Roosevelt, in the meantime, had gone on one of his Western trips but two weeks later he wrote, dating his letter "North of the Grand Canyon, July 29, 1913":

Now for the Harry White matter. I wish to adopt most of your suggestion; but to keep the statement that he was the best man in the service because that is the truth. How would it do to have it read as follows?:

"The most useful man in the entire diplomatic service, during my Presidency and for many years before, was Harry White; and I say this having in mind the high quality of work done by such admirable ambassadors and ministers as Bacon, Meyer, Straus, O'Brien, Rockhill, and Egan to name only a few among many. When I left the Presidency, White

272 IMPRESSIONS OF THEODORE ROOSEVELT

was Ambassador to France; shortly afterward he was removed by Mr. Taft, for reasons unconnected with the good of the service."

And that is the way the passage stands in the Autobiography except that someone—I do not know who—changed "Harry" White to "Henry" White; perhaps it was some punctilious lady proofreader who felt that it was impolite to call an ambassador in public by so debonair a name as Harry!

The facts which I have already related regarding his correspondence with Mr. Bryan while he was President, his preparation of his Guildhall speech, and his controversy with the Vatican, are illustrative of the caution and care with which he prepared himself for any important public act or utterance. His occasional appearance of impetuosity has often seemed to me to be analogous to that of the track athlete who is about to run a hundred-yard dash. The spectator sees a half a dozen young men at the starting line waiting for the pistol before they dart for their goal. They are on their toes, quivering with eagerness, sometimes making a false start in their overwhelming desire to accomplish their task. At the flash of the pistol they are off, like lightning. To the ordinary observer there is no more striking portrayal of rash impulsiveness than is found in the attitudes and actions of these swift runners. But the ordinary observer is unaware of the weeks, perhaps the months, possibly even the years, of arduous, exacting, tedious, accurate training that the athlete has subjected himself to before he may even venture to try to make a dash in less than eleven seconds.

So it was with Roosevelt. He studied, he read, he consulted, he thought, he deliberated, he put himself in the hand of trainers so to speak; but when the time for action came he was on his toes, ready to jump at the word "Go." It was at these times that the general public saw him, not during his hours of training. And thus it was that he got the reputation, quite an unjust and unfounded one, of being impetuous. It is not an insignificant thing that while he was accused of proceeding rashly along unconstitutional lines as a political executive, both during his governorship of the State of New York and his Presidency of the United States, no legislative act that he advocated and signed and no executive act that he performed without legislative coöperation has ever, I believe, been declared unconstitutional by any court.

The second quality which I would mention as typically characteristic of Roosevelt was his COUR-

AGE—not only his moral courage but his pugnacious courage. Although he was not rash he apparently had no sense of fear in physical danger. And his courage was tested, for his life was placed at great risk more than once. In his book describing his explorations in South America he tells very simply of the physical perils that he and his party went through in the canoe voyage down "The River of Doubt"—so simply, in fact, that the very great seriousness of the peril almost fails to impress the reader. In this adventure he became infected with the terrible jungle fever of South America which had much to do, I have always believed, with the illness that resulted in his untimely death. He narrates in a quite matter-of-fact way that the infection resulted in an abscess on his leg in which the surgeon had to place a drainage tube that would have kept the average man on his back in a well-equipped hospital. But he went on, struggling and stumbling over the rocks and through the matted underbrush of the jungle. I quote the story in his own words from his volume "Through the Brazilian Wilderness":

The men were growing steadily weaker under the endless strain of exhausting labour. Kermit was having an attack of fever and Lyra and Cherrie had touches of dysentery, but all three continued to work. While in the water trying to help with an upset canoe I had by my own clumsiness bruised my leg against a boulder; and the resulting infection was somewhat bothersome. I now had a sharp attack of fever, but thanks to the excellent care of the doctor it was over in about forty-eight hours; but Kermit's fever grew worse and he too was unable to work for a day or two. We could walk over the portages, however. . . .

Our men were discouraged, weak, and sick; most of them already had begun to have fever. Their condition was inevitable after more than a month's uninterrupted work of the hardest kind in getting through the long series of rapids we had just passed; and a long further delay, accompanied by wearing labour, would almost certainly have meant that the weakest of our party would have begun to die. . . . The previous evening Cherrie had killed two monkeys and Kermit one, and we all had a few mouthfuls of fresh meat; we already had a good soup made out of a turtle Kermit had caught. When a number of men doing hard work are most of the time on half rations, they grow to take a lively interest in any reasonably full meal that does arrive. . . .

The wearing work under the unhealthy conditions was beginning to tell on everyone. Half of the *Camarads* had been down with fever and were much weaker; only a few of them retained their original physical and moral strength. Cherrie and Kermit had recovered; but both Kermit and Lyra had bad sores on their legs from the bruises received in the water work. I was in worse shape. The after effects of the fever still hung on and the leg which had been hurt while working in the rapids had taken a turn for the bad and had developed into an abscess. The good doctor, to whose unwearied care and kindness I owe much, had cut it open and inserted a drainage tube; an added charm being given the operation and the subsequent dressings by the enthusiasm with which the piums and boroshudas, two species of stinging flies, took part therein. I could hardly hobble and was pretty well laid up. But "there aren't any 'Stop, conductor!' while a battery's changing ground." No one has any business to go on such a trip as ours unless he will refuse to jeopardize the welfare of his associates by any delay caused by a weakness or ailment of his. It is his duty to go forward, if necessary on all fours, until he drops.

It is true that Roosevelt did not jeopardize the welfare of his associates, that he got out safely, and that he had five years more of active and useful life, but he told me once on his return that at the climax of this experience he seriously considered, not from despondency but from a sense of moral duty, whether he ought not to end his life then and there in order to save his companions—who were being delayed by his disability—from the danger of death by starvation.

When an assassin shot him in Milwaukee during the Progressive campaign, making a wound that would have laid many a man low, he insisted upon going to the hall and completing the speech that he was engaged to make. He said: "It may be the last message that I shall ever be able to utter."

Roosevelt had just entered an automobile at the doorway of the Gilpatrick Hotel in Milwaukee on his way to make a political address at the Auditorium of that city about the middle of October, 1912. He was standing up in the car when the assassin drew a revolver and fired point blank. The assassin was immediately overpowered. Roosevelt's first thought was to save his assailant from bodily injury, for when the man Schrank was brought before him for identification the only reproach he uttered was: "Don't hurt the poor creature." Every effort was made to induce Mr. Roosevelt to receive immediate medical attention, but he refused. After his speech, which because of the circumstances of its delivery is unique in the history of oratory, he was taken to the hospital first in Milwaukee and then in Chicago and X-ray photographs showed that the bullet struck an inch to the right and an inch below the right nipple, fractured the fourth rib, happily did not puncture the lung cavity but ranged upward and inward four inches in the chest wall.

About a week later he was removed to his home at Oyster Bay and I saw him there very soon after his arrival. He was in bed, and there were still signs of blood showing on the bandages which his wound required. How, under the circumstances, a mortal man could have kept on his feet and spoken for an hour, it is almost impossible to conceive. He began his speech in Milwaukee in this way:

Friends, I shall have to ask you to be as quiet as possible. I do not know whether you fully understand that I have been shot, but it takes more than that to kill a Bull Moose [the slang term describing a member of the Progressive party, a term adopted as a badge of honour by the Progressives themselves]. But, fortunately I had my manuscript [holding up the manuscript and showing the audience where the bullet had gone through], so you see I was going to make a long speech! And, friends, the hole in it is where the bullet went through, and it probably saved the bullet from going into my heart. The bullet is in me now so that I cannot make a very long speech. But I will try my best. . . .

First of all, I want to say this about myself. I have altogether too many important things to think of to pay any heed or to feel any concern over my own death. . . . I want you to understand that I am ahead of the game anyway. No man has had a happier life than I have had, a happier life in every way. . . . I am not speaking for myself at all—I give you my word, I do not care a rap about being shot, not a rap. I have had a good many experiences in my time, and this is only one of them. What I do care for is my country. I wish I were able to impress upon our people the duty to feel strongly, but to speak truthfully of their opponents. . . . I say now that I have never said on the stump one word against any opponent that I could not substantiate . . . nothing that, looking back, I would not say again.

After Mr. Roosevelt had concluded that portion of his speech in which he referred to his injury, he turned to the concrete issues of the campaign, and spoke as if he had been delivering one of those addresses which were a matter of daily routine with him. After he had been speaking for some time he turned to the physician who, as a precautionary

Colonel Roosevelt in the Yosemite Valley

A hunting trip in Colorado

measure was sitting close by him, and said, "How long have I been speaking?" "Three quarters of an hour," replied the doctor, glancing at his watch. "Well," said Mr. Roosevelt with a smile, "I will talk for a quarter of an hour more." Actually he spoke altogether for nearly an hour and a half.

After he recovered, a group of us were discussing the event at one of our editorial luncheons. Someone reported that a newspaper despatch had stated that Roosevelt's motive in insisting upon keeping his engagement to speak was the desire to relieve his friends, especially the Progressives all over the country, from the anxiety of supposing that he was dangerously injured. Roosevelt laughed:

"That would certainly have been very considerate," was his comment, "but I must admit that it never occurred to me. I suppose my real feeling was an instinctive desire not to give up. Pioneers, soldiers, boxers, and men of that type—and I have had some of the experience of all three in my life— are trained not to give way under attack, not to let the other fellow for a minute think you are down and out." In other words, in the phrase of to-day, he wanted to "carry on."

The Milwaukee speech was a great and memorable physical feat. Nothing but the most perfect self-control and the highest kind of physical courage could have carried any man through it. But Roosevelt's moral courage was as striking as his physical courage.

Of this the Progressive campaign is perhaps a sufficient example. He sacrificed friendships and associations that were very dear to him. But the loss of them did not deter him from pursuing a course that seemed to him to be just and right. He also sacrificed the personal prestige which every man who has won it likes to preserve, and subjected himself to an extraordinary amount of contumely and abuse. The Philadelphia *North American*, on October 10, 1912, four days before Roosevelt was shot, published the following list of epithets applied to Roosevelt by a certain American newspaper of the opposition in the issues of a single month:

"Shrieks his hostility"; "ridiculous"; "contemptible"; "his antics"; "gnashing his teeth"; "eager to use fraud"; "unparalleled viciousness and dishonesty"; "a dangerous demagogue"; "insensate ambition"; "charlatanism"; "plain aberration"; "bad faith"; "unworthy methods"; "shocking demagogism"; "baseless and dangerous appeals"; "no scruples"; "revolutionary and subversive"; "horrible glibness"; "indecent performance"; "Aaron Burr"; "shameless"; "crazy socialistic scheme"; "blatant insincerity"; "hypocritical and dangerous"; "howling mobocracy"; "shabby tactics"; "damning proof of hypocrisy"; "hollow and untrustworthy"; "duplicity"; "shrewd political trickery"; "utter untrustworthiness"; "dangerous and self-seeking autocrat"; "unblushing effrontery"; "squalid bandying of words"; "no respect for truth."

One of the results of the Progressive campaign was a libel suit which at the time greatly interested the entire country as a *cause célèbre*. In October, 1912, a weekly newspaper of Michigan, called *Iron Ore*, published a scurrilous article which, after accusing Roosevelt of political and personal blackguardism, said: "He gets drunk, too, and that not infrequently, and all his intimates know about it."

Mr. Roosevelt instantly brought action for libel against the editor and proprietor of this paper and the case was tried in Marquette, Mich., during the week of May 26–31, 1913.

It has sometimes been asked why Roosevelt should have sued a small weekly publication in Michigan. It was because the statement as to his drunkenness, although a matter of rumour and gossip, was published in this instance for the first time by a responsible man of sufficient means to make the libel suit really effective. A large party of friends and supporters accompanied Mr. Roosevelt to Marquette, glad to go as witnesses in his behalf. This group of friends literally invaded the little town of Marquette, which is beautifully situated on the shore of Lake Michigan, and were received with cordiality and hospitality by Roosevelt's many friends in the community. The company included a large number of distinguished persons.

It is, I believe, a principle of trials for libel in this country that the plaintiff may make certain pleadings that will compel the defendant to open the case and prove his statement if he can do so. The plaintiff may then submit the case for judicial decision without introducing any evidence if the defendant fails to make good, thus avoiding what is sometimes an awkward inquiry into his, the plaintiff's, private life. This was not Roosevelt's method. He wished to go on record himself and have his friends on record in telling frankly all the facts about his alleged use of intoxicating beverages. He himself was the first witness and related with delightful frankness what his custom was as to the use of wine and stated that he not only did not use but disliked whisky, brandy, and beer. His testimony which showed his rather unusual abstention from alcoholic beverages was confirmed by his Cabinet associates, by his physician, and by his personal friends. For example, Dr. Alexander Lambert, his family physician, testified that he had known Roosevelt for twenty-two years; had been in and out of his household at all hours of the day and night; had been off with him on hunting trips; attributed his remarkable recovery from the assassin's bullet in Milwaukee "to his splendid, unpoisoned physique"; and declared that he "was an exceedingly temperate man, and an unusually abstemious one." This was the view of a great array of witnesses, whose accounts of Roosevelt really amounted to a delightful kind of biography of him.

When Roosevelt's lawyers rested their case the defendant actually threw up his hands. He could produce no testimony whatever, except hear-say evidence. In exculpation of his act he said that his article was written because of his, the defendant's, opposition to Roosevelt's candidacy; that his statement of Mr. Roosevelt's drinking to excess was based upon common gossip; and that he now in open court withdrew the charge. As a matter of fact, while this capitulation was expressed in legal terms it was evident, not only to the spectators but to the Court, that the defendant who had made the libellous accusation had not a leg to stand on.

Before the presiding Justice charged the jury Mr. Roosevelt addressed the Court as follows:

Your Honor, in view of the statement of the defendant, I ask the Court to instruct the jury that I desire only nominal damages. I did not go into this suit for money; I did not go into it for any vindictive purpose. I went into it, and as the Court has said, I made my reputation an issue because I wish once for all during my lifetime thoroughly and comprehensively to deal with these slanders so that never again will it be possible for any man in good faith to repeat them. I have achieved my purpose, and I am content.

Whereupon the presiding Justice, Judge Flannigan, of the Circuit Court for the County of Marquette, State of Michigan, charged the jury in these words:

The injury to the reputation and feelings of the plaintiff which naturally, proximately, and necessarily followed upon the false publication, would warrant a verdict in the plaintiff's favour in a substantial amount, and would sustain a verdict in any sum up to the amount claimed in the plaintiff's declaration, which is ten thousand dollars.

But, as the Court is advised by the plaintiff, the object of the plaintiff in bringing and prosecuting this action being the vindication of his good name and reputation, and not the recovery of a money judgment; and he having in open court freely waived his right to the assessment of his actual damages, it only remains for the Court to direct a verdict in his favour for nominal damages, which, under the law of Michigan, is the sum of six cents.

You are, therefore, gentlemen, directed to render a verdict in favour of the plaintiff for that amount.

It should be added as a matter of record that Mr. Roosevelt's case was entrusted to the firm of Messrs. Bowers and Sands of New York City who

after the trial refused to accept any fee whatsoever
on the ground that they believed they were performing a public service in defending an ex-President from slander.

It required moral courage on the part of Roosevelt to subject his private life to the kind of inter-
rogatory and analytical searching that takes place
in a libel suit, and his request to the Court that
the defendant, whose original publication had been
unusually vindictive and scurrilous, should be relieved of the final burden of his unjust act when
he virtually apologized for it, displays the warm-
hearted magnanimity of Roosevelt toward a van-
quished enemy—one of his marked characteristics.

No man that I have known liked personal approval more than Roosevelt. He had a kind of
childlike responsiveness to commendation and
praise. He did not wear his heart on his sleeve,
but I think he was really hurt when those to whom
he was attached were displeased with him. There
are people who thought he was thick-skinned. On
the contrary, he was highly sensitive; by this I
do not mean that he ever showed pique or irrita-
tion or resentment or hysterical sorrow which are
the things that come to mind when we speak of a
"sensitive girl"; I mean sensitive in the exact use

of the word—quick to receive impressions. But if this sensitiveness to mental or spiritual sensations pained him he rarely if ever gave any sign, except by depending more and more upon the devotion and affection of those who liked and trusted him. He was, as he says in his Milwaukee speech, a happy man. I never knew him to be "blue" or despondent or to complain of disappointments or an adverse fate. His courage was buoyant and unshaken to the last.

The third of Roosevelt's qualities which I wish to make note of—the quality that, to me, was the most appealing and engaging in his personality and that I most naturally and instinctively think of when I recall him to mind—was his SENSE OF HUMOUR.

A sense of humour is not merely an agreeable and pleasing social virtue of an ephemeral and superficial kind; it is a fundamental virtue. A man who possesses a sense of humour can be neither vain, nor conceited, nor a prig, nor a pedant. For if he falls into any of these errors, which are so apt to entrap men of great reputation who receive much public adulation, his sense of humour comes to the rescue and punctures the bubble of self-glorification.

One of the most beautiful and spiritual of all the

Mr. and Mrs. Roosevelt with their children, Theodore,
Kermit, Ethel, Archie, and Quentin at Sagamore Hill

saints in the calendar of the Church, St. Francis of Assisi, so appreciated the virtue of a sense of humour that he urged its cultivation, in one of the precepts of the Rule of his Brotherhood. Sabatier, in his delightful "Life of St. Francis," quotes this precept and remarks: "In the history of the early Franciscan missions there are bursts of laughter which ring out high and clear."

The precept, as Sabatier gives it, reads as follows:

Caveant fratres quod non ostendant se tristes extrinsecus nubilosos et hypocritas; sed ostendant se gaudentes in Domine, hilares et convenientes gratiosos.

As this Latin was the colloquial language of the mediæval Church, I venture to translate it into our own colloquial vernacular:

Let the brothers take care not to appear long-faced, gloomy or over-pious; but let them be joyous about their faith in God, laughing and good mixers.

Roosevelt certainly was joyous in his faith that there is a power that makes for righteousness in the universe and he was *convenienter gratiosus*, a good mixer in the best sense of the phrase. The characteristic falsetto intonation of his voice when he felt the humour of what he was saying was indescribably infectious in its cheerfulness.

This sense of humour crops out in much of Roosevelt's writing. It is especially to be found in certain chapters of his Autobiography and in the "Rough Riders." Take this example from the chapter entitled "The Vigour of Life" in the Autobiography. It is permissible, now that both men have gone on, to say that the "prize-fighting friend" about whom Mr. Roosevelt relates the incident was John L. Sullivan.

On one occasion one of my prize-fighting friends called on me at the White House, on business. He explained that he wished to see me alone, sat down opposite me, and put a very expensive cigar on the desk, saying: "Have a cigar." I thanked him and said I did not smoke, to which he responded: "Put it in your pocket." This I accordingly did.

Having thus shown, at the outset, the necessary formal courtesy, my visitor, an old and valued friend, proceeded to explain that a nephew of his had enlisted in the Marine Corps, had been absent without leave, and was threatened with dishonourable discharge on the ground of desertion. My visitor, a good citizen and a patriotic American, was stung to the quick at the thought of such an incident occurring in his family, and he explained to me that it must not occur—that there must not be the disgrace to the family—although he would be delighted to have the offender "handled rough" to teach him a needed lesson. He added that he wished I would take him and handle him myself, for he knew that I would see that he "got all that was coming to him."

Then a look of pathos came into his eyes, and he explained: "That boy I just cannot understand. He was my sister's favourite son, and I always took a special interest in him myself. I did my best to bring him up the way he ought to go.

But there was just nothing to be done with him. His tastes were naturally low. He took to music!"

What form this debasing taste for music assumed I did not inquire; and I was able to grant my friend's wish.

Or this, from Roosevelt's autobiographic account of his experiences as Police Commissioner at a time when he was carrying on a crusade against illegal liquor selling:

All kinds of incidents occurred in connection with this crusade. One of them introduced me to a friend who remains a friend yet. His name was Edward J. Bourke. He was one of the men who entered the police force through our examinations shortly after I took office. I had summoned twenty or thirty of the successful applicants to let me look them over; and as I walked into the hall, one of them, a well-set-up man, called out sharply to the others: "Gangway!"—making them move to one side. I found he had served in the United States navy. The incident was sufficient to make me keep him in mind.

A month later I was notified by a police reporter, a very good fellow, that Bourke was in difficulties, and that he thought I had better look into the matter myself, as Bourke was being accused by certain very influential men of grave misconduct in an arrest he had made the night before. Accordingly, I took the matter up personally. I found that on the new patrolman's beat the preceding night—a new beat—there was a big saloon run by a man of great influence in political circles known as "King" Calahan. After midnight the saloon was still running in full blast, and Bourke, stepping inside, told Calahan to close up. It was at the time filled with "friends of personal liberty," as Governor Hill used at that time, in moments of pathos, to term everybody who regarded as tyranny any restriction on the sale of liquor. Calahan's saloon had never before in its history been closed, and to have a green cop tell him to close it seemed to him so incredible that he regarded it merely as a bad jest.

On his next round Bourke stepped in and repeated the order. Calahan felt that the jest had gone too far, and, by way of protest, knocked Bourke down. This was an error of judgment on his part, for when Bourke arose he knocked Calahan down. The two then grappled and fell on the floor, while the "friends of personal liberty" danced around the fight and endeavoured to stamp on everything they thought wasn't Calahan. However, Bourke, though pretty roughly handled, got his man and shut the saloon. When he appeared against the lawbreaker in court next day, he found the court-room crowded with influential Tammany Hall politicians, backed by one or two Republican leaders of the same type; for Calahan was a baron of the underworld, and both his feudal superiors and his feudal inferiors gathered to the rescue. His backers in court included a Congressman and a State Senator, and so deep-rooted was the police belief in "pull" that his own superiors had turned against Bourke and were preparing to sacrifice him.

Just at this time I acted on the information given me by my newspaper friend by starting in person for the court. The knowledge, that I knew what was going on, that I meant what I said, and that I intended to make the affair personal, was all that was necessary. Before I reached the court all effort to defend Calahan had promptly ceased, and Bourke had come forth triumphant. I immediately promoted him to roundsman. He is a captain now. He has been on the force ever since, save that when the Spanish War came he obtained a holiday without pay for six months and reëntered the navy, serving as gun captain in one of the gunboats, and doing his work, as was to be expected, in first-rate fashion, especially when under fire.

Roosevelt greatly rejoiced in his experience with the Rough Riders—not only in the serious and soldierly part of it but in the human and humorous part, as will be seen from this allusion to some of the characters of the regiment:

The men speedily gave one another nicknames, largely conferred in a spirit of derision, their basis lying in contrast. A brave but fastidious member of a well-known Eastern club who was serving in the ranks was christened "Tough Ike"; and his bunkie, the man who shared his shelter-tent, who was a decidedly rough cow-puncher, gradually acquired the name of "The Dude." One unlucky and simple-minded cow-puncher, who had never been east of the great plains in his life, unwarily boasted that he had an aunt in New York, and ever afterward went by the name of "Metropolitan Bill." A huge red-headed Irishman was named "Sheeny Solomon." A young Jew who developed into one of the best fighters in the regiment accepted, with entire equanimity, the name of "Pork-chop." We had quite a number of professional gamblers, who, I am bound to say, usually made good soldiers. One, who was almost abnormally quiet and gentle, was called "Hell Roarer"; while another, who in point of language and deportment was his exact antithesis, was christened "Prayerful James."

One of the delightful qualities of his humour was that he enjoyed a joke at his own expense quite as much as one based on an oddity or quirk in someone else. Here is an example from the "Rough Riders":

There was a great deal of paper work to be done; but as I still had charge of the brigade only a little of it fell on my shoulders. Of this I was sincerely glad, for I knew as little of the paper work as my men had originally known of drill. We had all of us learned how to fight and march; but the exact limits of our rights and duties in other respects were not very clearly defined in our minds; and as for myself, as I had not had the time to learn exactly what they were, I had assumed a large authority in giving rewards and punishments. In particular I had looked on court-martials much as Peter Bell looked on primroses—they were court-martials and nothing more, whether resting on the authority of a lieuten-ant-colonel or of a major-general. The mustering-out officer, a thorough soldier, found to his horror that I had used the widest discretion both in imposing heavy sentences which I had no power to impose on men who shirked their duties, and, where men atoned for misconduct by marked gallantry, in blandly remitting sentences approved by my chief of divi-sion. However, I had done substantial—even though some-what rude and irregular—justice, and no harm could result, as we were just about to be mustered out.

Another instance of his enjoyment of chaffing himself that I often like to think of occurred in the early days of my editorial association with him. We used to meet at a weekly round-table confer-ence in which Roosevelt regularly took part. These meetings were generally held on Mondays at eleven o'clock in the forenoon.

One Monday morning he went to Brooklyn with some friends to inspect some model tenement houses in that borough, and did not reach the conference until between twelve and one. When he came in he was full of his experience and began to tell us about it. He had gone quietly and wished to avoid any publicity, "But," said he, "for some reason or other which I do not quite understand, the people recognized me, especially the children, and a crowd of the latter gathered around me."

We all smiled, for it should be explained that his characteristic feature, which was always seized upon by the newspaper cartoonists, was a mouthful of unusually fine and white teeth, which he unconsciously displayed whenever he laughed or talked emphatically.

Noticing the smiles on our faces he at once added: "Yes, I suppose there is something distinctive in my physiognomy. I remember that when I was running for the vice-Presidency I had to speak in a Western town where the crowd in the hall was so dense that the officers in charge had great difficulty in making a way for me through the packed audience to get to the stage where I was to speak. Mr. Dooley's comment was [Mr. Dooley as every contemporary American knows is the newspaper pseudonym of one of our most delightful and accomplished humourists]: 'And thin along came Teddy Rosenfeld and *bit* his way to the platform!'"

Roosevelt recalled this genial caricature with evident gusto.

In June, 1910, the Roosevelt party arrived in London very early in the morning, having travelled from Berlin during the night by the Flushing-Queensborough route. Mr. Roosevelt went to Dorchester House where he was the guest of Ambassador Whitelaw Reid, while I took up my quarters in a near-by hotel. Immediately after breakfast and after having removed some of the stain of travel, I went round to Dorchester House and by ten or eleven o'clock was engaged with Colonel Roosevelt over a great pile of accumulated mail, in a sitting room or "study" which Mr. Reid had placed at his disposal. It was a good deal of a task and one that was usually irksome to Mr. Roosevelt, although he performed it faithfully. A knock at the half-open door, accompanied by laboured breathing, showed that somebody was there in a state of suppressed excitement. I said "Come in," when one of the liveried, silk-stockinged footmen —a typical before-the-war English flunky—entered and announced in an evidently awe-struck voice— for kings were not in the habit of calling on private citizens at ten o'clock in the morning: "The King of —— is below, sir."

Mr. Roosevelt, of course, had to go down, not only because it was a king, but because it was a monarch (not the Kaiser, let me hasten to add!) for whom he had formed a real respect and friendship during his journey in northern Europe. Nevertheless, as the Colonel rose he threw down his pen, with a mixture of annoyance (at being interrupted) and amusement, and exclaimed: "Confound these kings; will they never leave me alone!"

Another royal or semi-royal anecdote comes to my mind. At Stockholm Mr. Roosevelt was a guest in the palace, a fine and spacious edifice of unusually large and impressive dimensions, where the hospitality extended to the party was of the most genuine and delightful kind. The suite of apartments which had been placed at the disposal of Mr. Roosevelt and his family was elaborate, and I had assigned to me on another floor a bedroom and a sitting room with a man-servant to attend to my wants. My bath was brought in each morning in a portable tub after the old-time European fashion, but while every comfort was provided, the palace, so far as I could find, lacked the modern plumbing upon which Americans are so accustomed to depend. When we left Stockholm by train, which had been equipped with a private saloon carriage and private dining car for Mr.

Roosevelt by his royal host, I asked him whether he had discovered any modern plumbing in the palace. He replied, with a quizzical look: "No; I don't like living in these palaces because you can't ring your bell and complain of your room!"

During the journey through Europe the English king, Edward VII, had died, and Mr. Roosevelt was appointed by Mr. Taft as special ambassador to the funeral. One of the things he had to do while in London was to attend the elaborate public ceremonies of this funeral. Captain (now Lieutenant-Colonel) Bentley Mott, then our Military Attaché at Paris, was assigned to Mr. Roosevelt as his personal attaché in the performance of his ambassadorial duties. The Earl of Dundonald and Commander Cunninghame-Graham were assigned by the King to perform for Mr. Roosevelt the functions of what I suppose would be called in the case of royal personages, "Gentlemen in waiting." The arrangements had to be made by these three gentlemen for Mr. Roosevelt's part in the solemn and splendid procession which proceeded through vast crowds from Buckingham Palace to Windsor. As Secretary to Mr. Roosevelt I was called into the conference. Captain Mott felt that Colonel Roosevelt should ride a horse, dressed in the conventional long riding trousers, frock coat, and high hat. The Earl of Dundonald and Commander Cunninghame-Graham courteously agreed that this was most desirable, but regretted that the Earl of Norfolk, the prerogative of whose family was to have charge of all English coronations and royal funerals, was insistent that Mr. Roosevelt should wear "ambassadorial dress"—this being, according to American precedent, a swallow-tail evening suit.

Finally, Captain Mott insisted that Colonel Roosevelt should be called into the conference. He came, the matter was laid before him, and he said: "Why, Mott, I appreciate your thoughtfulness, but I am here as an ambassador not to do what I like but what the English people like as the contribution of my country to the respect which the world is paying to the memory of the King. If the English people want me to, I'll wear a pink coat and green-striped trousers!"

The result was that he did wear American evening dress and rode in the procession in a carriage with M. Pichon, the French Ambassador, to the funeral, these two, I believe, being the only foreign representatives who were "commoners." Mr. Roosevelt told me that during the long drive he had all he could do to appease M. Pichon, because according to the exacting rules of precedence, their

carriage had been placed after that of the King of
Siam. This question of precedence gave Roosevelt no end of amusement. He saw its necessity,
for all social conventions are based on some kind of
necessity, but its extreme rigour struck him, as
it does every American I suppose, as sometimes
ludicrous.

He told me that at the funeral banquet given
to the foreign representatives in Buckingham Palace the evening before the procession and ceremonies at Windsor—a dinner which he somewhat
disrespectfully referred to as "the wake"—the
Kaiser told him an anecdote of precedence connected with the funeral, which indicates that the
Kaiser himself was capable of perceiving the artificiality of certain monarchical customs. It seems
that two royal personages of eastern Europe—I
think one was from a Balkan kingdom and the
other from an Austrian principality—met with their
private cars or saloon carriages at Vienna to take
the Orient Express for Paris and London. They
quarrelled as to whose rank entitled him to be first
on the train, but the aide-de-camp, let us say of the
Balkan personage, was clever enough to get his
master's car coupled directly on the engine. The
Austrian, therefore, had, willynilly, to take second
place. Then came the regular dining car of the

train.   When dinner was served the Balkan Highness sent his aide into the private car of the Austrian Highness with his compliments and might
he pass through to the dining car.   No, he might
not.   So he had to wait until the train came to a
station, get out, walk around his rival's car into
the dining car, eat his dinner, stay there until another station was reached, and then walk around
his rival's car again into his own.   As the Orient
Express makes very long non-stop runs it may
easily be imagined that although the Balkan celeb-
rity got the first place on the train it was not by
any means the most comfortable.   This incident
Roosevelt recounted with the greatest glee.

I have already referred to the fact that in the
summer of 1914, just before the European war broke
out, I returned from England, with a party of
friends on the steamship *Imperator*, in company
with Roosevelt.   We had been over to play golf;
he had been to England to lecture before the Royal
Geographical Society.   He was sitting with us one
afternoon in the smoking room, although he did
not smoke himself, and fell to talking on one of his
favourite topics—Americanism.   He was denounc-
ing a certain man in Boston who during the Spanish War, although purporting to be an American,
endeavoured to raise money to help Spain build a

battleship. The enormity of this offence grew upon Roosevelt as he talked and finally he raised his clenched fist in the air and almost at a loss for words, exclaimed, "Such a man as that should be — should be — should be — hanged, drawn, and quartered!"

One of the group, a great admirer and political follower of Roosevelt who had met him personally, I believe, for the first time on this voyage, leaned forward and said with a chuckle: "At least, Colonel!" Quick as a flash the Colonel turned, took his hand, and said: "I am delighted to meet a man, Mr. Erickson, who thinks my language is too moderate!" He did not go on with his denunciation.

Two years afterward Mr. Erickson, who had become actively interested in the formation of the Roosevelt League which was urging the nomination of Roosevelt for the Presidency of 1916, went to the office of the Colonel, who was then associated with the *Metropolitan Magazine*, to consult him about some campaign matters. He sent in his card, and when he entered the Colonel's room he remarked that, although probably the Colonel did not remember him, he had had the pleasure of crossing with him on the *Imperator* two years before. "Not remember you!" exclaimed Mr. Roosevelt, "I most certainly do—and most pleasantly. You are the man who thinks my language is too moderate!"

These rambling and detached stories, I am afraid, give a very inadequate impression of what I think was the most lovable of Roosevelt's qualities. I am not sure but that it was the most important of his qualities. He could be stern; he could be severe; he was occasionally biting although never bitter; he had a certain touch of bulldog pugnacity; but underlying it all was a reservoir of humour, not a careless or indifferent humour, not a mere jocosity, but humour which has its source in a spirit of sympathetic and joyous understanding of men and things—a spirit of which Emerson said in a Eulogy of Sir Walter Scott before the Massachusetts Historical Society: "What an ornament and safeguard is humour! Far better than wit for a poet and writer. It is a genius itself, and so defends from the insanities."

The fourth notable quality in Roosevelt's personality that impressed me was his GENTLENESS. Early in his presidential career he uttered one of those epigrammatic phrases for which he has become famous: "Speak softly, but carry a big stick."

The big-stick half of this phrase caught the public fancy and many people, forgetting that he put "speaking softly" first, pictured him as a kind of glorified Irishman carrying a shillalah in a universal Donnybrook Fair and joyously hitting every head he saw. Those who knew him best knew that this was a totally false conception—that one of his pronounced characteristics was a spirit of gentle consideration for others.

A man's general attitude toward his fellow beings can be pretty well determined if you can find out what he thinks of children and how he treats them. What Roosevelt thought of children is expressed in this paragraph from his Autobiography:

There are many kinds of success in life worth having. It is exceedingly interesting and attractive to be a successful business man, or railroad man, or farmer, or a successful lawyer, or doctor, or a writer, or a president, or a ranchman, or the colonel of a fighting regiment, or to kill grizzly bears and lions. But for unflagging interest and enjoyment, a household of children, if things go reasonably well, certainly makes all other forms of success and achievement lose their importance by comparison.

I am inclined to think that Roosevelt was generally regarded by the public as preëminently a man's man. He was so much in the public mind as a bear killer, a lion hunter, a jungle explorer, a Rough Rider, a "trust buster," and a fighter of malefactors that many people are astonished when

The Roosevelt Home at Sagamore Hill on Long Island

they are told that he was also a children's man. Nobody can detect a counterfeit child lover as quickly as a child itself. Normal children respect and admire their superiors, especially in physical prowess, without regard to age; but they despise and resent patronage. The man who assumes a patronizing air toward children is very soon avoided by them, but with magnetic rapidity they cluster round a man who understands them, who sympathizes with them—a very different thing by the way from sentimentalizing over them—and who can do things with them. This was the way Roosevelt treated children, and the result was that they often followed him as if he had been a modern Pied Piper of Hamelin. It is easy to imagine the atmosphere in which his own children were brought up in the family homestead, Sagamore Hill, at Oyster Bay. They swam, rowed, went barefoot, or camped in the woods or on the beach of Long Island Sound. They learned to shoot—for there was a rifle-range at Sagamore Hill. They made pets of the various animals on the home farm in the summer, and they coasted and skated in the winter. In this bringing up of the children in the vigour of outdoor life Mrs. Roosevelt was an active partner, as will be seen by referring to another passage in the colonel's Autobiography:

When their mother and I returned from a row, we would often see the children waiting for us, running like sand-spiders along the beach. They always liked to swim in company with a grown-up of buoyant temperament and inventive mind, and the float offered limitless opportunities for enjoyment while bathing.

All dutiful parents know the game of stage-coach. Each child is given a name, such as the whip, the nigh-leader, the off-wheeler, the old-lady passenger, and, under penalty of paying a forfeit, must get up and turn round when the grown-up, who is improvising a thrilling story, mentions that particular object; and when the word "stage-coach" is mentioned, everybody has to get up and turn round. Well, we used to play stage-coach on the float while in swimming, and instead of tamely getting up and turning round, the child whose turn it was had to plunge overboard. When I mentioned "stage-coach," the water fairly foamed with vigorously kicking little legs; and then there was always a moment of interest while I counted, so as to be sure that the number of heads that came up corresponded with the number of children who had gone down.

I am puzzled to know whether Roosevelt's attitude toward his youngest boy, Quentin, whose body lies in his soldier's grave in France, should be put under the head of courage or gentleness. The father who has the most gentle love for his child really wants that child to make the most of its life, not merely to vegetate, protected from every kind of danger, trial, or obstacle. Quentin's death was a blow to Roosevelt, but I think he never regretted the encouragement and support which he gave his youngest son in making the Great Adventure. Quentin, then nineteen years old, was completing his sophomore year in Harvard. When this country declared war on Germany he telegraphed his mother that he was leaving college to come to New York to enlist. During a visit at Sagamore Hill in the summer of 1917, after Quentin had gone to the French front, I asked Mr. and Mrs. Roosevelt whether they did not feel it to be a special hardship that, at so early an age, Quentin should have to give up his education and many of his associations at Harvard which he could never renew even if the war left him unscathed. They both replied that they were particularly glad that, on his own initiative, he had taken the exact course which would put him in one of the most dangerous branches of the service.

"I would not have stopped him if I could," added Mr. Roosevelt; "and I could not have stopped him if I would. The more American boys from nineteen to twenty-one join the army the better it is for the country. To take them out of our civil life entails the smallest economic loss upon the Nation, and because of their elasticity and powers of recuperation they are its greatest military asset."

Nevertheless, if Roosevelt could have given him-

self and saved Quentin he would gladly have done
so. Just before Quentin's death Mr. Stéphane
Lauzanne—the editor of the Paris *Matin*, then in
this country—was returning to Paris; he asked
Roosevelt for a message to take back to his countrymen. This was Roosevelt's response:

"I have no message for France; I have already
given her the best I had. But if, over there, they
speak of me, tell them that my only regret is that
I could not give myself."

One of my pleasantest recollections of Roosevelt
is connected with this gentle side of his character.
Preceding and during the Progressive campaign of
1912 he used to lunch weekly with his editorial
colleagues at the National Arts Club in Gramercy
Park. There were usually several guests. On a
certain one of these luncheon days there were to be
two distinguished foreign diplomats as the guests of
honour, the ambassadors from Brazil and Argen-
tina, and I had gone around from our office, a few
blocks away, to the club just ahead of Mr. Roosevelt, to make sure that all the arrangements were
complete. We did not often have foreign ambassadors at our table and I felt a desire, which house-
wives who read these lines will understand, to see
that the flowers and napery and spoons and forks
were properly arranged.

As I approached the club I saw a lady standing on the sidewalk stooping over to talk to a small boy about ten years old, who was crying bitterly. The boy was sobbing so convulsively that it was impossible to understand what he was saying; but on stopping to see if I could be of any assistance the lady, seeing that the boy was being attended to, went on her way. I managed to extract from the little, quivering figure the information that he was lost. His father was a Hungarian miner from Pennsylvania; that family had arrived that morning in New York on their way back to Hungary; the ship was to sail the next day; he had just stepped out of the house where they were stopping to see the street sights of the great, strange city. Further details were blotted out by another burst of weeping.

Just then Mr. Roosevelt came sailing around the corner of the iron palings of Gramercy Park, busily talking with his companion, General F. V. Greene, who, like Roosevelt, had been a police commissioner. He stopped and asked what was the matter. I told him what I had learned, and he said, half to the boy and half to General Greene: "We'll soon fix this. Let me see, General, isn't there a precinct station-house in Twenty-Second Street near Second Avenue? We'll take him there and they will send out a general alarm for his father and mother."

The little derelict stopped his weeping—he seemed to feel an instinctive confidence in the power of this strange man to do things—and we all started off to the police station half a mile away. Mr. Roosevelt hardly spoke to the boy, who plodded along contentedly beside him, while he continued his discussion with General Greene on, I think, some military subject.

When we got to the precinct station the lieutenant or sergeant in charge recognized the two former police commissioners. Mr. Roosevelt told him the facts, gave the boy a piece of silver to get some luncheon and, telling the little fellow that the police would find his mother and father before long, left him perfectly comfortable and contented. We returned to the club half an hour late, but the diplomatic guests were repaid for their delay by their interest in the story of the incident which I related as our excuse.

Late in the afternoon I called up the police station and found that through the medium of a general alarm, or some such police procedure, the frightened boy and the terrified parents had been happily brought together.

This little incident is a simple one but I think

it worth telling because it shows that Roosevelt was more interested in helping a small boy in trouble—not sending someone else as he might easily have done but doing it himself—than he was in greeting the ambassadors of two great foreign countries to which he was about to make an important visit. For he was then arranging his expedition to South America and his exploration of the Brazilian jungle. He had a warm-hearted human sympathy and a gentle, almost woman-like kind of tenderness of which thousands who admired his strenuous life knew nothing.

Roosevelt was not interested in dogmatic or metaphysical theology. Indeed, I doubt if he cared for metaphysics of any kind; I am inclined to think he would have sympathized with the wit who once said that the only use for metaphysics is to furnish arguments for the abolition of metaphysics; I am sure he would have agreed with Emerson that "metaphysics is dangerous as a single pursuit; . . . the inward analysis must be corrected by rough experience. Metaphysics must be perpetually reinforced by life; must be the observations of a working man on working men." But although not of the metaphysical temperament he was deeply interested in a philosophy of life and in the morals and ethics that underlie the finest, most beautiful, and most worth-while human relationships. I do not know whether he was a Platonist or an Aristotelian, a Trinitarian or a Unitarian, a Pantheist or a Deist, but I do know that he believed that there are axiomatic laws of virtue and goodness which we do not need to argue about any more than we do about the law of gravitation.

One of the most complete and satisfying creeds that was ever written is that of the Prophet Micah: "O man, what doth the Lord require of thee but to do justly, love mercy, and walk humbly with thy God?" Not long after Roosevelt's death, his sister, Mrs. Douglas Robinson, told me that this verse from the Book of Micah was his favourite. And a letter was published last February by the General Secretary of the New York Bible Society saying that when he asked Roosevelt in the summer of 1917 to send through that society a message to the American troops abroad, the Colonel chose Micah's text as his message, which he wrote out in his own hand with this comment:

Do justice: and therefore fight valiantly against the armies of Germany and Turkey; for these nations, in this crisis, stand for the reign of Moloch and Beelzebub on this earth.

Love Mercy: treat prisoners well; succour the wounded;

The last photograph of Colonel Roosevelt, taken shortly
before the serious illness which finally caused his death

© Paul Thompson

The hillside burial

treat every woman as if she were your sister; care for the little children, and be tender with the old and helpless.

Theodore Roosevelt's personality was an unsurpassed combination of the unterrified fighter of what he believed to be the worst, and the tender-hearted lover of what he believed to be the best in mankind. Whether he loved or hated, talked or read, worked or played he did it with zest and eagerness. The words of William James may well be applied to such a life:

Wherever a process of life communicates an eagerness to him who lives it, there the life becomes genuinely significant. Sometimes the eagerness is more knit up with the motor activities, sometimes with the imagination, sometimes with reflective thought. But wherever it is found, there is the zest, the tingle, the excitement of reality; and there *is* "importance" in the only real and positive sense in which importance ever anywhere can be.

CHAPTER IX

THE END

IF THEODORE ROOSEVELT could be asked what phase of his many-sided life seems to him the most important and gives him the most satisfaction, I am sure that he would say instantly that he wishes to be remembered most as the founder and head of a family. It was therefore peculiarly suitable that his funeral should have been that of a husband and a father rather than that of a statesman and a military hero.

He died on January 6, 1919. The services in his memory at the little Episcopal church in Oyster Bay, on Wednesday, January 8, were simple, unpretentious, and genuine, but they were profoundly impressive. There was no pomp, no ceremony. Four or five hundred of his personal friends gathered in the little edifice where he had been wont to worship. His son, Captain Archie Roosevelt—in his uniform and with his arm and hand still bound in the splint which was aiding to cure the serious wound he received in France—and his nephew, Theodore Douglas Robinson, met the friends as they entered, and aided in showing them to seats.

In accordance with the liturgy of the Episcopal Church, the coffin, draped in an American flag, was borne up the aisle preceded by the rector, Dr. Talmage, and followed by the immediate members of the family and of the household. The ceremony consisted simply of the reading of the burial service. There was no music. But the rector read as a part of the service what is believed to have been one of Mr. Roosevelt's favourite hymns: "How Firm a Foundation, Ye Saints of the Lord." There was no eulogy, no address. But at the close of the service the rector stepped forward to the head of the casket, and, instead of pronouncing in the usual words the beautiful benediction which will be found at the end of the Penitential Office for Ash Wednesday, recited it as follows:

Theodore, the Lord bless thee, and keep thee. The Lord make his face to shine upon thee, and be gracious unto thee. The Lord lift up his countenance upon thee, and give thee peace, both now and evermore. Amen.

After the brief service in the church Roosevelt's friends and neighbours followed his body to the cemetery, where it now lies. It is a village burial ground on a hillside, informal but neatly kept, and adorned with the native trees of which Roosevelt was so fond. His grave lies at the top of the hill, from which there is a charming view of the waters of Long Island Sound and of the rolling and wooded landscape which makes Oyster Bay a particularly beautiful spot.

There was solemnity during these last tributes, but there was no grief. There never was grief in the presence of Theodore Roosevelt, and although his body was gone there could not be in the presence of his spirit.

As I came down the slope from the hilltop where his body lies I thought of the requiem and epitaph by Robert Louis Stevenson:

> Under the wide and starry sky
> Dig the grave and let me lie.
> Glad did I live, and gladly die,
>   And I laid me down with a will.
>
> This be the verse you grave for me:
> "Here he lies, where he longed to be;
> Home is the sailor, home from the sea,
>   And the hunter home from the hill."

As time goes on Roosevelt's defects—for there never was a man of whom it could be more truly said that he had the defects of his qualities—will more and more sink into the background—his virtues and genius as a man and a statesman will more and more come forward into the light. Whether or not it will be possible at some time to make Sagamore Hill—his homestead at Oyster Bay—

a national memorial park I do not know, but since his burial there has been a constant stream of pilgrims to his hillside grave. This is not a little surprising, for Oyster Bay is off the main routes of travel and there is nothing about the country graveyard that forms his resting place to attract the visitor except the memory of the man himself. Even after death his magnetic spirit still draws people to him. This continuing power of his personality is set forth so appropriately in a poem by his sister Corinne Roosevelt, Mrs. Douglas Robinson, that I have asked and received her permission to close these pages with it.

> At Sagamore the Chief lies low.
> Above the hill, in circled row
> The whirring airplanes dip and fly—
>   A guard of honour from the sky—
> Eagles to guard the Eagle.   Woe
> Is on the world.   The people go
> With listless footstep, blind and slow;
>   For one is dead—who shall not die
>   At Sagamore.
>
> Oh!   Land he loved, at last you know
> The son who served you well below,
>   The prophet voice, the visioned eye.
>   Hold him in ardent memory,
> For one is gone—who shall not go—
>   From Sagamore!

THE COUNTRY LIFE PRESS
GARDEN CITY, N. Y.